THE TROUBLE WITH SNACK TIME

The Trouble with Snack Time

Children's Food and the Politics of Parenting

Jennifer Patico

NEW YORK UNIVERSITY PRESS
New York

NEW YORK UNIVERSITY PRESS
New York
www.nyupress.org

References to Internet websites (URLs) were accurate at the time of writing. Neither the author nor New York University Press is responsible for URLs that may have expired or changed since the manuscript was prepared.

Library of Congress Cataloging-in-Publication Data
Names: Patico, Jennifer, author.
Title: The trouble with snack time : children's food and the politics of parenting / Jennifer Patico.
Description: New York : New York University Press, [2020] |
Includes bibliographical references and index.
Identifiers: LCCN 2019039470 | ISBN 9781479835331 (cloth) |
ISBN 9781479845989 (paperback) | ISBN 9781479817214 (ebook) |
ISBN 9781479810062 (ebook)
Subjects: LCSH: Food preferences in children—United States. | Children—Nutrition—Psychological aspects. | Children—Nutrition—United States. | Food habits—United States. | Food—Social aspects—United States. | Middle class families—United States. | Parenting—United States. | Child rearing—United States.
Classification: LCC HQ784.E3 P37 2020 | DDC 613.2083—dc23
LC record available at https://lccn.loc.gov/2019039470

New York University Press books are printed on acid-free paper, and their binding materials are chosen for strength and durability. We strive to use environmentally responsible suppliers and materials to the greatest extent possible in publishing our books.

Manufactured in the United States of America

10 9 8 7 6 5 4 3 2 1

Also available as an ebook

CONTENTS

FIGURES

Introduction

Food, Parenting, and Middle-Class Anxiety

"Can I get this?" Eleven-year-old Tara holds up a small, sealed cup that contains chopped bits of pink grapefruit. "Wouldn't you rather get a *grapefruit*?" her mother asks. "No." Tara walks away from the produce section and apparently her mother, Renee, has relented, since the item stays in the grocery cart. Renee thinks aloud, "I need to decide whether to get grapes. They have really nice organic ones at the Farmer's Market, but when will I have time to get over there?" She decides not to buy them at the chain grocery store where they are shopping now. "Did you eat your plum yet?" she asks Tara. Tara affirms that she has, and Renee explains that Tara's little sister had wanted the plum, but Renee had refused it to her since it was a single plum that Tara had chosen for herself at the store. "I didn't know she tried to eat my plum!" Tara balks, seeming to confirm a shared understanding with her mother that her selection of the plum for her own consumption is something not to be violated.

Moving to a nearby section of the store, Renee continues to inquire about Tara's current preferences. "Are you eating hummus these days?" "I am eating hummus these days," the girl replies, picking the variety she prefers. Renee chooses an additional one since they are on sale: buy one, get one free. In the bread aisle, she considers the options briefly before grabbing a loaf of Sarah Lee Honey Wheat. "I'm never happy in terms of the bread thing. But I have to get something the kids will eat." She would like the bread to be less processed, and she tries to avoid high-fructose corn syrup, but she has had trouble finding something that meets those criteria that her daughters will accept. "And god forbid it should be the Farmer's Market bread where they make it fresh there!" Several items in Renee's cart—Cinnamon Toast Crunch breakfast cereal, Gatorade sports drinks, and frozen Lean Pockets meals that can be microwaved—are for her husband. Renee would prefer not to buy these more sugary and processed foods, particularly since the children end up eating them when they are stocked at home. "Stop making Dad sound so unhealthy!" Tara objects. "He's healthy!"

Renee's deliberations—and her shared concern with her daughter about being (and appearing) healthy—are far from unusual. Food for children has been cast in popular U.S. discourse as a crisis. The highly publicized rise in the percentage of children who are classified as overweight in the United States, also known as the "childhood obesity epidemic," is perhaps the most obvious example of how children's eating has been framed in crisis terms. Related to this, the last two decades have seen high-profile conflicts around school cafeteria nutrition reform and heated local debates about classroom cupcake parties (Crooks 2000, 2003; James, Kjorholt, and Tingstad 2009; Levine 2008; Moffat 2010; Schulte 2006; Isoldi et al. 2012). Books with titles such as *Cure Your Child with Food* (Dorfman 2013) speak to the considerable anxiety that runs through most discussions of contemporary parenting in U.S. popular media.

In her 2004 guide *Little Sugar Addicts*, for example, Kathleen DesMaisons advises parents that children who present seemingly inexplicable and intractable behavioral challenges may well be reacting to an excess of sugar in their diets.

> Do you have a smart, creative, compassionate child who is also spacey, inattentive, cranky, and sometimes obnoxious? . . . I know you really care for your child and that you know something is not right. The contradictions simply make no sense. . . . The pain you feel at seeing your gentle and loving child turn willful, frightened, and out of control is beyond words. The rage you feel in the midst of power struggles terrifies you. . . . You are tired of this and want your kid to be happy and well-adjusted. (DesMaisons 2004, 1–2)

This is one example of how contemporary experts propose dietary management as the solution to parents' most nagging frustrations and fears. But sugar is just one lightning rod in a wider conversation that is happening around childhood, parenting, and food; and "deceptively frivolous" debates over issues such as whether birthday cupcakes should be allowed in classrooms are diagnostic of much more (Abu-Lughod 1990).

Indeed, this book argues that such debates illuminate the fundamental ways in which people construe what it means to be a person: a conscientious, responsible, and likeable person. They also represent everyday struggles over matters of power and control, played out through minute instances of decision making and in the context of interactions among adults as well as between children and adults. An individual's eating—or guidance of another's eating—"is a basis for linking the world of things to the world of ideas through one's acts, and thus also a basis for relating oneself to the rest of the world" (Mintz 1996, 70; see also Biltekoff 2014). In this sense food and eating are potent embodiments of value, both economic/material and moral/emotional, through which "people represent the importance of their own actions to themselves" and situate themselves within a "larger, social totality"—that is, "society" as it appears in their own experience and imagination (Graeber 2001, xii, 45; see also Munn 1986).

In the United States particularly, children's food is a powerful, if mundane, nexus of value creation through which the meanings of childhood itself are defined and through which social differences such as class are perceived and reproduced, often very implicitly. To understand how this is the case, we need to defamiliarize nutrition: to, as food politics researcher Julie Guthman (2014, 3) has put it, "undo its taken-for grantedness in an effort to understand better its sociological and cultural underpinnings, as well as the effects that it has beyond improving or failing to improve dietary health." Highly concrete in their material forms and often framed through seemingly objective scientific discourse, children's food and nutrition are very much on the radar of public and private discourse in the United States; yet their implicit social meanings and effects often travel under it.

Those more implicit social meanings and unintended effects, not nutrition per se, are the topic of this book, though everyday understandings of nutrition in one community are discussed in every chapter. This book is about how, in the context of an industrialized food market and a capitalist culture that valorizes consumer choice and personal responsibility, adults' senses of their own and their loved ones' selves are at stake in the choices they make about food. This is especially true of the choices they make for children, who are seen as particularly vulnerable to unsafe foods and as in need of guidance toward proper selfhood. This guidance includes subtle training in how to interact with others, how to present oneself, and how to maintain appropriate physical and emotional boundaries between oneself and a potentially threatening physical and social environment. To see how all this happens in the material realm of children's food is to better understand how people are living a particular kind of economy in their—our—bodies and minds. It is to consider how we as individuals contribute to building a social world that reflects the exigencies of a certain historical moment and responds to its moral and practical demands.

The research upon which this book is based was conducted primarily from 2012 to 2015 at an Atlanta school I call Hometown Charter and in its surrounding homes and coffee shops. Over the course of many conversations and observations, I, a sociocultural anthropologist, heard how middle-class Hometown parents struggled to monitor and guide their children's development and behavior in a number of ways, including through food. I learned that they often worried that these attempts at control might be excessive and create new problems for their children. They looked for ways to practice "moderation," and implicitly or explicitly compared their own compromises to those struck by others. Moreover, I learned that "diversity" and inclusion—of race, class, sexuality—was highly valued by most adults here; yet "diversity" brought along with it divergent food practices, and Hometown parents' desires to protect children from what they perceived as low-quality, potentially toxic foods and to sustain "community" (which entailed close neighborliness and shared values) sometimes conflicted with their inclinations toward social inclusion.

This book is fundamentally about those struggles, including the ways that inequalities, particularly along lines of class, were experienced, communicated, and sometimes glossed over through conversations about food. While concerns about children's food in the United States are informed by complex and changing nutritional scientific information, this is not another book about how to do children's food or parenting "right." When I describe what parents said about how they fed their children and why, I do not seek to convince the reader of which approaches were better, more logical, or more in line with the advice offered by any particular school of nutritional or parenting thought. Instead, this study focuses on how those real but uncertain problems get thematized and amplified as they intersect with the other concerns parents have about their own roles as parents and about their relationships with one another and with their children. The tendrils of these concerns extend into many areas of life, including the activities through which people build a sense of community in their schools and neighborhoods.

This book contends that children's food is a locus for fundamental moral tensions in American middle-class life—particularly for the left-leaning, urban middle class among whom I spent time at Hometown—about how to live, how to present oneself, and how to be protected from harm. Children's food is a material realm in which people seek to balance and reconcile worries about regulating consumption adequately yet not excessively, and about promoting social inclusion while also protecting their families from substances and practices they deem unhealthy or otherwise undesirable. As we shall see, these tensions reflect the influence of an underlying ethic that is linked with neoliberal capitalism. In this ethic, middle-class parents take responsibility for protecting their children from an industrialized food system and for cultivating in them proper approaches to eating, but they do so in ways that ultimately and unintentionally tend to reinforce class privilege and the effects of social inequality. Listening closely to adults'—and children's—food concerns and contextualizing them both very locally and vis-à-vis a broader political economy, this book examines those unintended effects and asks how the "crisis" of children's food might be reimagined toward different ends.

The Politics of Parenting in the United States

Food and eating are heavily moralized in the United States, such that choices, preferences, and related outcomes (such as slenderness or obesity) tend to be treated as personal and voluntary successes or failures, judged by normative standards (e.g., Mintz 1996; Paxson 2008). Child rearing, which in the modern United States tends to be framed as a near-sacred responsibility and as a key determinant of full adult personhood, is also highly moralized (Katz 2008; Zelizer 1994; Anagnost 2004). Both of those things being true, the fraught nature of child feeding in the contemporary United States seems almost guaranteed (see also Curtis, James, and Ellis 2010; Coutant et al. 2011). But while it may be hard for many to imagine today, parenting—while obviously not new in its most general meaning—has been conceptualized and debated as such only since the 1950s, when psychologists, sociologists, and self-help experts popularized the term (Faircloth, Hoffman, and Layne 2013, 1). That interest in the practices of parents has exploded since the 1970s; and by the 1990s, sociologist Sharon Hays's (1996) analysis of "intensive motherhood"—a "time-and-emotion-expensive enterprise"—heralded a new wave of academic attention (Faircloth, Hoffman, and Layne 2013, 2; Lee 2014).

At the turn of the twentieth century, "intensive parenting" described a widespread approach that assumed parenting was difficult, requiring skills and expert input, but nonetheless properly experienced as emotionally fulfilling by parents (Faircloth, Hoffman, and Layne 2013, 1–2). Parenting has come to be understood as the source of—and the solution for—various social problems (1–2). Indeed, in the dominant discourses on parenting in the United States and other industrialized countries, parents are cast as highly responsible for the outcomes experienced by their children, from their long-term health to their future careers, while children are constructed in turn as highly vulnerable (Lee 2014; Furedi 2002; Faircloth, Hoffman, and Layne 2013, 3). Their surrounding physical and social environments are understood to be toxic, and parenting is imagined as the protection of children from their deleterious effects through careful monitoring (Bristow 2014, 211; Lee 2014, 12). Such discourses and practices are fueled by "individualized fears about uncalibrated risks," where threatening possibilities may loom large despite or apart from their statistical probabilities (Lee 2014, 11–12).

This climate promotes in parents a constant vigilance, "an attitude of constant alertness for possible opportunities, risks and shortcomings in their children's development" (Ramaekers and Suissa 2012, 33). Geographer and childhood researcher Cindi Katz (2008, 10–11) suggests that such intense concern about the vulnerability of children to multiple dangers may not only absorb parents but also "divert [their] attention from the political, economic and other sources of their insecurities"—such as job loss and home foreclosures—in order "to address their symptoms." Even so, parents' task is far from straightforward, not least because they have been criticized for absorbing the imperatives of intensive parenting all too well, falling into a double bind where the line between too much and too little seems terribly important but quite elusive (Bristow 2014, 200; see also Lareau 2003, 254).

In early January 2019 I received the *New York Times'* "Well Family" newsletter in my electronic mailbox. The newsletter was a curation of recent articles that had been published by the *Times* on parenting, children, and family health. In that first issue of the new year, I noticed two headlines that were somewhat contradictory to one another in tone. Yet together, they spoke to key aspects of what I had been observing about middle-class parenting in the United States during the preceding several years of conducting research and writing this book.

The first read "6 Ways to Be an Effective Parent in 2019."[1] Clicking on the link, I found that it was itself a repackaging of several more articles, whose themes included advice to parents on how to discipline their children using neither rewards nor punishments, how to raise resilient children (and be a resilient parent), and how to help teenagers "embrace stress" or become "college-ready." Additional essays emphasized the importance of not yelling at children, since yelling correlated with children's depression and lowered self-esteem, and advised parents on "The Confidence Gap for Girls: 5 Tips for Parents of Tweens and Teen Girls." The message offered by the *Times* was clear: American children were facing considerable challenges in a competitive, achievement-oriented environment, and it was up to parents to help them meet those challenges not only by giving them the wherewithal to hit achievement milestones, but also by preparing them to handle emotional turmoil, by protecting their vulnerable senses of self-confidence, and by making sure that parents themselves did not inadvertently become sources of pain and limitation.

Meanwhile, a separate headline in the newsletter addressed "The Relentlessness of Modern Parenting" (Miller 2018). This essay underscored how the widespread practice of intensive parenting—parenting styles characterized by heavy parental expenditures of time, money, attention, and energy—could be burdensome to parents but were appealing to them not least because of their sense of declining economic opportunities. "For parents, giving children the best start in life has come to mean doing everything they can to ensure that their children can climb to a higher class, or at least not fall out of the one they were born into" (Miller 2018).

Together, the *Times* articles pointed to the idea that parents were concerned about the future economic lives of their children. Moreover, they encouraged parents to think about the emotional skills children would need to meet those futures, and strikingly, they proposed that this was largely within the power of parents themselves to determine. The *Times* also pointed out ruefully that parenting these days had become "relentless," but it participated in telling parents that, according to the experts, there was still much they could and needed to do to save their children from unnecessary failures and suffering. What further struck me was the ambivalence the paper's headlines seem to represent when placed side by side: the recognition that expectations on parents were burdensomely high, that parents were feeling responsible for protecting their children from problems that were far larger and more structural, but also the impression that forging on ahead with a sense of individual responsibility for the world one's children would inhabit—and how they would inhabit it—still seemed the only imaginable option.

Neoliberal Selfhood?

Concerns about an insecure economic future and the conviction that its challenges can and must be met through individual initiative are part and parcel of what has been called a *neoliberal* moment. Though used relatively rarely in everyday parlance, at least in the United States, the term has become extremely common in anthropology and in other humanities and social science fields. It also has been critiqued for its excessive and harmfully vague use (e.g., Ganti 2014; Laidlaw 2015; Kipnis 2007). As we shall see, what anthropologists and others have identified as "neoliberal" influences on everyday life certainly resonate with the stories of Hometowners—for example, with their sense of individualized responsibility for protecting their children through acts of consumer choice—though there are other relevant frames that can be brought to bear as we consider these phenomena, and close attention must be paid to locally specific dynamics of class, race, and community life. My goal here is less to establish a singular definition of the "neoliberal" than to contextualize how the concept has been used in recent academic work and to clarify the cautious and selective way in which I use it in this book.

Classical "liberalism" refers to a broad set of beliefs including egalitarianism, individualism, and, often, the idea that society's flows and exchanges are best regulated through free markets; "neoliberalism," too, is linked with ideologies of individualism and the valorization of individual achievement (Ganti 2014, 92–93; Castagna 2014, 139). However, the term "neoliberalism" more specifically describes a political economic philosophy that originated in the years after the Great Depression and is hostile to the protection of working-class interests (Ganti 2014, 92–93). In current social science usage, however, "neoliberalism" is often used to denote not an explicit political economic ideology but rather a set of conditions, related to those sometimes described as "late capitalist": the situation of Fordist industrial economies having given way to the rise of postindustrial service economies; to flexible, insecure conditions of labor; and to government deregulation of markets. Governments' austerity in social spending, often linked with structural adjustment programs in economically "developing" countries, has impacted public health negatively through the curtailment of social welfare programs and the increasing privatization of health care (Janes and Chuluundorj 2004; Pfeiffer and Chapman 2010). Further, resistance to government regulation of environmentally detrimental and potentially toxic commodities and production processes leaves individuals largely responsible for protecting their own health through consumer education, decision making, and expenditures (Collins and Bilge 2016; MacKendrick 2018). The rise of obesity is one outcome of neoliberal development, as food and beverage corporations "effectively turn bodies everywhere into silos of high-fructose corn syrup" through the marketing and sale of branded products such as sodas (Sparke 2016).

Anthropologists use the term "neoliberal" not only to track those processes but also to describe how "subjectivities are formed or refashioned" through the inculcation of "values of individualism, entrepreneurialism, and market competition" (Ganti 2014, 94–96; see also Foucault 1984; Peters 2016). In other words, they have been interested to examine the ways in which the values that guide individuals' and groups' approaches to labor, personal success, and "correct" behavior are aligned with the needs of the current capitalist economy. These values do not necessarily signal people's deliberate support for neoliberal policies such as retrenchments of social welfare; rather, anthropologists have explored how such internalized values and goals reflect and accommodate the experience of making one's way through such an environment, as everyday experiences and expectations become steeped in moral discourse and ideas about proper personal development. Individuals become "responsibilized" in that they are expected "to make choices about lifestyles, their bodies, their education, and their health. . . . It is not simply 'consumer sovereignty' but rather a moralization and . . . a regulated transfer of choice-making responsibility from the state to the individual in the social market" (Peters 2016, 301). In other words, individuals with unequal resources are charged with countless choices, and if the outcomes for their health or prosperity are less than desirable, they become morally culpable for their own putative lack of conscientiousness or judgment.

It is important to point out that as social scientists use the term, "neoliberal" is almost invariably and automatically a critique of the situation to which it refers; in fact, some have argued the term is used indiscriminately and lazily to attribute too many phenomena to a big bad wolf of neoliberalism (Laidlaw 2015, 914; Kipnis 2007; Ganti 2014, 99; Borenstein 2019). As one cultural theorist most humorously put it, "'Neoliberal' is now a word used only by its opponents. It is just slightly more plausible to talk about neoliberalism positively than it is to talk about the unsung wonders of Ebola" (Borenstein 2019). While sensitive to that problem and foregrounding those meaningful reservations, I use the term to draw connections with other scholars' observations about trends in the ways American selves are being conceptualized and enacted, and how these are linked with broader arrangements of power. In most cases, I use it to refer to the ideologies that valorize self-responsibility, self-regulation, entrepreneurialism, and consumerism, along with the conditions and institutions (a relatively deregulated marketplace, curtailment of social welfare mechanisms) that are intimately related to those ideologies.

As societies across the globe experience similar shifts in their economies and accompanying social pressures, anthropologists observe how people absorb and cope with those developments on the ground. While distinct political economies and cultural histories make it impossible to identify some universal experience of a hegemonic neoliberalism, recent ethnographic studies from the United States and Britain to China and India do suggest that similarly intensive and newly "child-centered" parenting approaches go hand in hand with (both established and rising) capitalist economies, where parents are being tasked to produce "individualistic, risk-taking, entrepreneurial" and "happy" selves (Faircloth, Hoffman, and Layne 2013, 4, 12; see also Bialostok and Aronson 2016; Aronson and Bialostok 2016; Chua 2011; Kuan 2015). "Neoliberal" can serve, then, as a reminder of the political and economic moment in which this study takes place, the embeddedness of the most private consumer and child-rearing ideas within those experiences, and the connectedness—and, it must not be forgotten, specificity—of those experiences across the globe (see also Eriksen 2015). Indeed, this book is predicated upon the importance of local conditions, describing a community and its dynamics in ways that are versions of a bigger American picture, but also particular.

Of course, the ways in which contemporary Americans are thinking about themselves are not entirely new, springing into neoliberal form de novo. Social scientists have identified a deeper history of the connections between capitalisms, modernities, and ways of thinking about the self and about childhood, and they have used concepts other than the neoliberal to do so. For example, sociologist Viviana Zelizer's classic study (1994) argues that in the wake of nineteenth-century industrialization, the modern child was attributed a kind of moral pricelessness; children's sacralized status entailed their protection for their own sake, rather than treating them as working members of a household economy (see also Cook 2004). In the later twentieth century, Sharon Hays (1996) argued that intensive motherhood was responding to the ongoing intensification of capitalism inasmuch as it sought to combat the commercialization and perceived impoverishment of social life, in a context of rising work hours and outsourcing of care work (see also Faircloth, Hoffman, and Layne 2013, 2; Hochschild 2003).

In short, the subjectivities of children and of parents have taken form in relationship to an ever-evolving capitalist labor economy in the United States and beyond, reflecting how individuals and households accommodate themselves to labor conditions; how conceptions of morality and gender roles shift along with these; and how some practices, including consumption, serve as means to respond to, align oneself with, or even (perhaps simultaneously) protest the status quo. Thus some of the key experiences attributed to neoliberalism, such as the hyper-responsibilization of individuals for their own well-being, can be understood as extensions or intensifications of ways of thinking about selfhood and individuality that have earlier (industrial and preindustrial) roots.

For example, industrial capitalist modernity has been described as a context in which individuals are expected to forge their own paths rather than being able to depend upon "traditional" kin structures or presumed and inherited professional roles (Giddens 1991, 75–81). The modern self—an individual self, or what anthropologist Elizabeth Povinelli (2006) more recently has called an autological self—is understood as one that moves relatively independently through life, building a continuous, coherent, and linear life narrative. In this model, people create intelligible personae through work, through their choices of mates, and through lifestyles and material tastes. In an earlier era, French anthropologist Marcel Mauss (1938/1985) described Western understandings of personhood as having been shaped by Christian belief in a unitary being (God as Father, Son, and Holy Spirit) as well as by secular, Enlightenment thought, particularly as expressed in contract law and other legal institutions that frame individual persons as distinct, unique, and bounded entities. This stands in contrast to cultural and historical settings whose practices, ideologies, and institutions emphasize the ways in which people occupy social (such as kinship) roles and are intimately, inextricably, rather messily connected to others around them through affiliations, obligations, and shared social experience (Mauss 1938/1985; Lutz 1988).

Those messily embedded aspects of personhood are more often acknowledged, even idealized and promoted, in some cultural contexts (such as Kondo showed for late twentieth-century Tokyo) and social encounters (as in Carsten's account of a British woman's contested legal claim to her dead husband's frozen sperm) (Carsten 2012; Kondo 1990; see also Munn 1986). Indeed, "neoliberal" styles of responsibilization are never completely hegemonic but are nested within other models for thinking about responsibility, care, and the social contract across institutions (Trnka and Trundle 2014). Ethnographic attention to parenting and to what sociologist of childhood Daniel Cook (2008) has called "co-consumption," or consumption for and with another person, provides one way to see how individuals work through ideologies of individualism and self-responsibility precisely through their interactions with others, through acts of exchange and care that continually belie the clarity of the boundaries between actors.

Hence this book examines how middle-class parents in the United States live particular versions of self-responsibilization and individualism, but it does not take those models and values of selfhood for granted. Rather, it draws attention to their historical and local specificity and—harkening to the longer history of the anthropology of self and personhood briefly described above—starts from the notion that the boundaries between these selves and others, whether within the family or across households, are never natural and established but are always in the process of being drawn and redrawn, not least through food practices and discourses. I analyze these activities flexibly using intersecting terms including "neoliberal," "middle-class," and "postindustrial," shifting according to which framings are most apt and illuminating for particular scenarios and themes I observed at Hometown.

Listening to Parenting Anxiety

As parents consider the best ways to provide for their children, they not only are creating child selves but also are at work producing themselves as proper adults. Indeed, children are not the only objects of discipline; parents, too, meet discipline, often becoming targets of public pedagogy concerning food and parenting (Allison 1991; Pike and Leahy 2012). The feeding of children not only is a means of child socialization, then, but also is a way that adults—especially women—perform normative gender roles, showing themselves to be responsible, loving parents in the terms defined by reigning discourses (Ochs, Pontecorvo, and Fasulo 1996; Ochs and Shohet 2006; DeVault 1991; Miller 1998; Namie 2011). Something like neoliberalism as personal responsibilization is emotionally *felt* precisely through "the anxiety, guilt, and frustration experienced by many mothers who feel they are individually responsible for protecting their children from harmful food additives and chemicals" (Cairns and Johnston 2015, 34).

Indeed, a consistent thread of this book is the sense of anxiety and conflict that I found to characterize Hometown parents' (and to some extent, children's) efforts to do well with food. Literary theorist Sianne Ngai describes "anxiety" as associated in the continental philosophical tradition with a male intellectual stance. She identifies anxiety as a kind of fear of, and fleeing from, something rather indefinite, with the act of fleeing itself imagined as a kind of self-liberation and a quest for knowledge (2005, 232, 246). Reading Ngai's description helped define for me how very different the anxiety I am talking about at Hometown is. For one thing, this anxiety is not gendered as masculine. It is not strictly feminized nor exclusively experienced by women, but it is more practiced by women through the highly gendered work of grocery shopping, meal planning, and cooking. It is not marked as particularly "intellectual" (though it requires a good deal ongoing mental labor) nor as removed from the daily or the mundane. It is more associated with hands-on modes of care and planning: the attitude of the daily decision maker, the line drawer and compromise maker, the winnower of information.

Ngai (2005, 213) observes that identifying something as an anxiety, whether a "middle-class anxiety" or a "millennial anxiety," usually signals distaste and an implicitly skeptical attitude that links up with "the general prominence of phobia as a signifying economy in modern culture." Yet in naming parental anxiety as a key thread of this book, I want to fend off the assumption that what is called "anxiety" deserves to be met with doubt about the groundedness of the fears expressed. There are very material, sensible reasons for people to focus on the things they discuss in this book. For example, sociologist Norah MacKendrick (2018) describes "precautionary consumption" (in which parents engage to protect their families from environmental toxins) as "more than just expressions of upper-middle-class anxiety"—she seems to imply here that "anxiety" would represent something frivolous, a failing both personal and class endemic—but a "response to ubiquitous environmental pollution and a poorly regulated food system and retail landscape." In a broader vein, philosophers of education Ramaekers and Suissa (2012, 128) identify contemporary parents' concerns as part of an inevitable existential experience, seeing parenting anxiety as a "human response to the real, and morally significant, existential experience of being a parent."

Thus I do not name "anxiety" to imply that the parents described in this book are in any way pathological, unreasonable, or unbalanced (though as we shall see, the fear of being called such ran through many conversations about food and children at Hometown). In fact, I am thinking about anxiety not primarily as an individual emotional or psychological experience, but as part of a shared affective milieu; it is something in the air, something in which people are immersed and that circulates through conversations—and through things left unsaid (Richard and Rudnyckyj 2009; Stewart 2007). It is also meant to invoke the kinds of mental and emotional labor parents take on, individually and in conversation with one another. Consumption is not a passive act of reception nor a mere practice of display; it involves physical and emotional work, particularly when performed on behalf of others. This is labor that reproduces the family and is part of the fabric of relationships among households and between families and institutions such as schools. Children's food is a key means through which people are working out the nature and the contradictions of American individualism—symbolically, discursively, and in the most concrete, material ways. They are endeavoring to draw boundaries between children and adults, and among communities and institutions, as part of the everyday work of living in a particular kind of political economy.

Middle-Class Ways of Being

While approaches to children's food in the United States are shaped by broad norms and aspirational discourses such as those disseminated in media like the *New York Times*, countless parenting and cooking blogs, and self-help books, they are also differentiated in practice—especially by class, despite the fact that Americans often lack ready language for explicit discussion of the role of class. Households enjoy divergent outcomes (as well as variable access to other resources, such as time and education), but class as identity and positioning is more than a question of material resources immediately at hand. It also refers to the more immaterial ways in which class *habitus* shapes people's tastes and dispositions (Bourdieu 1984; see also Inglis, Ball, and Crawford 2008; Julier 2005; Mintz 1986).

Habitus is eminent social theorist Pierre Bourdieu's (1984) term for the ways that individuals and groups embody their historical experience in the present. Individuals acquire (through socialization) and exercise habits, aesthetics, and preferences over time. These are repertoires of taste and practice that are not random but tend to be coherent across realms. That is, because of their shared conditions of access (resources), conditions of life (such as educational training and labor experiences), and contexts of socialization, it is no accident that two consumers with similar class backgrounds might prefer both locally grown produce and vegan shoes—as well as, for example, similar approaches to child discipline.[2] Different class backgrounds produce different tastes and desires, but they all exist in relation to one another in hierarchical systems of power, where some people's tastes are concordant with institutions such as schools and museums while others are not legitimated by such affiliations. Thus while tastes in food, art, or clothing can be perceived as individual, innate, and/or freely chosen, they also work quietly to sustain and naturalize systems of inequality.

This kind of class differentiation applies not only to consumer decisions but also to styles of parenting (Kusserow 2004; Pugh 2009; Lareau 2003). Intensive approaches are dominant currently in the popular media, but they have been associated most closely with middle-class parents. For example, sociologist Annette Lareau (2003) has described the U.S. middle-class approach to parenting as one of "concerted cultivation," an intensive approach characterized by highly scheduled extracurricular routines. In such contexts, children not only participate in many scheduled activities but also learn to converse and negotiate with adults, learning a sense of entitlement for adult attention and interacting with adults as relative equals (2). By contrast, she found that working-class and poorer families espouse "natural growth" approaches that involve more unstructured "hanging out" with kin, tolerate less negotiation and whining, and instill a sense of powerlessness vis-à-vis institutions (31).[3] In these ways, practices that enable the reproduction of class inequality can be misrecognized as signs of natural talent, individual merit, and personal initiative (or lack thereof). Lareau notes that middle-class parents tend to see these tasks of intensive or concerted parenting as an obligation beyond question (rather than a matter of choice or strategy), not fully understanding either the costs or the social benefits of these expenditures but benefiting from them nonetheless (64–65).

Of course, these classed practices are not just ways of reinforcing the status quo—even if they ultimately may have that effect—but also represent ways for people to navigate, negotiate, and make sense of their lives, their moral worlds, and their own identities (Patico 2005, 2008; Liechty 2002). They are entangled with dominant moral ideals concerning selfhood, including what it means to live well, what it means to be human, and what it means to parent a child (Ramaekers and Suissa 2012, 11). Different kinds of selves get framed as either more or less deserving, and having the "right" kind of self can "become a resource for middle-class parents to consolidate their advantages and ensure the reproduction of privilege through the generations" (Gillies 2005, 836; see also MacKendrick 2018, 141). Meanwhile, working-class women must work harder to enact the same priorities due to a lack of the same resources (MacKendrick 2018; see also Cairns and Johnston 2015, 81). Poverty comes to be blamed on "poor selfmanagement" (Gillies 2005, 837). In this way, "structural and other constraints on action are dismissed in this model of the agentic, reflexive self, with appropriately raised citizens assumed to be able to negotiate and transcend obstacles in their path by exploiting opportunities, developing skills and managing risk. . . . Class is thus obscured by its re-framing in terms of an included majority of reasonable, rational, moral citizens who seek the best for their children, and an excluded minority who are disconnected from mainstream values and aspirations" (Gillies 2015, 840).

Thus while appearing as acts of individual will, efforts to be a certain kind of self-responsibilized self or to feed one's children in such a way as to avoid known health risks actually depend upon structural arrangements. With access to education and available discretionary time for learning about the latest research, middle-class parents make their children's bodies through their application of specialized knowledge; the child's body becomes "a sign of the parent's devotion—or neglect," depending upon how the middle-class mother acts on that knowledge (Strathern 2005, 4–5, cited in Faircloth, Hoffman, and Layne 2013, 7). Further, the ability to express "devotion" is a product of class privilege, given that it requires resources of time, money, and cultural capital.

But who is included in this middle class, and what does membership in it signify? In the United States, certainly, the middle class seems to be a rather capacious and vaguely understood category, a colloquial designation of some "normal" or "average." In a classic Marxian sense, class refers to one's relative position vis-à-vis the means of production; that is, in an increasingly polarized system of labor and ownership, one either owns the means of production and accumulates capital or sells one's labor for the profit of those owners. More loosely, contemporary U.S. class identities often are understood to be connected with a person's (or one's spouse's or parent's) paid occupation (professional and white-collar positions, as well as relatively secure labor conditions, conventionally signal middle-class status, though the designation can be broader) and by relative income. For example, according to data posted by the Pew Research Center, the median income among those Americans grouped by income as "middle class" was $78,442 in 2016 (Kochhar 2018; see also Leonhardt 2019).[4] Yet harkening back to Bourdieu's (1984) analysis of class habitus, anthropologists and others have recognized consumer tastes and sensibilities as part of a system of differentiated, stratified class identities that are contextually linked with—but do not necessarily map easily onto—income or current profession (see also Holt 1998).

In the same vein this book, while taking note of demographic markers including income and current employment among Hometowners, treats class as a matter not only of labor relations but also of styles of consumption, parenting, and other lifeways that are differentiated and stratified in a capitalist economy. Attending to class is less a matter of establishing rigid categories of membership than of foregrounding how those dynamics of stratification are enacted and reinforced in everyday life. At Hometown, middle-classness manifested as a broad set of sensibilities, including certain "intensive" parenting and feeding practices, that were linked with high levels of education and engaged in by individuals and households relatively protected (in the immediate or long term—usually both) from experiences of extreme material need. Hometowners' activities also resonated with descriptions of middle classes given in ethnographic accounts of diverse contemporary locales; recurring themes in this literature include middle-class interests in personal health, intensive attention to children, and attraction to self-help programs emphasizing individual responsibility for success and well-being (Patico 2016; Salmenniemi 2016; Kuan 2015).

Anthropologists have worked to theorize the commonalities that seem to unite contemporary middle-class ways of being around the world without losing sight of the particular ideologies and material circumstances that shape them in each setting (Heiman, Liechty, and Freeman 2012; Liechty 2012; Patico 2016). Still, certain themes recur, and concerns that have been dubbed part of "neoliberal" culture around the world (self-help, intensive parenting) parallel those characteristics that have been attributed to the "middle classes" globally. This suggests that our understanding of what the neoliberal condition is may be inordinately shaped by our observations of its fallout for *middle-class* workers and consumers, and accordingly that we should consider explicitly how experiences of class inform what is often framed as a generically "neoliberal" condition. By the same token, what we construe as "middle-class" identity perhaps can be read as a shorthand for the strategies and values through which people are marshalling their discretionary time, money, and emotional energy toward coping with the new instabilities and opportunities represented by today's capitalist economies and state retrenchments, always in locally contextualized ways.

Gentrification and Difference at Hometown

I use the pseudonym of "Hometown" to refer to a charter K–8 school near downtown Atlanta and, secondarily, to the neighborhoods that immediately surround it, where many of its students live (though some reside in other areas of the city). It is an area of Victorian and bungalow-style homes primarily built around the turn of the twentieth century. In the 1950s to 1970s, "white flight," in part a reaction to school desegregation, contributed to low housing values in this and similar Atlanta neighborhoods, but in the 1980s and 1990s gentrification transformed them from mostly lower-income and Black into places where increasing numbers of white, middle-class families purchased homes (Kruse 2005; L. Martin 2007). Reflecting broader shifts in the U.S. political economy, inner-city areas have been "rediscovered" by the middle class—increasingly by middle-class families with children (Hackworth 2007; Hankins 2007). Though the area is still primarily residential, gentrification has brought amenities such as cafés that feature vegan baked goods (styled in low-key hipster messy, artsy industrial, or sleeker tones) and a weekly farmers' market showcasing local cheeses and charcuterie. As we shall see, this is an area where many residents are relative newcomers who value the urban, racially and economically diverse vibe of the area and embrace a kind of small-town, naturalist aesthetic that values locally grown foods and home vegetable gardens.

In Atlanta, as in many other cities, the gentrification process has been shaped by long-standing racialized politics that have been intimately connected to schooling (Bayor 1996; Henry and Hankins 2012). In the Hometown area, a local charter school, imagined as a neighborhood school to which local children could walk each day, was formed through the activism of middle-class, primarily white gentrifiers with children. This development is part of Atlanta's experience not only of gentrification but also of neoliberal political economy more broadly; as geographer Katherine Hankins (2007, 114) has observed,

> As the state transforms itself from a protector and provider of services for its citizens to a protector of and provider for the market, new resources are required to fulfill the role of the retrenching state. Community, as an ideal for private actors to create, becomes just such a resource. Ultimately, gentrifiers are taking advantage of the retrenching state (and its neglect of inner city neighborhoods) in the form of undervalued housing stock, but these gentrifiers are in turn spending private time and money participating in the community-based provisioning of (public) education.

In the case of Hometown, the K–8 charter school (serving children aged about five to fourteen years) purports to offer education devoted to project-centered learning, with emphases on social-emotional learning and on qualitative over quantitative assessment of student achievement. In one school newsletter, a lead administrator offered talking points for adults who might have acquaintances curious about applying to the school's lottery. Her roughly five-hundred-word summary of what made the school distinctive included a number of points related to their educational approach, constructivism, which she described as involving "small, personalized instruction, depth of content over breadth, interdisciplinary instruction, 'real-world' learning experiences, and performance-based assessment." Traditional subjects such as science and writing were interwoven in their curriculum, and teachers were to emphasize process over product and to work to foster student collaboration. Amid these points, the administrator also highlighted, "We are inclusive of each child. We celebrate our differences and that each individual has something valuable to offer our community." Moreover, the school expected consistent involvement by parents in the life of the school (for example, through volunteering in classrooms or helping to organize fund-raisers), exemplifying one norm of intensive parenting.

Hometown's leadership described diversity as central to the school's mission and identity, but as we shall see, attracting and maintaining class and racial diversity could be a challenge. As Hometown was a public charter school, admission was free, but due to high demand it was governed by a lottery (students from a zone immediately surrounding the school were given first priority, but all Atlanta Public School system students were eligible to apply). Circa 2013, the elementary school was composed of about 30 percent African Americans and 57 percent Caucasians, per school records; in the middle school grades, 50 percent were African American while 33 percent were Caucasian (and about 10–11 percent at both levels were recorded as multiracial). As a measure of relative incomes among Hometown Charter School families, approximately 20 percent of students qualified for free or reduced-price lunch in 2014. Notably, that percentage had been twice as high just four years earlier, a fact that demonstrated rapid change in the neighborhood's demographic makeup, perhaps, but also indicated that white, relatively affluent residents were those more likely to apply to Hometown, given that the close-by non-charter public elementary school had far higher percentages of free/reduced lunch and of African Americans.

My own interview sample skewed toward the whiter and somewhat more affluent end of the parent population. My goal had been to recruit parents, teachers, and administrators who roughly reflected the demographics of the school as a whole, with awareness of race and ethnicity but with special attention to class. Like the school itself, I used qualification for free or reduced lunch as a proxy for determining which households were on the lower end of the school's income spectrum. I gave most interviewees a survey form to fill out that included a space for self-reporting annual household income before taxes, whether

they qualified for free or reduced lunch, and their racial and/or ethnic self-identifications. To recruit individuals, I (and occasionally my
graduate research assistants from Georgia State University) approached
people personally at school-sponsored events such as parent coffees and
beginning-of-the-year orientations. I also sent out an announcement
in the school newsletter seeking interviewees, explaining clearly that I
wished to have a broad variety of Hometown perspectives included. Ultimately, self-selection played an important role in determining which
individuals came forward and carried through with the interview:
Which parents were most interested in the project? Who had free time
to participate? Who attended school events, many (but not all) of which
were held during school hours? Who replied to my follow-up emails?

In the end, we conducted interviews with fifty-two adults, of whom
thirty-nine completed my demographic survey. Of these, three indicated
that their households qualified for free or reduced lunch. This was a significantly smaller percentage than the roughly 20 percent who received
free or reduced lunch at the school. Nonetheless, those who responded
reported a rather broad range of annual incomes: from about $12,000 to
$340,000, with a median of $104,000.[5] According to one recent definition, these values indicate that using income on its own, some of the
households might well be defined as "upper middle class," while many of
them would be just "middle class," or in a few cases, below middle class.[6]
Yet class as identity and social positioning includes more than income.
Most, perhaps all, of my interviewees (irrespective of race or income)
were college educated, and by occupation they included academics, art-
ists, teachers, lawyers, and other professionals with graduate degrees, as
well as stay-at-home parents. Most were parents of Hometown students,
but some were teachers and administrators at the school (and several
were both; just two interviewees were staff members who did not have
school-age children at either Hometown or other schools). Teachers and
administrators represented some (though not all) of the lower end of
reported incomes.

In short, while a few interviewees reported relatively limited incomes,
I refer to the group at large as middle class in recognition that most of
them shared concerns that reflected high levels of education (at least college) and that were not shaped presently by experiences of great material
need or of extreme wealth. Furthermore, their stories reflect many of the

themes other researchers have identified as part of intensive, middle-class parenting, such as great attention to minimizing health risks and to protecting and furthering the social-emotional well-being of the child as individual. More specific than this, Hometowners' perspectives were shaped by an urban, gentrifying environment in which racial and class diversity was an acknowledged, often explicitly valued, and sometimes thorny part of the immediate neighborhood experience.

Of the forty-two adults whom I (or in a few cases, one of my assistants) interviewed at least once (some were interviewed twice), thirty-nine can be identified as white, Caucasian, or European American (including five who identified as also Hispanic, Chicano, Jewish, or Filipino); nine as African American, African, or Black (at least one of whom was also Jewish); and four in other ways (e.g., Mexican American or Middle Eastern). Throughout this book, wherever possible, I identify individuals using the racial/ethnic category they offered to me for themselves in the survey that was administered at most interviews. This explains why my categorizations appear to be inconsistent: for example, one person is "white" and another is "Caucasian."

I made this choice out of awareness that my own perceptions might not always be reflective of individuals' own experience, or might dull certain forms of diversity that existed in tension with the rather bifurcating categories of Black and white that dominate U.S. discourse. Thus in one case, an interviewee I might have described as white described herself as Filipino American. Another whom I perceived as African American called himself African and Jewish. For lack of another option, I do fall back on my own perceptions at times: because my survey was introduced midway through the research, when some interviews had already been completed, a quarter of my respondents did not complete it and so did not answer that particular question. Of these, I guessed that about a quarter would identify as Black/African American; the remaining appeared to me as white, based on phenotype as I perceived it. As the examples mentioned above remind, these categorizations likely reflect assumptions made by other social actors in the community but may not necessarily line up with the individuals' own sense of identity.

My goal is to provide a general sense of the range of backgrounds and social identities included at Hometown and particularly within my interview sample, without flattening that range any more than necessary for brevity. To this end, I mention the race/ethnicity of each interviewee as they come up, along with other details such as professional status, household makeup, and/or marital status. For individuals discussed repeatedly in the book, I reiterate their racial/ethnic and other identifiers at least once in each chapter to assist the reader in keeping track; each person has been given a unique pseudonym. Occasionally I omit a person's race/ethnicity or school role (or do not use an interviewee's pseudonym when discussing her unique administrative role) when I feel that inclusion of that information could make her too readily and specifically identifiable to readers within the community. A few individuals mentioned only passingly are not given names. Throughout the book, I omit specific information about household incomes for the sake of interviewees' confidentiality, though I often offer additional details that speak to households' relative resources, including their professional occupations or (where relevant) qualification for subsidized school lunch. I generally include marital status as well because it speaks to the relative security of economic and other resources in households (through the presence of either one or two potential wage earners and caregivers); notably, the overwhelming majority of parents in my interview group were married.

To be clear, I do not attempt to map cleanly what people of one race or professional affiliation believed or did as opposed to those in other categories. Rather, I seek to provide detail that gives a grounded sense of a community conversation that was rich with shared beliefs and experiences as well as unsettling conflicts and divergent affiliations. And while, as we shall see, race certainly was a relevant form of social difference in this community, I found, similarly to Lareau (2003, 4, 240), that in many cases my white and African American interviewees described very similar sensibilities concerning parenting and specifically children's food. A few African Americans described feeling somewhat marginal to, or learning to become more aligned with, the culture of food that seemed broadly normative at Hometown, but others were quite inside it. Thus it did not seem to me that these differences could be attributed to racial identity in any simplistic way. Race cannot be, and is not here, ignored as a component of people's experiences of social difference in this community, but its relevance to particular social conflicts is always intersectional: not experienced in isolation, but always entangled with factors such as class and gender in individuals' lives and in their talk about food and about others in their social worlds (Collins and Bilge 2016). In this book, I strive to keep all of these aspects in view, but I often choose to highlight the significance of class because it describes most efficiently the forms of difference that seemed to *make* the most difference in this community when it came to children's food.

Finally, I must note that my interviewees included forty-two women (of whom all were mothers of school-aged children) as compared with only ten men (of whom eight were parents of school-aged children). I entered this project aware of the feminization of the work of childcare and feeding in the United States (DeVault 1991), even as I sought to interview both male and female parents, teachers, staff, and caregivers. The feminization of food work can be understood as a burden—the famous "second shift" that falls disproportionately to women—but it can also be a source of satisfaction and a means to demonstrate resource-intensive forms of "good mothering" (Hochschild 1990; Cairns and Johnston 2015, 11, 21; Maher, Fraser, and Wright 2010). Because women in the United States often *care* a great deal about food, recruitment for a research project on food organically slants toward women (Cairns and Johnston 2015, 4). Moreover, the teaching profession is dominated by women, meaning that they were more likely present at the school than were men, whether in their roles as involved parents or as teachers and administrators. Thus self-selection through people's differential presence at the school and interest in the topic yielded me far more women than men as interviewees.

Yet while it is crucial to acknowledge that child feeding and the broader labor associated with school volunteering and other community activities rests unevenly on women, the concerns I describe are not exclusively women's. Men who volunteered for my study were often the primary cooks for their families, whether due to professional schedules, convenience, interest, and/or talent. A few were not primary food preparers, yet they were involved intimately enough to speak knowledgeably and thoughtfully about how food decisions were carried out in their families. A few were chefs. Though I did not specifically ask people about their gender or sexual identities, a few were in same-sex marriages or long-term relationships. A few were divorced or single, but most were married and all, to my knowledge, were cisgendered. As with the topic of race, I indicate the gender identity of individuals as they are introduced, but I do not attempt to differentiate "male" versus "female" approaches to nutritional discourses that appeared to me rather shared among interviewees.

In fact, parents with whom I spoke at Hometown by and large shared—across race, gender, and a fairly broad swath of income levels—many ideas about how to be. They presented a certain brand of middle classness: one that leaned toward a preference for the nonpretentious and nonjudgmental, that valued a "neighborhood" experience and a politics of inclusion. They tended to show an attunement to issues such as the environment and animal welfare, the importance of social-emotional learning for children, and a desire to be sensitive about racial, ethnic, and class difference. Even so, I draw out how awareness of differences within and just beyond the community came forth and created discomfort and occasional conflict, not least in talk about food.

An Ethnography Close to Home

There is much that I share with my interviewees from Hometown. For example, I am a white, highly educated, middle-class, cisgendered woman with two school-aged children who is concerned and often frustrated about their nutrition. Thus when people ask me whether I have pursued this research because of my own experience as a mother, the short answer is yes: inevitably, my own experiences as a mother of two children living in a community similar—but not identical—to the one that is the focus of this ethnography shaped my feeling that there was something important to be said and understood about the way parents engage with children's food. The longer answer is a bit more complex: previous anthropological work based in Russia, conducted well before I became a mother, had already gotten me interested in how consumer choices are tied up with class, morality, and self-fashioning (Patico 2005, 2008, 2009). Being a mother subsequently taught me about the many choices that were to be made for children, the many books and articles available for guidance, and the relentless and ongoing nature of trying to decide what was "good enough" while balancing concerns of time, money, and energy.

I embarked upon the study thinking that a central question of my research in Atlanta would be to see how parents balanced the "priceless" value of their children with the very materially bounded possibilities of consumer choice, and how this differed by class and income among working families. While those questions remained relevant, what really got my attention among the middle-class parents I later interviewed at Hometown was that, even if some were more concerned than others about saving time and money, the main axis of tension seemed not to be about providing what was "good enough" for the children versus deciding what was "too much" to spend. More accurately, it was a tension between (what felt like) controlling their children too much and not controlling them enough. On another level, as we shall see, it was a tension between their desires for safety and comforting sameness versus their embrace of a more challenging kind of diversity and inclusiveness in their communities.

Ethnographic research is rigorously, deeply empirical but also highly and inevitably personal since the researcher herself is personally involved in drawing people out through conversation or observing them informally, always having some effect on the situation through her presence. The Hometown neighborhood and school were located about a fifteen- to twenty-minute drive, depending on traffic, from my own home and the public schools my own children attended. Parents' clothing styles, their worries about food, and their political beliefs (often left implicit in our conversations, but generally left leaning) were all familiar to me from my own communities and often quite similar to my own. Even so, I listened to these parents in a different way than I listened to the parents of my own children's friends: with a different kind of curiosity and a distinct form of engagement as an ethnographer. I had made a conscious choice to choose a school that included class and racial diversity, which was part of the rationale for my choice of Hometown as a research site, but I also had made an intentional decision not to work at the schools my own children attended. In this way, local players and debates were fresh to me and discussions about school policies did not affect my own children, which made it easier to engage with a sense of impartial curiosity.

In addition to conducting audio-recorded (and subsequently transcribed) interviews that averaged about an hour to an hour and a half with each adult who consented to participate (as noted, some participants were interviewed twice), I engaged in participant observation in a wealth of Hometown contexts. I was welcomed to share family dinners in several households, which created the opportunity not only to see what families really prepared at home, but to have more organic contexts for discussion of food, meals, and parenting that triggered different thoughts than an interview in a café might do. I asked some of my more eager interviewees if I could go grocery shopping with them, but as this was difficult for them to schedule I ended up doing so with only one mother and her middle-school-aged daughter, Renee and Tara. A few individuals agreed to submit to me food journals that recorded what they had fed their families over the course of one week and how they (the adults journaling) had felt about what had been consumed.

I also spent a great deal of time on campus at Hometown. One of the primary jobs I gave my two research assistants was to help me help the school by providing extra supervision and staff support during the elementary grades' lunchtime. We took turns so that one of us was there daily. These sessions also provided informal chances to see how children were interacting among themselves and with adults around food. In addition, I spent a few afternoons observing lunchtime at a close-by public elementary school, the school I call "Englewood" in this book. I attended a healthy food fair held during school hours at another public school in the greater neighborhood. While these observations were too slight to give me a basis for extended comparisons among schools, they did help me to contextualize what was distinct and notable about Hometown's food service and other routines. Further, I observed and helped out with a middle school enrichment class on food education at Hometown, which was linked to the care of a vegetable garden that was being maintained on school grounds. I also sat in on middle school nutrition classes. Later, I co-led a course on food and culture together with the school's new chef for an entire term, and I was able to collect written and oral materials from some of the students as part of this study.

Importantly, I attended events such as parent coffees at Hometown, where I listened to the content of workshops on topics such as internet safety and child discipline techniques. I often spoke with parents afterward, sometimes meeting new people willing to be interviewed. I frequented parent groups that met in the evenings, such as a Conscious Discipline group and a Health and Wellness parent group. In these contexts, in addition to discussing potential events, school policy issues, classroom snack guidelines, and so on, we discussed our own children and our ongoing challenges with them or their recent successes. I participated in kind, sharing when it was my turn about things that had been going on with my own children, such as a disciplinary issue or a food allergy test. I did, however, alert members to the fact that I was playing a dual role there as not just an interested parent but also a researcher working at Hometown.

Where did my informal, more personal interactions end and the research in a relatively "objective" mode begin? This line is difficult, even impossible, to draw in any ethnographic research context, but perhaps especially so in a case where the researcher and her "subjects" share so much. On the other hand, anthropologists working in their "own" societies may be considered "native," but they never fully share the subject positions of those whom they study, who are variably positioned by gender, class, race, education, and the intersection of all these factors, or even just by the fact that being engaged in research creates a different perspective from that which comes with the practical immersion others experience in the same contexts (Narayan 1993). Still, such research "is challenging because it requires those who are already embedded in particular cultural and social processes to subject themselves and their most intimate surroundings to the same forms of critical analysis as they would any other . . . there is no possibility of a truly uncontaminated point of view. But in highlighting one's positionalities, which may shift radically over the course of one's career, one hopes to make explicit the social and structural parameters at play" (Young and Meneley 2005, 2–3).

In the course of my research at Hometown, I often found myself simultaneously jarred by critical, scholarly realizations about what I was observing *and* being moved in far more immediate ways because of my shared experiences with those in the room. For example, when parents discussed the importance of teaching children moderation in eating and we learned about the importance of "self-regulation" in parent workshops, I reflected on the ways these concerns instantiated the emotional self-management that has been highlighted in other studies of neoliberalism and affect; at the same time, I shared experiences about my own children in these settings and often found myself thinking, *That's a good tip! That way of talking empathetically about feelings really is helpful in moments of conflict with my daughter.* Or I might compare my own practices with those of Hometown parents, thinking to myself during an interview, *I should be emphasizing to my son that fresh fruit is a wonderful everyday dessert, just like this other parent says she does.*

I also needed to pay attention to how people's perceptions of me as a university researcher and/or as a relatively local mother influenced their responses. In interviews, I attempted to leave my questions open-ended enough that interviewees did not feel unduly guided to a seemingly expected answer. Other questions were highly specific (for example, Where do you do grocery shopping? What do you look for in a breakfast cereal?), since asking concrete questions is often an effective way of inviting individuals to think about their decision-making processes. Each semistructured interview traveled similar but unique territory, depending upon the responses of the interviewees and the follow-up questions these prompted in me. Occasionally interviewees asked me for my own opinions or experiences with food and parenting. When asked, I answered truthfully though fairly briefly, hoping to keep the focus on their opinions (and not mine) but also to engage in meaningful reciprocity and transparency. In one case I recall, an interviewee I had grown to know pretty well acknowledged that she had begun to feel acutely self-conscious talking so much about herself, and she asked me to speak to my own experiences. I felt it was important to do so when asked, as part of my human relationship with those who were entrusting their thoughts, feelings, and experiences to me.

A final note: One of my children has a severe food allergy. I made a decision that while I would include similar experiences of Hometown parents as they came up, the topic of allergies would not be a major focus of the book. A "truly uncontaminated view" of any of these phenomena of food and parenting, in any cultural context, is impossible; this is inherent to the nature of ethnographic research. Many of the conversations I had with parents were ultimately about their children's safety, health, and happiness and how parents could best nurture and protect those. I certainly shared many of those concerns, yet I felt able to introduce critical distance in my work as an ethnographer, to listen closely and to gain new perspectives through listening to these others so attentively. I felt less able, or perhaps simply less willing, to do so when it came to a topic that was, for me (like many other food allergy parents), linked with memories of the ER and with fears far more immediate than those raised by most other food concerns. Certainly the world of food allergies deserves more research, particularly because of the ways that they escalate parents' (and children's) senses of risk in connection with food. But for the purposes of this book, I take up questions of food, anxiety, and parenting through a broader lens, focusing on topics to which all parents in my sample could speak.

Overview of the Book

Chapter 1 draws upon ethnographic data to examine concretely the primary food concerns of parents in this community, contextualizing these against historical trends in nutritional recommendations in the United States. Rather than using "neoliberalism" as the frame for Hometowners' concerns, this chapter homes in to consider parents' experiences of what Ulrich Beck (1992) has described as "risk society," where people confront and manage the uncertainties and dangers inadvertently created through industrial production. The Hometown milieu is best described as postindustrial, in that it is both of and deeply resistant to the highly commodified economy of children's food. By trusting or rejecting certain foods and brands, adults worked to understand and to address fears and challenges they experienced with and for their children.

Chapter 2 moves beyond nutritional discourse to consider the more social and emotional content of parents' food talk. Much of this talk was oriented toward the concern to socialize and to train but not to overly limit children, project a negative adult persona, or come across as judgmental of others' choices. The popular concept of the overprotective "helicopter parent" was an expression of these ambivalences, visible in national media and parenting blogs as well as in the ongoing commentaries of Atlanta parents; overattentiveness and food anxiety were seen as potentially negative influences on children. This chapter explores how food and feeding are wrapped up with models of personhood, that is, with conceptions of the kind of person one should be in order to be a good parent or a healthy child and socially attractive to others. In particular, we shall see how power struggles around children's food reflect ideas about individuality, relationships, and the fuzzy boundaries of the self.

Chapter 3 listens not only to parents' discourses but also to children themselves and the ways that they engaged with adults' food meanings. My participant observation in the elementary cafeteria yielded examples of the questions children asked about food and nutrition, the ways they monitored one another's engagements with food, and how they performed their own healthiness or lack thereof in a collective setting. While co-teaching a middle school enrichment class on food and culture, I learned how students were quite aware of "junk" foods such as chips and candy as transgressions. Yet by the same token, they understood these transgressions as expected and normal for children in ways they were not for adults. Likewise, adults spoke of children as naturally enjoying sugars, simple foods such as macaroni and cheese, and other less explicitly healthful foods. In this way, the qualities attributed to foods also provided means for children and adults to recognize childhood and adulthood; "healthy" food was associated with the knowledge, discernment, and self-control of maturity, while childhood was associated with pleasure and lack of moderation. This immoderate space of childhood was under extreme scrutiny, yet also valued and defended in ways that invite us to consider how adults ambivalently relate to "neoliberal" prescriptions for consumer self-discipline.

Chapter 4, the final ethnographic chapter of the book, considers how concerns about children's food are part and parcel of people's participation in and recognition of their urban, gentrifying community: a means of creating their urban, middle-class civic identities. As a general rule, parents who participated in my research held inclusivity and diversity (understood primarily but not only in terms of class and race) as explicitly valuable and beneficial to their school community. At the same time, after-school childcare programs and other school events were sometimes cause for consternation to food-aware parents: bags of snack chips, cupcakes with bright blue frosting, or Rice Krispie treats sometimes circulated through classroom birthday parties, illicit lunchroom trades, and impromptu cooking classes. Food comparisons across families and observed differences between school and home were often fraught by concern for children's physical well-being, but these concerns and their expression were also constrained by the preference for nonjudgmental, politically circumspect and socially aware attitudes. These sensibilities themselves index socioeconomic status and reflect class cultures, but explicit talk of status or prestige was submerged in this urban child-rearing vision, where the language of whole foods and wholesomeness coexists carefully with that of progressivism and social inclusivity.

The book's conclusion reflects further on how Hometown conceptualizations of parental care and engagement bespeak the neoliberal labor burdens middle-class parents take upon themselves as individuals, and how these practices can work at cross purposes with their politics of inclusivity. I draw comparisons between contemporary U.S. discourses and postsocialist European perspectives to raise questions about how those burdens and challenges might be differently imagined.

That, ultimately, is the provocation presented by this book: when we interrogate the assumptions that link our constructions of childhood, nutrition, and neoliberal responsibility, what new avenues for conceptualizing well-being and community might open up?

1

Discerning the "Real" from the "Junk"

Managing Children's Food in the Postindustrial United States

Many of my very first encounters with Hometown parents took place at the school's monthly morning coffees. Here mothers and fathers gathered to chat and to be informed, their informal conversations often bookending featured presentations by teachers, counselors, hired consultants, or the school's executive director. I met Jan one morning as parents drank coffee and milled outdoors in front of the elementary school, and her impromptu narrative conveyed—albeit in brief, crystallized, and personal form—how Hometown parents' efforts to protect their children from unhealthful industrial foods constituted rather intense forms of mental and emotional labor.

Introducing myself and describing my research to her, I highlighted that I wanted to explore "what parents worried about" when it came to feeding their children. Jan was in her element here, offering quickly, "I worry about sugar" and about all the "non-food" children seem to eat; "I worry a *lot*." Jan, a white married mother, continued that artificial sweeteners were even worse than sugar. She had seen something in the news about the artificial sweetener aspartame being added to milk and not being required to be listed as an ingredient on the label ("I'm not sure if it was regular or flavored milk, which you [already] kind of know is not healthy"). Her elementary-aged son, after recently finding a worm in an apple, had complained that he did not want to eat raw fruits anymore. Jan had explained to him that when you get fruit from the can, the worm has already been mashed in there and you don't have a choice but to eat it without knowing; and she explained to me that her own food awareness had been shaped by her parents, who were farmers. Now Jan and her husband owned a successful food business in an upscale Atlanta neighborhood.

Jan worried about sugar, about foods that were not really food, and about foods that were misrepresented or underexplained by their labels: "I worry a *lot*." Some readers of this book might find concerns like Jan's so familiar and identifiable as to be unremarkable; others, on the contrary, may find them more unfamiliar or striking, and either commendable or distasteful in their high degree of awareness about ingredients, processing methods, and labels. This chapter sets the scene for the broader discussions of neoliberal selfhood, class, and community that are to come in this book by providing an overview of some of the shared food worries and objectives of Hometown parents. Immersing in these details, readers to whom these concerns feel close to home may begin asking new questions about why they are so compelling after all. Others may find them newly legible and identifiable, as I endeavor to show how such food worries are organically (no pun intended!) interrelated with many other aspects of parents' and children's everyday lives, including the day-to-day rhythms of work, school, and extracurricular activities. Hometowners' talk about material and mundane food choices is depicted here not to document what these families (self-reportedly) ate, but rather to provide a vivid impression of the ongoing mental and emotional effort that they focused on food, particularly for their children.

In addition, this chapter frames food as one of the key ways in which adults confront and manage the uncertainties and dangers of living in a moment of postindustrial modernity. If industrial modernity was oriented toward solving the problem of *lack* through technological ingenuity, a more recent form of modernity—what noted sociologist Ulrich Beck (1992) has called risk society—is oriented toward identifying and minimizing the risks to human health and well-being that have resulted from those very efforts at "progress," such as industrial food production. Thus, Beck argues, while a previous generation was concerned primarily with the ideal of ensuring equal *opportunity* across categories of class, gender, and race, risk society is preoccupied with the ideal of *safety*—in a context where one's material and cultural resources can offer a relatively greater or lesser degree of (perceived) protection from risk. In this way, a generalized situation of risk is refracted through, and tends to reinforce, existing relations of class inequality, even as it dwells in the language of protection rather than that of prestige or propriety.

The United States is postindustrial inasmuch as it has shifted from industrial production to service industries as the main locus of economic growth and employment. Beyond this, I use the term "postindustrial" to refer to a situation in which many American consumers—including many Hometowners—inevitably engage with industrially produced foodstuffs and incorporate these into their food repertoires, even as they also push "beyond" industrial production in their cautious, cynical judgments about these foods and their explicit valuation of practices such as home cooking and local farming. These practices can appear traditional or preindustrial but are, as articulated and managed today, inherently in counterpoint with and in response to risk society's industrial ills.

Hometown beliefs and practices are not universally shared by Americans, of course, nor do they represent any generic U.S. middle class. Yet inasmuch as most of my interlocutors were highly educated people who tended to pay a good deal of attention to food, it is not surprising that their concerns tended to reflect the warnings and guidelines set forth by standard-setting media sources in the United States like the *New York Times*, popular parenting blogs, and high-selling parenting books. Over the course of the twentieth and early twenty-first centuries persistent and intense attention has been paid to nutrition in the United States, but there also have been significant shifts and discontinuities in terms of which concerns are most foregrounded, which foods most praised or vilified. These shifts do not represent just changes in fashion nor simple advances in modern nutritional science but inevitably take form vis-à-vis evolving systems of industrial labor, emotional labor, moral frameworks, and governance.

Nutritional Trends in the United States

The Industrial Revolution brought changes in the ways Europeans and Americans ate. Noted anthropologist Sidney Mintz (1986) illustrated this famously for the case of sugar: slave labor in the Caribbean yielded new supplies of inexpensive sugar in England, and what was once a luxury enjoyed only by elites now became part of the British industrial labor force's quick fix of calories and energy, particularly in the form of sweetened tea and bread with jam. "As the first imported luxury food to become a cheap daily necessity of the masses," writes Mintz, "sucrose epitomized the success of a rising industrial economy in tying the consumption of the workers to their increasing productivity" (Mintz 1996, 63). Having all the sugar you wanted was considered "eating like a king," given its continuing signification of privilege at the time; but in line with today's concerns about excess dietary sugars and carbohydrates and the championing of more complex starches and whole grains for health, Mintz (1986) links the rise of sugar with the impoverishment of the British working-class diet.[1]

Beyond sugar, the Industrial Revolution promoted new ways to construct social identities through food and other consumption. In the realm of nutrition, consumer discernment was guided by a new set of nutritional experts who were oriented especially toward the prevention of nutritional deficiencies (Scrinis 2015, 12, Bentley 2014). In the United States, the early 1900s was a time of growing awareness of the role of vitamins in human nutrition, which yielded new attention to the importance of consuming fruits and vegetables (Bentley 2014, 26–29). This was also an era when the nation's first school lunch programs were created to combat malnutrition and to encourage immigrant families to adopt the foodways of the established middle class; this form of food socialization functioned as "basic civics training" (Levine 2008, 5–6). By 1946, the National School Lunch Act had been passed under Truman (Levine 2008, 71–72), triggering ongoing debate around how school lunches could address poverty and how this project could be balanced against concerns about local and federal costs. Much responsibility for nutrition was still based within the household, of course: the early twentieth century also gave rise to the ideal of a "mother consumer." Along and in conjunction with the provision of emotional care, her tasks included choosing the proper things for her family from the expanded array of available consumer goods, guided by expert advice (Bentley 2014, 7). Industrially prepared foods, including jarred baby food, promoted both through nutritional guidelines and as a convenience commodity, had taken the fore by the mid-1940s and 1950s, eclipsing breastfeeding and scratch cooking (Bentley 2014).

Yet the 1960s saw the beginnings of risk society, ushering in an increase in public mistrust of industry and government as well as rising concerns about food components such as sodium, sugar, and preservatives, including in baby food (Bentley 2014, 74). In turn, the championing of "natural" motherhood, which emphasized women's instinctive and intuitive knowledge, and "natural" (nonindustrial) foods surged in the 1970s through the 1990s, even as nutritional experts remained important and the roles of government and public health institutions—as well as the food industry's marketing strategies—all intensified (104, 117; see also Levine 2009; Scrinis 2015; Rothman 2016). The USDA's Dietary Goals (later Guidelines) for Americans were established in 1977, advocating limits on foods containing sodium, cholesterol, saturated fat, and sugar (Hite 2014, 6). Meanwhile, direct marketing of foods to children expanded, employing tactics such as placing popular cartoon characters on packaging (Elliott 2008, 2010).

Food science historian Gyorgy Scrinis (2015, 12) characterizes the late twentieth century as the era of "good and bad nutritionism," a time when the attention of nutritional experts shifted away from the risk of vitamin deficiencies and toward the definition of "good" and "bad" foods as such, judged so for their roles in the prevention or causation of conditions such as heart disease (see also Hite 2014, 6). In the 1980s, sugar was one of the first food villains, to be replaced by fat in the 1990s (Scrinis 2015; McKay 1993). In *The Picky Eater*, a parenting help book of the 1990s, McKay (1993, 16) railed against what she described as the extremism and oversimplicity of such trends.

> Remember the 1980s and the Big Sugar Scare? It seemed that everywhere we looked we were being told to hold the sugar. As it turns out, sugar isn't all that evil after all. True, we don't need it and it's a good idea to reduce the sugar in our children's overall diet, but it's not the major health concern we were told it was. But now we're in the 90s and we have the Fat Scare. Yes, it would appear that the evil fat lurking in our food is gonna get us. Hang on. Adults should reduce the amount of fat in their total diet, but parents *must not* eliminate fat from a child's diet. About 40 to 50 percent of the energy spent by a baby and toddler should come from fat. Children over two years of age should have a diet composed of 30 to 35 percent fat.

Scrinis likewise calls the low-fat diet craze "the pinnacle of this oversimplified, decontextualized, and exaggerated interpretation of single-nutrient advice" in which scientists and laypeople alike were "encountering food primarily as a collection of nutrients," as opposed to thinking in terms of integrated meals and food traditions—the broader contexts of foods that are chosen and that interact in a person's diet and in food absorption—or about issues of food processing and production (Scrinis 2015, 7, 13). By the 2010s, low-fat diets had waned and sugar (alongside, for some, carbohydrates more generally) had returned as the primary foe, in what had become a "contested nutritional space . . . occupied by a host of competing expert and lay nutrition *sciences*—ranging from the governmental assertions of the DGA [USDA Daily Guidelines for Americans] to the weight management guidelines of Jenny Craig, Inc." and beyond (Broad 2014, 11).

Since the mid-1990s, Scrinis observes, the demonization of isolated food components has coexisted with attention to the benefits of certain foods seen as *optimizing* health. In this way the food industry further fetishizes the power of isolated food components to determine health; "superfoods" and omega-3 fatty acids are actively promoted in this new ideology of "functional nutrition." This approach still "constructs and preserves scientific authority," even as it more effectively commodifies certain nutrients (Scrinis 2015, 12–13). In a complex media environment, sources from governmental guidelines to countless health websites convey "a host of contradictory, targeted, and often profit-driven messages—and not an unquestioned conventional wisdom" (Broad 2014, 12). This is risk society in full force, where an excess of information is presented to the public, who in turn works to winnow and assess the data in the hopes of protecting their own (and their children's) well-being. In this context, experts such as nutritionist Kelly Dorfman (2013) have emerged to advise parents on how specific food decisions—either eliminations or supplements—may be used to treat health and behavioral problems on the rise in children, including attention-deficit/hyperactivity disorder (ADHD) and anxiety. (In fact, a few Hometown parents had had personal contact with Dorfman to explore such solutions for their own children.)

Whereas public concern in the United States in the early twentieth century had been focused on eliminating rickets, anemia, and low body weight, obesity—particularly child obesity—became a primary concern in the late twentieth century and early twenty-first. According to the Centers for Disease Control and Prevention (2018a), the percentage of children classified as obese has tripled since the 1970s, with about 20 percent of children and youth aged six to nineteen affected in 2015–2016. Obesity has been linked with long-term health consequences including diabetes, heart disease, high blood pressure, and cancers. The crisis has been blamed, in part, on the prevalence of food advertising aimed at children that promotes highly processed, high-sugar, and high-fat foods (Pomeranz, Lobstein, and Brownell 2009). Alarm about childhood obesity has also been linked with concerns over lost "family meals," maternal negligence, and the putative effects of women working outside of their homes (Maher, Fraser, and Wright 2010). Michelle Obama's "Let's Move" campaign set a goal to eliminate childhood obesity by 2030, but it was criticized by some for encouraging self-regulation by the food industry and voluntary partnership rather than mandating constraints on food ingredients or production (Huber 2012).

The application of the term "epidemic" to the observed rise of child obesity has brought about large increases in funding for obesity research (Moffat 2010). Yet the term also provokes panic and results in defining obesity as a disease, leading to emphasis on biological factors rather than environmental (such as local unavailability of grocery stores carrying fresh foods) and economic ones (such as poverty); and quantifying strategies such as BMI (body mass index) measurement can lead to the diagnosis of obesity in children who may or may not be seen as obese by their parents and teachers (Moffat 2010; Wright 2009; Broady and Meeks 2015; Guthman 2011).[2]

If approaches to obesity reduction tend to depend upon the nutritionist paradigm that prevails overall, in tension with it is a newer "food quality" approach that emphasizes the role of production processes and values traditional experience (Scrinis 2015, 22, 215). In one highly popular example, food writer Michael Pollan's *In Defense of Food* (2008) argues that much of what is sold and eaten these days is actually not food at all, but what once would have been called imitation food.[3] Though Pollan's philosophy counters what is understood to be a more mainstream, highly processed U.S. diet, anthropologists have attributed related views to contemporary Americans rather broadly: "good food" is "whole, pronounceable, identifiable ingredients, grown, cooked, eaten in moderation, shared, sociable, slow, hunger, vegetables, wild, omnivore, diversity, colorful, ethical, farmers' market. Safe. Rural associations"; bad food is "processed, unpronounceable, hidden ingredients, ready-made, bought, eaten alone, anti-social, fast, temptation, meat, domesticated, carnivore, uniformity, drab, unethical, supermarket. Risky. Urban associations" (Crowther 2013, 233; see also Counihan 1999).

In this scheme of value—which has clear anti-industrial and class tones but is not necessarily rarefied since it is echoed in best-selling books—"good" food is simple, "traditional," "safe," and "slow," as opposed to "unethical," "anti-social," and highly available "fast" food. These are not simply evaluations of nutritional components; they are moral evaluations directed at individual eaters and provisioners, and they speak more broadly to the ways in which different foods are understood to be part of, and to influence, the flow of social life. While contemporary American depictions of "good" and "bad" foods tend to focus on the nutritional content and, for some, the processing techniques and environmental impacts associated with particular food commodities, the moral valence of foods is not limited to these aspects but can also be shaped by questions of family or ethnic tradition, conceptions of the "local," and standards of sociability (e.g., Wentworth 2017; Mintz 1996). Notably in the United States, "good" foods are often those that require more investment of time by caretakers, and in some cases they also cost more; they are not necessarily easily accessed through the consumer marketplace but require more intensive resources, whether of time, knowledge, or money. As we shall see throughout this book, classed aesthetics of taste tend to link up material aspects of foods with far more abstract judgments having to do with understandings of proper selfhood and comportment as well as individual and community identity (Bourdieu 1984).

At Hometown, desires to have children eat "good" food were also tempered by awareness of how "good" intentions could go too far. Pollan (2008, 62) observes—commenting on a food fervor of which his own work undoubtedly must be considered part—that "orthorexia," or obsession with correct nutrition, has been considered by contemporary psychologists for status as a recognized pathology. Among many parents at Hometown, as we shall see, there was a great degree of concern about nutrition but also an explicit awareness that such concern *could* move into pathology for parents or children, whether in terms of an overattention to physical appearance (perhaps leading to eating disorders or self-esteem issues) or through other forms of food obsession.

Rather than assessing where the lines between pathological and prudent may lie, we will listen carefully to the terms through which parents themselves assessed the nutritional impacts and psychological healthiness of different approaches to food. As adults took up ideas from popular nutritional science as well as "foodie" critiques, they engaged in material, moral, and social labor that deployed not only nutritional knowledge—gleaned through a winnowing and stylizing of the diverse sets of dietary advice available—but also perceptions of their local social environment and their hopes and fears for the long-term health and emergent selfhood of their children. Parents' food talk exposed not individual pathology, then, but rather some of the recurrent pressure points of postindustrial, urban life.

Postindustrial Food: Defining and Advocating for the "Real"

Concerns that exemplified both nutritionist trends and critiques lodged by the likes of Scrinis and Pollan threaded through nutrition talk at Hometown. Parents spoke in terms of nutritional components such as carbohydrates and proteins; for many adults, the general category of "carbs" was suspect, devalued or less valued than proteins and vegetables. Conversely, vegetables were the category of food most universally understood as desirable and, perhaps, as most difficult to get children to eat enough of, though some parents were also concerned about getting their children adequate protein. In addition, some worried about specific additives such as artificial food dyes and reported avoiding these. There was broad consensus on sugar as one of the most problematic of food components, and a few parents noted that their families—usually their extended families—had histories of diabetes that made them particularly aware of their own sugar intake and of their children's. Excessive sugar intake has been linked with childhood obesity in the public imagination, and in these parents', but obesity was not their most explicit concern in most cases.[4] More common and explicit was their wariness of industrial food producers, as adults questioned the substance and safety of food commodities.

Their food milieu was postindustrial in that industrially processed and commodified foodstuffs were omnipresent and at least selectively used, yet also questioned, feared, and devalued.

Rebecca, a white, married parent active in the school's parent Health and Wellness Committee, was particularly attentive and informed on these issues. A transplanted New Englander, she was cheerful and casual yet intense in her demeanor. She told me that she was a "label reader" and that she was especially aware of trying to avoid sugar as well as soy. She thought her son might have a sensitivity to soy and that more generally "now the trend is kind of moving away from soy. I don't know what's right and what's wrong but soy is processed, so just avoiding that processed food I think is a good choice for our family." Concerns for her family's bodily health were intermingled with environmental and political ones:

> I also try to do humanely raised meat products, so. [JP: Can you, I know this might seem kind of obvious but what is your concern there in terms of humanely—is it for your family's health, is it for the animals, all of the above?] For the animals [JP: yeah] and for the environment. [JP: Uh-huh] Yeah, that's my concern. I don't really know if it affects us or not but I don't want those hormones going into my kids' bodies or the antibiotics being transferred, you know, by them ingesting the meat, so I don't want that for sure. But for me it's more just supporting a method of supplying our meat that is humane, so. . . .

Patronage of farmers' markets and community-supported agriculture as well as enthusiasm for home gardening and chicken or goat raising were not uncommon at Hometown, though not all families found such practices appealing, affordable, and feasible. More consistently, they mentioned avoidance of highly processed and packaged foods and set them in opposition to "real," homemade, or higher quality foods.

For example, Lila, a single working mother educated at one of Atlanta's historically Black colleges, explained that she had cut much of the sugar from her family's diet "because I just felt like the children didn't need it. I felt like everything that was in it—it wasn't real. It didn't taste right so let's just stop." When I asked her to explain to what degree she had eliminated sugar, she responded, "For me it's more or less natural sugar." She did a lot of juicing. Her children could have cookies or candy upon occasion, but not every day, and "it's still back to the quality, so we'll eat at [the local ice cream shop] before we eat at Zesto's [a fast-food chain] when it comes to ice cream." Lynn, a white former professional no longer working outside the home due to health issues, explained that her own illness had raised the whole family's awareness about eating and the importance of a low-sugar diet. She and her husband had "gotten their bluffing in early" by "brainwashing" their children to enjoy foods such as yogurt, avocado, and sweet potato when they were small. As a result,

L: I think they prefer real food for the most part. Except sweetened cereal. They really do like sugared cereal.

JP: What were the other examples of "unreal" food, if you will?

L: Tater tots . . . you know, frozen, prepackaged things. Not that they won't eat tater tots but they prefer potatoes made in the oven.

Highly processed and sugared foods were less "real," and Lynn suggested that sage and consistent parents could and should shape their children's tastes in favor of the real.

Even fresh produce could become less than real thanks to industrial agricultural processes. Pete, a Caucasian, married stay-at-home dad who volunteered frequently at Hometown, recounted that he recently had heard a report on National Public Radio that described how mass-produced fruits and vegetables, presumably not grown in the elements (wind, rain) that usually required and selected for hardiness, did not develop a protective shell and for that reason had lower vitamin content. "So certain apples like . . . I couldn't, I can't remember if it's Golden Delicious or which one it is, have . . . you know, the risk of being sugar water. Isn't that interesting?" While Pete was intrigued if perhaps concerned by this knowledge, other conversations about processed foods carried tones of disgust, sometimes mitigated by laughter.

For example, Noelle, an African American mother who worked from home and was highly involved as a volunteer at the school, emphasized how preservatives and other additives impacted the healthfulness of many foods. By way of explanation of her preference for organic and fresh products, Noelle connected industrialized food production with a poorer quality of life and expressed her own revulsion.

> I don't ever buy canned anything, not even beans, it's just—I just don't, 'cause it's gross! [laughs] [JP: You mean they just, like, look gross?] It's just gross once you put it in your body. It's so many preservatives. So it's just, I don't know, I wanna live a little bit longer and I look at—before us, you know, so long ago there weren't canned anything. Like a nature vibe and people lived long lives and all of sudden we found this easier way to preserve food and make it quick and it's like now we have all these illnesses, and I think they coincide together. . . . I see a lot of people [through her professional work] that [eat] TV dinners and then the next time I see them, they have high blood pressure . . . and the next time I see them they have diabetes and it's like: yeah, 'cause you're just having white sugar all the time with your coffee like every time I see you. White sugar, coffee, and Sweet'n Low [a saccharin sweeter]. It's like at some point these quick fixes to things, they do affect your body 'cause they're quick fixes and it makes your body say, "hey, what are you doing?" So I just think that we lived a really good life before all those things were put into it and you can live a life without those things and have a really good life. So I try not to even entertain it, you know? Some people, it's like, three for a dollar, so what? [laughs]

Noelle watched expenses and planned her family's menus carefully but rejected the notion that "three for a dollar" would be a good rationale for buying any low-quality, processed foods. Faye, in a similar mode, spoke of the past—"our ancestors" or "great-grandparents"—as representing more optimal nutritional practices than those encouraged by the contemporary industrial food system. She was a married working mother of two who placed special emphasis on avoiding processed, quick foods in favor of homemade meals.

> We don't even buy things out of cans. I wouldn't buy can broth or a box of broth. I would make it myself and put it in the freezer and I would

store it away. We don't eat, like, a box of macaroni and cheese. We don't usually eat a lot of grains either. However, I will, every once in a while, I will make some. If I do they are either soaked or sprouted before. If we are going to have rice, I'll soak it in whey . . . I know it's a bit extreme . . . and water at least for the morning, if not the night before. We do a lot of traditional food preparation. So we follow the Westin A. Price dietary guidelines.[5] It is kind of turning back to how our ancestors ate . . . probably how our great-grandparents ate before modern food and modern processed food.

Faye explained that people were surprised that she worked and still had time to cook in this way, but she said she simply made a routine of it and enjoyed it. "I feel like our family in general . . . for our health . . . I feel like it is a really important thing to do. See, I make everything from scratch . . . it's not hard."

Faye's comment seemed to place the moral onus on parents, emphasizing that parents are capable of choosing to provide wholesome food for their families since "it's not hard." She did mention, however, that she was able to arrange her work schedule so that she could come home a bit early in the late afternoon, when she started the family's dinner. Moreover, parents like Faye often did acknowledge at other times that their incomes allowed them to buy high-quality foods that not all families could attain. To paraphrase Beck (1992, 35), what seemed like individualized consumer responses to generalized risks inevitably did reflect and sustain existing socioeconomic inequalities as people brought resources of time, money, and knowledge to bear in the project. "A sufficiently well filled wallet puts one in a position to dine on eggs from 'contented hens' and salads from 'pampered heads of lettuce.' Education and attentiveness to information open up new possibilities of dealing with and avoiding risks." At Hometown, I often perceived that adults were mindful of the economic privilege and time investment some of their food choices reflected; yet those same choices held moral value that made them seem primarily *conscientious*, in this way also bypassing or seemingly transcending issues of material privilege.

Parents like Faye had the opportunity to mark not only their practical, moral, and (more implicitly) financial capabilities through avoidance of highly processed foods, but also their commitment to home and family as valued contexts for balanced eating. Meredith, a teacher and a white married mother of two, spoke in particularly emotional terms about what happened when a teenager who was her temporary ward insisted on eating Hot Pockets, a standard grocery store brand of frozen pastry with savory fillings. He ate it along with a medication he needed to take daily, and for him nothing else would do; no healthier substitute brand could be found.

> It was a challenge for me the first time I bought the giant pack of . . .'Cause it doesn't feel like that's . . . even though it's hard, I feel like one of the things that I'm tasked with as an adult person in this world is feeding my family healthy food. And so, when I can't, when I'm too busy, or when I'm pulling a frozen pizza out of the freezer, there's that little bit of heartbreak for me. I don't wrap myself around it. And so, there's that little bit of heartbreak, when I smell that smell of the microwave food in the morning. But, it's okay. That's how it works. I don't think I'm a food snob. I sometimes might be. . . .

Meredith struggled to reconcile herself to the compromises made due to time or to other family members' desires. She preferred not to think of herself as a "snob," yet she had deep emotional reactions to the idea of household members consuming ready-made foods on her watch.

One of the places where the threat of undesirable, packaged, unhealthful foods emerged as a special concern was in discussion of scenarios where adults other than the speakers were providing foods eaten by their kids. When I asked Irene, a married Caucasian mother of two who worked in communications technology, whether her daughters talked about the snacks they were given in their classrooms at Hometown, she responded,

> Less this year, but they have in the past. Snacks used to be one of the first things when you ask them about their day. Here is what I did at recess and here's what I had at snack. [laughs] And, yeah, I was a little appalled sometimes. Sometimes it was great, and sometimes

it's like. . . . They kept telling me they have gummies and I'm like, who the hell is bringing in gummies for a snack? And then, I realized that they meant those little gummy fruits. [JP: Fruit snacks.] The fruit snacks, yeah. It still kind of appalled me, but at least I get why someone thought that was a snack instead of like gummy bears. [JP: Right.] But, still. [JP: So what do you find appalling about that?] They are just rubbery fakeness. [laughs]

Irene said she was "appalled" by "rubbery fakeness," though she noted that the fruit snacks (highly processed but containing and marketed as "fruit") were better—or at least more understandable—than gummy bears (categorized as candy) would have been.

Fakeness was at issue, too, when Meredith, both a mother and a teacher at Hometown, talked about the snack foods that middle school students at Hometown seemed to favor.

Everything's red, red, red, red. I've noticed that, and I noticed that they often eat them in the morning, so they arrive eating them. If a package is opened anywhere in the vicinity of the other children, children flock to the small package. So I'm not sure that kids are getting a whole serving of it, 'cause they seem to share it with their friends. So there's lots of sharing around it. . . . I don't see what's in their lunch boxes as much. But in terms of snacks, the snack preference tends to be chips of some sort, a bunch of salty things. Nobody cares. No.

Fakeness and unnaturalness were seen as problematic themselves, but particularly notable is that these mothers were concerned that certain other parents evidently were unaware of or did not care about this.

Indeed, hints of conflict emerged when parents talked about items that were shared across families at the school, such as birthday treats or shared daily classroom snacks. Concerned parent volunteers and an administrator had collaborated to compile a list of suggestions that was distributed to Hometown parents to guide their snack contributions. In addition to highlighting various logistical concerns, the handout instructed parents that "the best snacks have simple, recognizable ingredients."

Figure 1.1: Annie's gummy fruit snacks (photo by author).

Figure 1.2: Takis Fuego, the red, spicy chip popular among students at Hometown (photo by author).

Thanks to our wonderful parents, Hometown Elementary students are provided with a healthy afternoon snack to keep their brains and bodies energized for the remainder of the school day. Parents volunteer to bring snacks for the classroom based on a schedule coordinated by your teachers or a snack coordinator parent.

Our Favorite Snacks

Based on teacher feedback, these are some of the most popular snacks among our students: 1. Fruit Pre-washed and cutup (if needed) 2. String Cheese 3. Crackers 4. Gold Fish 5. Graham Crackers 6. Carrot / Celery Sticks 7. Applesauce 8. Mini Bagels 9. Yogurt "squeezers" 10. Mini Sandwiches: Cream cheese & Jelly, Turkey & Cheese, Cucumber & Cheese

The best snacks have simple, recognizable ingredients. Whenever possible please try to avoid artificial colors and sweeteners, high fructose corn syrup, and partially hydrogenated oils. You may also super-charge your snacks by combining a protein with a complex carbohydrate. Combinations such as cheese and whole grain crackers, mini sandwiches, graham crackers and nut butter (providing the class has no nut allergies), or fruit or veggies with a dairy-based dip or hummus can provide a great source of balanced nutrition and sustained energy. Your teachers may provide you with additional snack ideas based on class preferences.

Convenience!

Convenience is very important to our teachers. Snacks should be easy to serve and quick to clean-up. For this reason teachers commonly use school-supplied coffee filters to distribute snacks. For snacks that require the use of plates, bowls or utensils (such as dips, yogurt, cottage cheese, etc.), or anything that needs additional prep before serving, ask your teachers ahead of time if they can accommodate. Students love creative snacks, but we want to be sure that it can work based on the available time and resources in the classroom.

Serving Size

School-aged children require 100–200 calories per snack. You may refer to the Nutrition Facts on a packaged item for serving size and caloric information. For produce, the typical serving is a small piece of fruit (such as a small apple or pear) or a half-cup of a cut-up fruit or vegetable (carrots, pineapple, or melon, for example). There really is no one-size-fits-all rule for serving size so we leave it to you to use your best judgment. Your teachers will ensure that the snack is distributed to the class based on the quantity provided.

Preparation and Storage

Fresh fruits and vegetables should be thoroughly washed. Ideally, anything requiring a knife to portion should be cut-up in advance. Some of our classrooms have a mini-refrigerator, but all teachers have access to refrigeration and can keep 1–2 days of fresh items stored. For pantry items, available storage space can vary in the classroom. Please speak to your teachers if you would like to store more than 2 days of snacks.

Allergies and Special Dietary Considerations

Allergies and special dietary considerations vary by classroom. You will be notified if there are any ingredients to avoid entirely due to food allergies. Depending on the allergy, food sensitivity or special diet, some parents may choose to provide their own snack or a backup snack for their student on a daily basis. Please follow the allergy guidelines set up for your classroom.

Figure 1.3: Hometown class snack guidelines.

While ideals like Irene's and Meredith's were broadly shared among parents I got to know at Hometown, some took note of compromises that needed to be made when balancing concerns for personal health, the environment, time, and money or described how they needed to negotiate with partners whose priorities were not quite the same. Kristin, a self-employed professional who identified as "Caucasian (European) and Chicano," talked about the role of money and conflict she had experienced with her husband about the cost of organic products.

> It's certainly not as important [to my husband] as it is to me to do free-range, organic, grass-fed. . . . He's—to him it's not worth the money. But because I do most of the meals, he's supportive of it. . . . I don't really know if we've compromised . . . I've kinda gotten my way on that [laughs] but . . . so that is something that it definitely plays a factor. And again I'm still kinda wrestling to find that balance. . . . There's still a lot of it that I feel like it's *wayyy* too much packaging. It's way too much sugar. It's way . . . this and that, but it's just convenient, so I definitely sacrifice more on the edge of convenience than I would like to.

Parents' food knowledge, orientations, and levels of concern varied as well as their resources. Rita, an African American mother who had three children and had recently completed her bachelor's degree, explained that she had worked two jobs while doing so. One of these was at a regional grocery store chain where she also did her shopping, bought house brands, and received discounts.

> JP: There are certain things that a lot of people seemed to be concerned about these days: high-fructose corn syrup or um, yeah, antibiotics and . . . you know, chemical additives or whatever. Are any of those types of things you worry about?
>
> R: I do, especially if there's a recall, but the good thing about working at [that grocery chain] is that we get the full recall list of everything that's been recalled from day to day . . . so I kind of like know what foods are and lately I have been, 'cause the five-year-old did a task in the after-school program about healthy eating, so now he's into like recognizing sugar, which is kind of a weird kid. [laughs] "You can't fry fish anymore, you can't fry chicken anymore!" So he's into that, yeah.

Rita did not seem highly conversant or concerned with problems such as antibiotics in meat or chemical additives that concerned some Hometown parents, but my question to her prompted awareness of food safety recalls. Further, she observed that her five-year-old son, a student at Hometown, was bringing lessons from Hometown back to his family, drawing attention to sugar (which she said had been on her radar already due to diabetes in her extended family) as well as fried foods. She called this food awareness "weird" for a child his age, though she seemed to be more pleased, if amused, than disparaging about this. Indeed, she described his newfound interest as part of a general (and, to her, positive) learning curve her family was on, since the neighborhood and school community in which they were now ensconced differed from the ones in which she and her husband had grown up and their older children had been raised. There, by her description, fried foods, chips, and sodas had been more normative choices, particularly in festive contexts.

Worries about sugar, chemical additives, and other foods could be particularly thorny for the parents of children with food allergies or with other health challenges that parents were seeking to treat through food choices. One married white mother, Courtney, had mentioned her preference for organic and non–genetically modified foods, and when I asked her to explain why she thought those were important, she told me,

> I think because we know that [our daughter] has kind of a sensitive digestive system and she tends to react to things. Kelly Dorfman says the GMO [genetically modified] stuff has been linked to kind of neurological issues, um, and so that makes me want to stay far away from them 'cause we're having issues in so many other areas anyway and then you know pesticides and whatnot, um you know, still the food dyes and stuff too, I'm definitely trying to avoid those but you know, that happens. . . . But yeah, just trying to avoid the chemicals in general and you know, corn syrup, I try to avoid that, but I think there's just so much that [she] is sensitive to that I try to read the labels.

Another day, she told me that her family had gone gluten-free, and when I asked her at a subsequent meeting about whether that was still the case, she said that she had started it herself out of solidarity with her daughter but had seen some benefits for herself too. I asked whether she felt she now had the food part pretty much figured out for her daughter's needs. She shrugged noncommittally, saying that she thought "we could do more, for sure," and we talked about how challenging it was to keep track of one factor such as gluten and the isolated impact it could have, and how it was hard to say what was worth it when there were so many things that needed attention. We discussed how I had experimented with gluten elimination briefly for my own daughter, who had been experiencing frequent stomachaches. Courtney believed that eliminating gluten indeed had been helpful to her daughter, whose challenges included anxiety and sensory sensitivities, but she also thought that her sugar consumption had gone up when eating gluten-free foods—and that *that* may have been detrimental in turn.

Thus some parents pursued time-consuming paths of discovery that involved a great deal of knowledge acquisition, trial and error, emotional involvement, and money in the attempt to ameliorate physical, behavioral, or emotional difficulties through the management of food. Those who were not sleuthing out the effects of foods on specific conditions often nonetheless went to considerable trouble to assess the foods marketed to them by an industrial food system and to shore up the home as a space for "real" food and the protection of children. Throughout this book, we will consider these activities from angles other than their ultimate and somewhat uncertain nutritional and medical efficacy. For example, how did wishes to regulate children's nutrition and to protect them from the ills of industrial production go to war with potentially conflicting wishes to appease children's apparent tastes and desires, and to what ends? How did these provisioning activities shape adults' perceptions of the other households and institutions that collaborated—or, more threateningly, seemed to compete—to form their children's bodies and selves?

Deception and Discernment

In the postindustrial consumer context, a significant part of the work of parenting lies in properly categorizing foods: through discernment, parents need to see through deceptive marketing strategies, recognize "empty" foods for what they are, and protect children from them.

Boxed breakfast cereals often came up as particularly problematic. Noelle, an African American mother who had spoken about her avoidance of canned foods, noted that she did not really eat cold cereal, but she bought Frosted Flakes and Froot Loops (a brightly colored, sweetened breakfast cereal) for her husband because he requested them and because "he pays the bills" (though she also was employed). She said she sometimes tricked her family by buying the smallest box available and saying it was all they had at the store. For herself, she preferred "real" oats or Cream of Wheat cooked with a bit of cinnamon, butter, and milk. Meanwhile, Faye acknowledged, when I asked whether her kids ate cereal, that they sometimes did and that she accepted that this was just "reality." Yet she wanted them to understand what was healthy, despite the fact that "something may sneak in that you normally wouldn't get."

> I explain to [my son] when I'm getting something . . . or a cereal commercial comes on and he's like "hey can we try that?" I explain why. It's not just a "No, we don't eat that." It's, "Here's the rationale behind that." [JP: So what do you tell him?] Umm . . . most cereals are made with horrible ingredients. There's a lot of chemicals fake flavors and the colors in it . . . and it's loaded with sugar . . . and even if they did clean it up, it's not necessarily giving your body what it needs.

Robin, a Caucasian married mother who was a professional nutritionist, described the cereal aisle in the supermarket as "crazy." Her son didn't get a chance to try most of those items, she said, though he did comment on cute graphics on boxes and ask to try them. "Right now he's had Cinnamon Toast Crunch. That's his cereal. Mm, that's alright. [laughs] Not what I picked. [laughs] But he'll eat Raisin Bran. He'll eat Cheerios. He eats fruity Cheerios." When I asked how she decided which cereals she was willing to buy, she noted that the choices were determined in part by who did the shopping—her or her husband—and she laughingly allowed that Cinnamon Toast Crunch was really her husband's fault.

> I'm gonna throw Bill under the bus. [laughs] [to Bill across the room:] I love you! . . . But Bill is usually the line. Like if he brings something home that it wouldn't usually be something I'd buy. [JP: Yeah. You'll respect it.] Yeah. I mean, I, you know, I think there has been a time where I'm

like, hey, can we cut back on the food—the sugary cereal thing and he's like, alright I'll go back to, I don't know, Raisin Bran or whatever. [JP: Uh-huh.] And that was the end of that. But it's usually just like cereal or cereal bars. I'm not a big—you know, but [my son] likes them. I just think they're like—they have a lot of sugar . . . I feel like they have a lot of sugar in 'em. But you know, Bill will get 'em and that's fine. It's more about—so it's also control in the way that I do most of the shopping that way with the groceries, and then I just don't buy it. It's just not here.

When I asked Irene about her morning routine with her daughters, she said that they had a rotating roster of breakfast cereals that they enjoyed, changing them every few weeks.

Right now, it's Special K with yogurt and fruit. Sometimes it's the Mini-Wheats. There's one called Cinnamon Roll, which sounds horrendous until you look at the nutritional thing and you see that it is the same as the granola [chuckling] that we were buying. Granola is something that's always in the rotation. Sometimes when I have . . . I eat Cheerios every morning because it's just plain, and I'm not awake yet. Sometimes one of them will eat that or the Multi-Grain Cheerios. Yeah, it's an array of usually whole grain. I would say they're lightly sweetened because I think that the Special K and stuff are hiding the nutrition, but I really think they're lightly sweetened.

For Irene, the names and marketing attached to foods were often deceptive, so it took attention to place things into the right categories ("I really think they're lightly sweetened") and to assess whether they should be considered healthful or not.

JP: If they pick something that you're not that familiar with, how do you decide whether to buy it or not?

I: Well, I look at the nutrition thing and I usually compare it to what they have been eating. And I'm often shocked at what they have been eating. Like you would think that just plain granola would be a good thing until you put it up next to a sugar cereal and you realize that it has—

JP: It has a decent amount of sugar.

I: Yeah.

JP: Is sugar the main thing that you are watching out for?

I: I watch the sugar, but also whole grains. If it has whole grains, it gets a good leeway. For cereal, I realize it's going to be pretty processed. We'll just go with that.

Whole grains redeemed more processed, sugary foods, and here Irene adhered to the advice of contemporary nutrition experts who advise providing whole grains and proteins to children at breakfast to sustain their energy levels throughout the day (e.g., Aubrey 2006). Jane, a married, Caucasian mental health professional, explained that she worried about her children not getting enough protein "because cereal's—really? I mean, what's in cereal? Like not a whole heck of a lot."

These stories illustrate how breakfast cereals occupied the position of a kind of deceptive non-food, presenting themselves through marketing and by virtue of long-standing cultural norms as appropriate for breakfast, yet suspected of being "empty" and "not real," a sort of lazy but possibly indispensable solution to the problem of quick morning food ("I realize it's going to be pretty processed"). It took knowledge and attention for a parent shopper to know which of these commodities were relatively acceptable and which were "horrendous." Some players—such as children and less-than-totally-conscientious husbands—were understood to be more likely than others to be drawn in by marketing, to succumb to their sweet teeth, or simply to have different priorities. Renee, a white former academic, described how her middle-school-aged daughter and she disagreed about whether Special K with Strawberries was a "sugar cereal": "There's this like marginal zone sort of arbitrated by the sugar content [laughs] . . . nine is sort of the marginal breaking point, anything with nine grams of sugar or above is sugar cereal, yeah um but then there's stuff like Raisin Bran where the raisins are literally loaded with sugar." When I asked Pete, a stay-at-home father, about his family's morning routine, he commented that his husband did not necessarily understand, like he did, that eating a lot of cereal in the morning was no different than eating cookies for breakfast. "You are just fooling yourself if you think it's any different. You know, it might be sprayed with vitamins or something like that, but it's the same thing, you know?"

In addition to such discernment of deceptively empty foods, parents also could engage in their own alternative kind of marketing: strategizing to present "healthy" foods as sufficiently "junky" to please their desirous children, who were not expected to discern in the same fashion as adults. Through projects of adult food management, label reading, and food planning, solutions could be identified whereby the "junk food" children wanted could be provided—from the perspective of the children's putative pleasure—yet could be relatively "healthy" simultaneously. For some parents, there was a sense that eliminating "junk food" altogether was not feasible, but that they could at least choose items that were less bad than others. "I try not to keep too much junk in the house, I mean . . . even if I buy junk food, I always get healthy junk food [such as cheese and crackers from Trader Joe's] . . . I mean it's still junk food." Another mother explained that she felt that if she started baking more, she would be able to give her son foods that satisfied his desire for junk as well as hers to minimize it. "If I made him a chocolate chip muffin that had just a few chocolate chips in it, it looks like junk food even if I made it with just eggs, butter, coconut flour and maybe a little bit of maple syrup or something, but not a lot. . . . Where I could control the sugar content, so it looks a little bit like junk food, but it's got really healthy ingredients." Faye had already carried out such a plan, observing that she did not buy packaged cookies but, "I make them so I have all the control over it. I'm pretty particular about the sweetener I use too. . . . We use maple syrup, honey, and I use coconut palm sugar for almost everything . . . and we are pretty particular about what chocolate. If we are going to eat chocolate chips . . . we don't eat any soy in our house. I just try to eliminate as many variables as I can and get it down to what I think is the most acceptable of everything." She said she occasionally would buy organic lollipops without artificial flavoring. "It's not perfect, but you can have a lollipop." She talked about going to a local health food store and choosing treats from their bulk aisle that she believed at least weren't "horrific." Her son liked macaroni and cheese, but she said she would never use a boxed mix; she made it from scratch using pasta "that meets our standard" and fresh cheese from "our farmer."

Through such resource-intensive tactics, what was accepted as children's possibly inevitable desire for rich and highly sweetened treats could be held in balance with parental concerns about lower quality sweeteners and other industrial ingredients. In the process, one could demonstrate specialized knowledge and dedication—though these also could be played down and normalized as just basic care, common sense, or "not that hard," which implied in turn that perhaps all parents should be able to do it if they simply chose to.

Contestation and Comfort: Brands and Health Borderlands

Packaged and processed foods were, as we have seen, generally disfavored by Hometown interviewees; at the same time, they were sometimes desired for qualities such as speed of preparation or portability. Specific products and brands popped up repeatedly in parents' narratives and seemed to do so because they occupied some borderland of convenience foods. They were "not as bad as" alternatives or, like Faye's mac and cheese and another mother's homemade chocolate chip muffins, represented acceptable versions of something generally considered nutritionally undesirable. These foods constituted compromises among competing factors for some, while for others they fell more clearly into the categories of either acceptable or unacceptable foods. As such, they concretized shared domains of concern, the territories upon which adults daily managed meanings and judgments concerning what was good enough.

One of these was Goldfish, the small, orange, cheese-flavored crackers shaped like smiley fish, sold by Pepperidge Farm since 1962 (though as the product website highlights, the smile was added only in 1997). In my own experience, Goldfish are, for many American families, one of the first packaged snacks (preceded only by Cheerios, the classic oat cereal shaped into tiny Os) offered to small children as they become able to eat crunchy foods. In addition to the original cheese-flavored fish, the Goldfish line now includes variants such as Pizza, Pretzel, Whole Grain Cheddar, and Princess Cheddar (colored pink). At Hometown, parents of elementary-aged children were asked to provide snacks for their entire class for a total of two weeks per school year, and this was one context in which Goldfish commonly were mentioned.

For example, Renee, an academic currently at home with her younger child, named Goldfish as among the snacks she had brought for her older daughter's class at the elementary school, along with "lit-

Figure 1.4: Two varieties of Goldfish crackers (photo by author).

tle Cuties clementines things [a branded whole fruit] and bananas and cheese sticks." She noted that it could be expensive bringing snacks for a whole week for twenty-four children and remembered, "Oh yeah, I got like Nutri-Grain [brand cereal bars] which I usually consider junk food, but they were on sale! [laughs] I try to do things that are pretty healthy but . . . ." For Renee, Goldfish was among those foods considered to be reasonably healthy enough and reasonably priced enough; by contrast, a parent interviewed by my assistant Liz Barnett said that while she sympathized with the fact that bringing school snacks could be quite expensive, especially for families with multiple children at the elementary school,

> I get really ticked off when I'm like "What'd you have for snack today?" And [my daughter] is like "Oh, I had pretzels" and I'm like, "How is that even going to energize you or give you a pick-me-up in the middle of the day?" [LB: I know some parents have had Goldfish, issues with people bringing Goldfish and thinking it's healthy.] It's not. I always. . . . We bring Pink Lady, little mini apples that you get from Costco, bananas, and then usually I'll make a huge thing of fruit and they just heap it onto little cup holders.

Pete, who spent many volunteer hours at the school, remarked that "you end up bringing in crappy food, you know," since you have to buy a lot at once, and it is expensive. And it has to be "allergy sensitive" as well, he noted, so it could not be anything like homemade brownies, and so "that means it's another kind of day that my child's eating junk, you know, it's gotta be easy for the teacher to dole out." When I asked which foods were too junky, he replied,

> Well so they have crackers, or they have their little, um you know . . . star . . . fish or whatever they are. You know, Goldfish . . . they end up having . . . you know, parents will bring in apples or carrots sticks and all that kind of stuff . . . but your kids don't eat it, you know, like if you watch them . . . because that's not the only thing they're putting in front of them, you know. It's usually—they have the choice of that box snack or the fruit and you know what they're choosing. . . . Once in a while though, I'll hear [my daughter] say she had a banana for a snack, so that's kind of cool.

When Robin explained that she was not happy with the snacks that were being provided in the after-school childcare program at her child's school (which was the local non-charter public elementary school—they were on the waiting list at Hometown), she cited too many packaged sugary snacks and chips, including Doritos, and sometimes Goldfish. "I mean I feel like Goldfish would be better," though she rued the fact that fruit was never provided, and "never some carrot sticks and ranch [dressing]."

Goldfish crackers thus illustrated a certain loosely agreed-upon hierarchy of foods operative in this community: whole fruits and vegetables were preferable to anything processed or starchy; simple cracker products were preferable to artificially colored and flavored chips such as Doritos; and depending upon the circumstances—expense and the amenability of children to actually eat these things—middle-ground Goldfish could comfort a parent or "tick them off." Foods like Goldfish were where these negotiations and line drawings took place, as were boxed macaroni and cheese mixes.[6] Recall Faye, who said she let her son have only homemade macaroni and cheese that was up to her standard. Other parents noted that it was worth it to "pay fifty cents more and get the Annie's versus the Kraft or something," while another said that her children did not generally ask for packaged foods marketed to children, though they might ask for "Annie's macaroni and cheese with the bunnies or whatever." Generally they did not ask or were told no, and "we try to do as much real food" as possible. Robin offered that she preferred buying Annie's macaroni and cheese because the cheese was less processed than Kraft's, though she admitted that "that's one of those things that I'll slide on every once in a while. [laughs] Probably because it reminds me of my childhood. [JP: The Kraft?] Yeah."

Annie's is a company based in Berkeley, California, acquired by General Mills in 2014, "with the goal of bringing more of our great tasting, organic products to more stores and more people across the country, with zero compromise to our company mission."[7] Their most iconic product is a line of macaroni and cheese boxed mixes, some of which are labeled organic, and according to the brand's website the emphasis is on organics and sustainability. "We ride bikes to work, snatch veggies from our back-office garden, and stock that scratchy, recycled toilet paper. Anything to make the world a little better."[8] By contrast, while Kraft also features organic varieties, it stands as a mainstream childhood classic rather than an environmentally friendly brand, proudly declaring on its website its "iconic cheesy flavor and classic macaroni shape" even as "now it has no artificial flavors, preservatives or dyes. You know you love it."[9] Kraft's website also played to the idea that its macaroni and cheese served the needs of stressed parents: Kraft macaroni and cheese was

> the part of parenting that's impossible to mess up.
>
> We don't always get the parenting part right. Late nights, missed games, having to be in a hundred places at once—it's hard. But getting the mac and cheese part right? That's nothing. Because Kraft Mac & Cheese is made with no artificial flavors, preservatives, and dyes.
>
> They'll remember how much they love you by dinner.[10]

In this advertisement, macaroni and cheese takes the stage as a food that serves as an appeasing treat, calming sustenance, or even way to win the affection of kids—"They'll remember how much they love you by dinner"—as well as, for the benefit of cautious parents, a healthy (or at least non-harmful) food and an attractively easy solution to the problem of providing quick meals that children will eat.

Indeed, companies such as Annie's and Kraft position their products, if with distinct aesthetics (environmentally aware hippy versus comfort food traditionalist), to be what anthropologist Robert Foster (2007) has called "lovemarks": brands with enduring emotional meaning, infused with personal and familial memories created by consumers themselves as well as through the marketing ploys of corporations. Packaged convenience items considered to be "healthy" versions of popular children's foods—based upon their ingredient lists as well as their marketing messages—occupied a special niche among processed food products: they promised solutions to parental conflicts around balancing nutrition, time, the food desires of children, and cultivating the affection and satisfaction of children.

Lara, a white married mother who worked from home, talked about how she was buying more packaged snacks than she used to now that her children were in school. One of these was fruit strips from Trader Joe's, a national chain that emphasizes low prices based on buying direct from suppliers and whose products contain no artificial flavors, artificial

Figures 1.5 and 1.6: Kraft versus Annie's macaroni and cheese (photos by author).

preservatives, MSG (monosodium glutamate), genetically modified in-gredients, or partially hydrogenated oils.[11] "I actually feel good about [the fruit strips]. Um, the ingredients are like fruit and—something. But—I stopped getting those because he loved them and he has cavities. So he can't have any dry fruit. Which is really a bummer 'cause it's usually a snack that I totally—can keep in my purse all the time when we're out, you know?" She seemed to present it as counter to her own expectation that she could "feel good" about a convenient packaged snack, so it was a "bummer" that dried fruits' natural sugar content was off limits to her cavity-prone son. She had discovered a seemingly elegant, though tem-porary, solution to a problem—finding a healthy snack that was easily portable—and Trader Joe's presented Lara with other solutions, as well.

> Well, for the first time I just recently bought these packaged chicken nug-gets. Which I had never bought before. But they were at Trader's Joes and they were organic, so I was like, hmm, why not? And um, that was hilari-ous. I had to post it on Instagram. Like, "hooray for Mommy for making such a wonderful dinner!" [both laugh] Like all you do is put the chicken nuggets in the oven for ten minutes, and I put raw carrots and raw grapes and that was it. That was their—they were both over the moon. Cleaned their plates. [laughs] I was like, I should do this every night! [laughs] It was great. Um, another one they really loved was also packaged food. Swedish meatballs with barbeque sauce. . . . [JP: Is that from Trader Joe's too?] Yes. And I just noticed the other day that it has dairy in it. [JP: Hm.] And I was like, oh great. But I don't think it's bothering them. But I'm really trying to go completely dairy free for me anyway. [sighs] So I gotta find something else for that. But, um, I could make like my own meatballs but that would be like actually cooking. [laughs] Like actually—actually cooking.

Vera, a white Hispanic artist, meanwhile commented that Trader Joe's had a lot of packaged foods and that she did not generally like a lot of packaged foods, but the location was convenient on her weekly routes and there were certain things she liked there, such as their hummus and the fair trade organic chocolate that served as her husband's "sweet fix." Food shopping had become a bit more complicated since one of her children recently had discovered he needed to avoid gluten. Mostly she preferred the larger grocery chains as well as a local health food co-op, but she described her own solution-finding on a recent trip to Trader Joe's:

> Trader Joe's just the other day, I did get some sweet potatoes and some yellow, I think they're Yukon gold organic potatoes, 'cause I know they spray pretty heavily on potatoes, you know a lot of pesticides on potatoes so, in trying to think of different things 'cause [my son] likes pasta so that was sort of one of those things where I could sort of make like a little pasta thing on the side and then he would—that was something that we all would enjoy, so the whole trying to figure out the starch side of it that satisfies them.
>
> . . . I try not to be overwhelmed, you know, and sort of take it on as a project [JP: Right, ongoing]—yeah, because it is an ongoing process. My husband said you know, "here's a bag of rice sitting on the counter." I had gone to the store and it was just the grocery store, you know, I didn't go to like [the health food co-op] and get organic rice 'cause it was like, we had to have rice for this thing. And he's like, "oh yeah you hear about the [recent news coverage concerning] arsenic in the rice?" I was like, great. . . . [laughs] [JP: Another thing to put on my list.] Right, right or just to think about. And then you know I was down at Trader Joe's and saw the potatoes and thought: there's a starch fix and it's organic [JP: so that works] so I'll do that and it's a whole food.[12]

What is highlighted here is that the process of problem solving to find convenient and nutritionally acceptable options is ongoing and part of what it meant to live in the context of risk society. Lovemarks and relatively trusted grocery chains could provide temporary solutions—ones where nutritional contents and emotional pulls combined to make something feel good enough or safe enough—though discoveries of arsenic or cavities could undo these tactics, and dependable, long-term strategies for minimizing health threats seemed far more elusive.

Sugary Food as a Threat to Psychological and Behavioral Well-Being

Sugar uniquely linked parents' worries about nutrition with their worries for children's behavior and emotional well-being, particularly in terms of sugar's understood link with hyperactivity in children. Research studies actually have raised questions about the link many parents assume to exist between hyperactivity and sugar consumption in children, though sugar consumption, associated with unstable blood sugar levels and increased adrenaline levels, has been suggested to impact a child's ability to focus and to produce "normal" behavior, especially in the case of children diagnosed with ADHD (Huynh 2010; Hammond 2013; DiSalvo 2012; see also National Institutes of Health 2014; Sears 2019b). Robin spoke about her son and his reactions to sugar. A nutritionist by profession, she was aware that some research indicated that the popularly accepted connection between sugar and hyperactivity had been thrown into question, but her own experience contrasted.

> R: After he finishes his meal and some nights, you know, we can just—we see that face. You know, I know that they say that too much sugar or any sugar at all doesn't affect kids [JP: Mhm] but—I don't know who "they" is, but I've kinda read that that the be—supposedly the sugar does not affect, but *I don't know.* Sometimes—
>
> JP: Doesn't affect how?
>
> R: Like, um, hyperactivity [JP: Uh-huh] or lead to—
>
> JP: Oh, that's what they say now?
>
> R: Mmmhmm. I've read that and I disagree. [JP: Hmm.] I don't know. I definitely watch [my son] like run circles sometimes.

Parents spoke of not giving sugar close to bedtime, as when Lila noted that when she took her two children out for Thai food, she gave them the choice of having a soda with dinner or going out for ice cream afterward. "You're choosing the sugar but there's no way in hell I'm giving you both. You know? You're going to bed after this. How are you gonna run off this sugar?"

Others described their children's experience with the "sugar crash," especially with younger children: "They'll go to bed in tears 'cause they're so tired but they can't get themselves to sleep." Kristin explained that her son had impressed her by voluntarily giving up sugary drinks and desserts when she and her husband had explained to him that they themselves were doing so while participating in a "thirty-day [health] challenge."

JP: So do you think he understands about sugar and why it would be good to give it up?

K: That's a good question. . . . I don't know about that. That's a really good question. I don't think he fully has the grasp because I haven't felt the *need* or the comfort level to talk to him about things like obesity or things like that. What he does understand is what it means to crash. And he's experienced that—I'll point it out. If you have a lot of sugar, you're not gonna have energy. You're gonna feel really great, you're gonna fly around the room and then bounce off the walls and then you're gonna crash. And that he's able to really grasp and under-stand and witness and feel for himself and I think that's part of why he was really open to cutting that out.

The school day was a time when sugar was recognized as particularly problematic. White married couple Diane and Robert talked about what they did for classroom birthday parties for their elementary-aged daughters.

R: . . . maybe we bring some brownies or something to the school.

D: Well we don't generally, 'cause the school asks us not to and I under-stand that.

JP: Because of the allergies and everything?

D: Well the sugar and. . . . [R?: The sugar daze.] It's hard for them to—we did a mystery reader one time with a book about donuts and I took donuts in but we always—we check with the teachers and say, can we do this? It's totally fine if not, I understand. You don't want sugared up kids at ten o'clock in the morning. You know, you just gotta slow down and do some math now.

When Irene talked about not wanting her kids to get fruit gummies for snack during the school day, she explained further that "that's not going to give a kid any energy for any amount of time. And, to me, that's kind of the point. It's not so that you can have something sweet for a second. It's so that you have energy to get through the time until lunch. Or until the end of school." Though she was not concerned about hyperactivity, she acknowledged that for her children, remaining well tempered for a day's activities depended upon eating properly: "When they have low blood sugar, they're big jerks. . . . It's a big driver in their moods."

Irene was frustrated, further, that if her children were given sugar during the day, it placed a limit on the sugar she felt she could give them herself.

> Someone brought in Oreos as a snack, and again, the same thing . . . I mean, Oreos at least have enough fat that they'll stay with you a little bit. But kids will eat anything. They're hungry. Why are you giving them Oreos? It's not a party. Yeah. That's one thing that actually kind of appalls me is when the amount of sugar that they are exposed to outside the home and it's to the extent where I feel like I can't give them that many desserts at home. I can't make cookies with my kids this weekend because someone gave them candy, and then someone else after school gave them a cookie, and then someone loaded them up with . . . I don't know. Something else. It's like their sweet allotment for the day. They could have had only cookies, but they already had. . . . [JP: But they have already had it. Right.] Yeah, which is taking a little bit of the fun out of it, but. . . .

Parents observed behavioral disturbances in connection with sugar, but also salient was that sugar was wrapped up with parents' more general concerns about low-quality foods and about their own potential lack of control over regulating how their children entered the industrial food system (or how it entered them). Moreover, Irene expressed her preference to be the one who gave her children the occasional, allowable sugary treat, speaking both to many parents' concern to limit the influence of *other social actors* in their children's lives and to their ambivalent, conflicted feelings about sugar as a source of pleasure, as we shall see further.[13]

Some Hometowners spoke more deeply about their individual children's special predilections for sugar or about the meanings of sugar in children's emotional lives, and here similar concerns about external influences and the management of pleasure resonated, escalating to concern about sugar as addiction. When I asked Fran, a married Caucasian health professional, whether she viewed her children as picky eaters, she spoke about each in turn and observed that one of them used sugar as a "quick fix" for addressing emotional discomfort:

They all like bread a lot. But, um, my son—one of my sons . . . he's a real—so he's I—he's a sugar addict. So he looks for that to—I think to suppress some of the anxiety. He's a stressed kid. [JP: Mhm.] So he goes for the quick fix. Sugar. He's skinny as a rail. [JP: Mhm.] Um, he is really thin. He's the thinnest of them all. Um, they're all slender, athletic children but he's, ya know. He worries me because he will not tell—sometimes he'll come home and he'll choose what he wants me to put in his lunch box. Sometimes he comes home and it's full. And he will hide it and he will try to get to the trashcan and dump it out before I can see it. 'Cause he knows that I want him to eat his food and I've given him a choice to what he wants and we've discussed strategies of him packing his own lunch so he can put it exactly in there what he—he just goes for the sugar. This kid. And he—I think it's just to, to—it's like a quick fix for his little brain. Ya know, he's lookin' for those, um, for some relief and that's the food he goes for.

Experts too have treated sugar as an addiction with behavioral impacts. Recall DesMaisons's (2004) appeal to parents to consider that sugar may be the cause of their children's alarming behavioral problems in *Little Sugar Addicts*. DesMaisons argued that such behaviors are the result of sugar's effect on some children's biochemistry, "*not* . . . your parenting skills," thus positioning sugar as a potential solution to unwanted behavioral dynamics—and removal of sugar from the diet as a solution to some children's troubled emotional lives (20).[14]

The addiction issue came up in relation to a middle school vending machine some parents and staff complained about, which sold packaged honey buns and other treats (the honey buns being the most maligned, as we shall see later in the book). Lisa, an active volunteer at the school who identified as Caucasian, complained that the children got enough sugar otherwise, and "you have kids getting three [packaged honey buns from the vending machine]. I know my son will be begging money off people so that he can get three, because he's such a sugar addict." She joked about these items being "dope for kids," though her concern was real. When I asked Noelle to explain her concern about sugar, she offered that it was akin to "giving your kid an alcoholic beverage":

Because I don't think it does anything to recharge your body, I don't think it—it's not a natural product and that's why, 'cause you're already eating something that's artificial, cereal's artificial, and on top of it there's going to be sugar on it, so it's like two plus two, is like—it's nasty, you know, it's like, you're just poisoning your body, you know? It's almost like giving your kid an alcoholic beverage because you're doing something to them that—you're permanently addicting the body to something. And then to go through the course of trying to take them off of something that you addicted them to is not easy.

Parents worried about losing control of physical and psychological aspects of their children's behavior and growth that would be hard to redirect once off track.

Barry, a lawyer (and self-dubbed "white guy" married to a Black woman), did most of the cooking for his family. He talked about the addictive power of sugar and other foods when discussing the middle school's vending machine, digging further into what he considered to be the psychology of addiction.

I think that the vending machines should go. I think that if you put it out there, you're basically saying that, you know, this is okay to choose . . . I mean you wouldn't put a vending machine that had alcohol or drugs or cigarettes, right? . . . All those things, you know, honey buns, cigarettes and beer are all . . . potentially addictive on some level . . . and some of them are more patently addictive than others, but the idea that you would have a—I just, I really don't like the idea of having the vending machine. . . . I mean if you go to school and use your allowance at the vending machine and get some donuts, it's kind of like somebody, you know the guy going to the street corner to get a fix or a kid stealing his parent's cigarettes. . . . If I walk into my house on Sunday morning with donuts, with Krispy Kreme donuts, and say "look, I've got donuts," that's me saying: it's okay for you to have these. It's an indulgence, we're going to share it and have it as a family, we're all going to have a little bit of fun. We're all going to indulge ourselves and do something that gives us a little bit of glee, but when it's all over with, we're going to go back to the family that tries to eat properly. If I say, you know, here's your allowance and do with it what you want and they run down to the corner store, to the vending machines, get something and eat it secretly, you know it's like encouraging a pattern of behavior [of] self-indulgence in private.

Figure 1.7: A commercial honey bun similar to those carried, in plastic packaging, in Hometown's vending machine during the 2013–2014 school year (photo by author).

Sugar thus was menacing not only for its inherent properties, but because it might lend itself to behaviors that escaped and avoided parental attention. Recall Irene's disappointment in finding that her children were given so much sugar by others that she could not be the one to bestow the fun of it at home. The decadent pleasure of sugar was understood as safer when modulated by parents in the flow of family life; this modulation could also be preferable, as Irene demonstrated, because it yielded parents the reciprocal pleasure of having provided it, and reinforced the idea that the home was a more desirable space for the modulation of dangerous if pleasurable substances.

Indeed, the meanings of sugar were not all negative. Since sugar was associated with childhood and with pleasure, it also had positive connotations. Irene associated her own childhood with greater sugar consumption, in both negative and affectionate lights:

> I think we probably did eat a lot more sugar than we eat now, because my dad's mom always put sugar in the canned vegetables when she cooked them. There would be green beans, but you had to put like a spoonful of sugar in there, and the corn and everything. And so my mom did that too, because my dad thought that's how you eat. It was disgusting. . . . And then my grandfather was just crazy about giving grandkids sugar. That was like his fun in life, so he had the sugar bowl on his table, and when we walked in the door, he'd just hand a spoonful. . . . So yeah, probably my kids eat less sugar than I did. I hope so. That's great stuff.

Another mother acknowledged her own "soft spot in my gut for the Hostess prepackaged, chemical cakes. For some reason. I think I grew up with those and I really liked them with my lunches," though her children "don't even know them really to be an option." Most poignantly, Lynn, a married white mother of two, worried that since she had a potentially terminal illness, she should also allow her children to have sugary birthday cakes so that they would have "happy childhood memories . . . so their world isn't so stark . . . just to have their childhood feel like a normal childhood." Lynn allowed that even within her household—where the children thought apples could be a dessert—occasional sweets were permitted, including ice cream as a reward for doing well on a test. "I don't think it hurts to eat junk food. I think if you eat enough health food, then that's what you actually physically crave. I mean, they really like healthy food I think. That's my fantasy."

Conclusion

Lynn's "fantasy" was the hope that her children voluntarily and authentically enjoyed what she considered to be healthy food, so that she did not have to force them to eat these things nor deprive them of pleasure.

By calling this a fantasy, she implied her fear that the dream was unrealistic or unattainable, perhaps that her children had not incorporated her lessons as seamlessly or deeply as she hoped they had, or that those lessons inevitably would be overridden by other desires and impulses. In a broader sense, Lynn's reflections spoke to many parents' fantasies of resolving contradictions: for example, to find meal and snack options that were healthful, were convenient, *and* would be eaten eagerly by their children, despite the fact that the "healthy" category often seemed at odds with the other two. Acknowledging that the judgment calls could ultimately seem rather arbitrary—as well as provisional and relentless— did little to relieve the strong emotional pull many Hometown parents felt toward the task.

This was a moral activity and a mode of self-definition, a delineation of the household's values. These choices reflected on individuals' knowledge, their conscientiousness, and—often indirectly or implicitly—their social standing and class identifications. As food anthropologist Sidney Mintz (1996, 82–83) has put it, "The repudiation of a desired good bestows virtue, while opening the door to additional consumption of different kinds. Exercise of choice heightens the illusion of individuality. . . . Individuals learn to consume with more discipline; morality . . . becomes a new consumable." Even so, these choices—at least in the postindustrial food context of Hometown—tended to be framed in terms of concerns over children's safety and well-being. Certainly they were discussed with tones of disgust and discomfort at times (Bourdieu 1984; Lavin 2013), but generally they were not expressed in terms of competition, prestige, or explicit social prejudice; rather, the salient and acknowledged wishes were for a child's health, bodily integrity, and emotional regulation.

In a de-traditionalized, post-scarcity society, as sociologist of modernity Anthony Giddens (1995, 4) has pointed out, "everyone must confront, and deal with, multiple sources of information and knowledge, including fragmented and contested knowledge claims"; this brings new forms of autonomy as well as new anxieties, since we know that we must make many decisions and that these can impact our short- and long-term health. These pressures are all the weightier when children are felt to be in need of special protection; and by highlighting that parents' strategies for dealing with them were both morally weighted and resource-intensive in ways that inevitably linked them with class politics, I mean to take nothing away from the (not unfounded) fear and sincere care that informed their efforts to feed their children well.

In many ways, the consumer discourses of Hometown parents were voiced as anti-consumerist (wary of consumerism and marketing) and anti-industrial (wary of production practices and artificial food components). For the most part, they valorized what was homegrown, home-cooked, consumed at home, or at least not highly processed and filled with chemical additives. At the same time, they depended upon—and certainly were in conversation with—an array of packaged, processed, variably denigrated (non-)foods. While these aspects are distinct to the later twentieth and early twenty-first centuries with their intensified regimes of industrial production and proliferation of scientific information, taking care of one's health and lifestyle is also part of the deeper history of the U.S. middle class, for whom self-purification has long been posited as the solution to social problems and self-control has been constructed as a form of freedom (DuPuis 2015, 10, 101; see also Biltekoff 2013, 2014). Correct eating promises a seeming escape from contradictions: "Nature can save us from culture; local can save us from globalization; the artisanal can save us from the industrial; and detoxification can save us from a toxic world" (DuPuis 2015, 117).

Even as Hometown parents entertained this fantasy of resolution, safety, and hominess, they often were concerned not to overdo it by controlling their children excessively, by becoming overly anxious, or by appearing to be intolerant of others and their consumer choices in a diverse urban environment, as we shall explore further. In this fashion, the morality of the individual, her personal consumer style, and her relative safety from harm—and ability to be a "good parent" by protecting her loved ones in proper measure—intermingled and were continually problematic.

2

Helicopters and Nazis

Projects of Regulation, Control, and Selfhood

The elementary lunchroom at Hometown Charter was located on the ground floor and had the feeling of a basement, though it was cheerful enough. Mass-produced nutrition posters and school announcements adorned the walls, and a shelf unit full of cubbies displayed lost-and-found sweaters and water bottles in an ad hoc fashion. Three rows of round tables were arranged by homeroom class: one row per class, three or four tables in each row, each table hosting several students. The space was airy and dim, especially when the lights were turned down, which they often were during the lunch periods my graduate assistants and I observed. Dimmed lights served as a signal to the children that their *"voices should be off."*

Typically, once students had settled at their assigned tables and once those who were purchasing school lunch had moved through the food line and back to their seats, the lights would be turned on—that is, if teachers on duty deemed the children's volume and activity levels acceptably moderate. The students were allowed to chat while they ate; but over the course of the half-hour lunch period, as eating subsided and talking intensified, the din often became more clamorous and teachers turned off the lights—sometimes calmly, sometimes with frustrated commentary and reminders of possible penalties to be imposed, such as an entirely "quiet lunch" the next day. One teacher pointed out to me that the grade he supervised had a specific time each day (to the minute, he believed) when the tide turned and the noise suddenly but predictably slipped out of control.

The turning up and down of lights and voices was in many ways what structured the lunch period for these students and their teachers. Indeed, from teachers' positions, the noise level and how manageable or unmanageable it had been on any given day seemed to be the primary gauge of how smoothly lunch had gone. Over time, I learned that so much emphasis was placed on modulating noise not only as a general disciplinary standard nor to ensure that socializing did not prevent eating, but (also) because there were classes in session on the same floor; staff said that noise carried readily to those rooms from the cafeteria. From time to time, supervising teachers would remind the children at lunch that keeping their voices down was a matter of respect for the learning that was happening elsewhere in the school. These acoustical matters, in addition to age differences, seemed to explain why the middle grades were far less regulated. Middle schoolers spoke freely and noisily throughout the lunch period, in a far more crowded room, without comment from teachers on duty.

Elementary teachers who wanted to adjust the noise level spoke to children of their ability to follow rules and to sit more quietly, casting this as a form of maturation in urgent need of acquisition. On the last day of school before winter break, some of the teachers organized a "flash mob" for the fifth grade during lunch. Holiday music suddenly played through a boom box and several teachers entered, dancing among the tables and singing along to the music. The children become excited, some of them getting up on top of tables and benches and singing too. The atmosphere was exuberant; it seemed the teachers had departed from the usual drill for the sake of some holiday festivity. Yet a few moments later the music was turned off and one of the teachers told the children that they, the teachers, had wanted them, the students, to have something fun but now saw that they could not handle themselves and their bodies in that situation. "It makes me sad," the teacher added, admonishing them to think about the coming year (when they would move up to middle school) and what would be asked of them then.

Though teachers at this school did not use the more conventional, authoritarian language of punishments or detentions, they did work hard to use the tools (such as the lights) at their disposal to manage the human environment. Sometimes the room would be told to sit in complete silence for a few minutes until students gained back the right to talk quietly among themselves, or they would be informed that there would be a certain number of quiet minutes the next day to make up for today's noise. Students who, even under such conditions, were not silent might be warned that they would need to write a "reflection" (in which they would explain how their behavior had been in conflict with one or more of the school's guiding principles; for more serious cases, a "referral" could send a student to the principal's office). One day when a wave of loud noises from popping plastic bags rolled through the fifth grade, the teacher on duty warned, "I have no problem making seventy-two copies of reflections," suggesting that every student in the room would be required to sit down and write one if the behavior did not stop. One administrator came in from upstairs on a particularly noisy day to say that she was "*embarrassed.* And I'm going to be honest, if your parents saw this behavior they would be embarrassed too, because I know you're not allowed to act like that at the dinner table at home. You've been doing this since kindergarten, so act like it."

Indeed, teachers spoke to children about the importance of showing responsibility and "making good choices," along with making more agitated statements such as "I'm serious, voices off!" One noisy day, a male teacher who had been speaking sharply to students walked by me and remarked ruefully, "I hate having to be the Wicked Witch of the West." Other days were easier: I observed a teacher walk through the room when the children were quiet, and she beamed, "This is *amazing.*" Catching my eye then, she revised her statement—seemingly for the children's benefit, though perhaps the fact of my observation had reminded her of how the lunchroom was "supposed" to be: "This is *normal.*"

As these scenes illustrate, the settings in which children eat, whether at school, at home, or elsewhere, are structured by adults' more general concerns about socialization and discipline, not only nutrition. Having examined some of Hometowners' nutritional concerns and ideologies, here we will consider the broader context of child-adult relationships, particularly adults' understandings of their own efforts at control and how they shaped children's personhood. In past scholarship, linguistic anthropologists have made significant contributions along these lines through close observation of the social interactions that take place at family mealtimes. This work often thematizes issues of power and control, how these are played out between parents and children in negotiations over food at the table, and how such dynamics vary cross-culturally (Paugh and Izquierdo 2009; Ochs, Pontecorvo, and Fasulo 1996; Ochs and Shohet 2006; see also Pike 2008, 2010; O'Connell and Brannen 2014).

Though I had several opportunities to observe family mealtimes, some of which are described in this chapter, instead of dwelling mainly on family food interactions I observe a variety of social settings (including the school cafeteria and after-hours parent support groups) and draw upon parent interviews to understand adults' ambivalent attempts to regulate children's behavior, including but not limited to their eating. Nutritional discourse intersected with the more broadly social and emotional content of parents' food talk, much of which was oriented toward socializing, training, and protecting children without excessively limiting them. In other words, many adults felt responsible both to regulate children's nutrition *and* to enable children's growing autonomy. Overattentiveness and food anxiety were seen as potentially negative influences on children, and adults evinced a sense of conflict about the need to teach children self-control while also allowing them some space for childhood (which, as we shall see later, connotes pleasure, desire, and precisely a lack of mature self-restraint). Indeed, adults were not only talking about fostering their children's physical health and psychological maturity, but also setting standards for adults themselves, who were held responsible for setting those processes in motion.

More particularly, in this urban community parents wanted not only to teach their children moderation but also to appear as appropriately moderate (attentive, but low-key) themselves. Adults did not want to be wicked witches nor, as we shall see below, "food Nazis." They often came across as rather diligent in monitoring what their children ate (or at least could talk extensively on the topic), usually with an interest in maximizing fresh produce and limiting sugar (especially high-fructose corn syrup) and highly processed foods. However, at another level many were concerned, too, about the meaning of monitoring itself: that is, they were self-conscious about the possibility that they might be overmonitoring or overregulating. Similar worries have been observed elsewhere in the American middle class; anthropologists Amy Paugh and Carolina Izquierdo (2009) observed that in dual-earner, middle-class Los Angeles households, parents and children often negotiated and bargained about which foods would be allowed and in what portions; they argue that these struggles reflected parental ambivalence about their own authority versus the autonomy of their children. In the process, parents transmitted a kind of individualism to their children, in a mundanely agonistic way (see also Cook 2009b; Ochs, Pontecorvo, and Fasulo 1996; Backett-Milburn et al. 2010; Grieshaber 1997; Ochs and Shohet 2006; Maher, Fraser, and Wright 2010).

At Hometown, as I have said, discussions about children's food intake shared concerns with seemingly unrelated workshops and meetings concerning child discipline and development. Both demonstrated middle-class values and preoccupations—expressed in specific ways in this urban, gentrifying community, no doubt, but also voiced and problematized in national media. Together they point to what might be called a distinctive "emotional style" (Illouz 2008),

> the combination of the ways a culture becomes "preoccupied" with certain emotions and devises specific "techniques"—linguistic, scientific, ritual—to apprehend them.
>
> An emotional style is established when a new "interpersonal imagination" is formulated, that is, a new way of thinking about the relationship of self to others, imagining its potentialities and implementing them in practice. (14)

Such imaginings of self and (inter)personhood are always part and parcel of their broader cultural and political economic contexts, and anthropologists have situated many projects of self vis-à-vis contemporary capitalism. Sociologists Steve Bialostok and Matt Aronson (2016, 96), for example, note that emotional awareness is being modeled by teachers for U.S. elementary school students, and they link this trend with the neoliberal labor economy inasmuch as the ability to identify and discuss emotions "corresponds with late capitalism's needs for workers who are reflexive and emotionally adept" (see also Hardt 1999; Hoffman 2009). Anthropologists in contexts as varied as Kerala, India (Chua 2011), and Saint Petersburg, Russia (Matza 2012), have described how the behavior of children and youth becomes problematized in contexts of rapid political and economic transformation. The work of parenting and pedagogy has been invested with the responsibility to alleviate anxieties about the future, particularly the widespread financial insecurity of neoliberal capitalism globally (Katz 2008; Liechty 2002).[1]

At Hometown in particular, power struggles and anxieties surrounding children's food revealed a contemporary American middle-class emotional style that dwelt upon monitoring the fuzzy boundaries of the self and idealized the "self-regulating" individual often associated with neoliberalism. This style was one means through which adults grappled with (and took onto their own shoulders and into their own senses of self) the stresses of living in an industrial economy and urban environment. Those conditions presented constant challenges to parental efforts at control, even as such efforts themselves were questioned and often denigrated in private talk and public discourse alike. In this way, parenting through food expresses what we might think of as classically neoliberal ideals but from a variety of angles, showing the tensions, conflicts, and ambiguities of such ideologies as they are put into practice. While individuals positioned themselves variably vis-à-vis these ideologies, and while as we shall see, judgments about over- and underattention to children's food sometimes spoke explicitly or implicitly to perceived class and race identities, this chapter focuses on the axis of ambivalent concern about matters of regulation and control around which many middle-class Hometowners' food worries revolved.

Socializing a Regulated, Autonomous Self

A local influence on the ways teachers and (at least some) parents understood their responsibilities to children was the "Conscious Discipline" philosophy formally espoused by Hometown Charter. Though its teachings bear kinship to other popular texts (including some mentioned to me by parents and staff, such as Cohen 2002 and Siegel 2013) and academic discourses on child development, psychology, and education (e.g., McClelland et al. 2015; Mooney 2013; Maccoby 1992), Conscious Discipline is the specific approach of Becky Bailey, a PhD in early childhood education and developmental psychology. The approach focuses on how to nurture a child's emergent ability to handle her own emotional reactions in order that she may interact with the surrounding social world in ways that are not socially or physically destructive. The learning of these skills is recognized to be a matter of socialization, not a developmental inevitability, but like other popular works I heard cited or recommended by staff and parents at Hometown, Bailey's teachings also dwelt upon how a child's brain and its emergent development provided the neural context for self-management.[2]

A representative from Becky Bailey's organization ran a workshop for Hometown parents one morning in the elementary cafeteria. After leading us in a sunny greeting song ("Hello, Buenos Dias, What's Up") complete with hand motions and interactive components (shaking hands with the person next to you), our guide showed a video in which Bailey explained that Conscious Discipline was a model for emotional intelligence and that it involved teaching people to respond from *this* part of the brain—she tapped to indicate the top front—rather than reacting from *this* part (the lower back brain). Conscious Discipline was not a model for obedience and compliance, Bailey explained in the video; it was a relationship-based model. Its principles included that you could not "make" people change; you could only change yourself. It was dependent less on rules than on relationships and on the idea of "seeking willingness" so that people were motivated to resolve conflicts. It also viewed conflict as an opportunity for growth, rather than as bad.

When the short video had concluded, the workshop instructor explained that before learning Conscious Discipline, she herself had lacked composure in dealing with her own children; she had not acquired the necessary skills in what she described as the chaotic, angry environment of her own natal family. Encouraging parents in the room that they were seeking to act from a place of peace and calm in interactions with their children, she showed a slide that depicted how different brain states were responsible for different kinds of emotions and behaviors: the "survival" or "fight or flight" mode that reflected activation of the brain stem; the blaming, emotionally overwrought state of the limbic system; and the calm, learning-oriented executive state governed by the frontal lobe.

Citing another influential child psychologist, Daniel Siegel, a Hometown school administrator portrayed similar content in a newsletter to families. She wrote that the executive state "looks like time management, working memory, impulse control, empathy, task initiation, and goal achievement. We want children and adults to function in the Executive State as often as possible but that is easier said than done!" She went on explain that adults at Hometown Middle used strategies such as measured breathing and a focus on "reflection rather than punishment" to keep all members feeling "safe and connected." Finally, the newsletter entry pointed out that children were not able to work at a level "above" where the adults in their environment were operating; if the goal was for children to function in the executive state as much as possible during the school day, adults needed to be in that space as well.[3]

Back in our morning workshop, the leader encouraged everyone to think of a time, "I'm sure there is at least one, when you said something to a kid and they just complied. You didn't get hooked into their upset. You maintained calm and your brilliance shows up." She linked this kind of skill with the brain's executive state and pointed out that it was not fully formed until age twenty-four, maybe even twenty-seven, so that parents must "loan" these skills to their children until they can be learned effectively. She showed a video about "neuroplasticity" and emphasized that even adults can "rewire" new thought and behavior patterns, so it's "not too late" to adopt these practices, whether with older children or for adults themselves.

A number of things stood out to me in this model, in part because I had noted that similar values and tensions ran through talk about children's food. Authoritarianism was disavowed; the workshop instructor told us that according to Bailey, "discipline is not something we *do* to children; it is something we develop within them." Emphasis was on the relationship between parent (or teacher) and child. The relationship was understood to go both ways; this was not a simple top-down flow of power, though the adult (ideally) had greater skills of self-management that could be "lent" to a child. In Bailey's published work (e.g., 1997), she emphasizes that adults should validate children's feelings, thereby recognizing the emotional (and neural) basis of misbehavior, but must not get pulled into the child's crisis state themselves.

Rather than giving vague directions such as "be nice" that speak of a parent's misguided desire to control a child's behavior, the adult must communicate expectations concretely. This can be done by offering the child two *acceptable* and positive choices (Bailey 1997). "Sand is not for throwing. You could fill the cup and turn it over to make hills or use the water wheel. What is your choice?" (Bailey 1997, 210). In a similar way, Hometown parents talked about the provision of choices as a strategy for managing conflict with children, including when it came to getting them to eat nutritionally desirable foods. In both cases, adults considered it to be important to allow children to take agentive roles—to *choose*—even while acknowledging that children's brains were not yet developed such that they could be expected predictably to make the choices adults construed as socially functional or as physiologically healthy. Adults were to assist children in making acceptable choices, even as they were encouraged to maintain a boundary between themselves and the child whereby the emotional state of each could be seen as remaining separate rather than as fluidly intermingled (cf. Lutz 1988; Povinelli 2006).

Parents at Hometown with whom I discussed it generally were approving of the Conscious Discipline approach, though they were informed about it and attempting to practice it themselves to varying extents. (One white/Caucasian mother who will figure prominently in this chapter, Wendy, expressed her approval in the negative by explaining why she had not felt confident about another charter school her son had attended before Hometown. She had heard from a neighbor who had visited that school that there was a lot of screaming at the children. "I don't know how to say this politically correctly, but it was an old school teacher mentality—I'm going to scream at you." She allowed that "we all do sometimes, but it shouldn't be the MO [modus operandi]. It really made me nervous.") In addition to school-provided workshops like the one described above, a few parents had organized a voluntary support group that met roughly monthly to discuss Bailey's books and to share their own experiences in implementing such strategies with their own children. Attendance was strong early in the year with perhaps twenty or more parents at one meeting, though as the year wore on I found myself to be one of the most active members, along with the group facilitators and a few others. (It was at one of these meetings that I encountered Robin, a white, married working mother whose son was attending the local non-charter public school because they had not been successful yet in Hometown's lottery; she explained to me that she still hoped to get him in, and she was here to hear more about the approaches espoused at Hometown. She had been unsettled by experiences with teachers at her son's school, who seemed unable or unwilling to learn about her son's experience rather than simply imposing shaming terms of evaluation; and she rued the fact that candy and ice cream had been used to reward students for academic performance.)

We would meet on weeknight evenings, sometimes on school grounds, other times at casual local restaurants or at someone's home, where we might have glasses of wine as we alternated between discussion of an assigned text by Bailey, reports of recent episodes or ongoing worries with our own children, and observations about events and procedures at Hometown. Participants talked about the special challenges of helping children diagnosed with ADHD or those with as-yet mysterious food sensitivities, and they shared about the daily ins and outs of handling discipline, emotional upsets, and boundary setting with their children.

At a café bar near downtown Atlanta, three of us—two Hometown mothers and I—met to talk about a chapter from one of Bailey's books. One attendee was a first-generation (though long settled) migrant to the United States; the other was the parent facilitator, who first shared about some cooking she had done for her family that day and about a local yoga class where she had been offering administrative assistance in return for a free class (though she had a professional background, she was married with four children and currently was not employed for pay). To begin the meeting in earnest, she led us in a sensory exercise in which we spent a few minutes concentrating on just one of our senses, whichever the individual chose, observing what we perceived with it. The parent leader explained that this was to promote presence and the ability to be in the moment, which could be useful when dealing with stressful encounters with one's children.

Next, we turned to discussing the chapter that had been assigned. One of the topics was Bailey's recommendation to give a child two positive choices. The facilitator and I discussed how it could be difficult to discern between positive choices and "false choices" or punishments. For example, telling a child to "clean up your room or lose TV for a week" is not providing two positive choices equally acceptable to the parent; rather, it offers the choice to comply or to earn a penalty. Our leader offered that she had been practicing the strategy of giving two positive choices recently but had found it was not very well received by her sixth grader, who would respond by saying things like, "I'm going to do both of them, okay?" She reminded us, too, of Bailey's teaching that one cannot *make* another feel a certain way; hence a parent should avoid modeling language such as "you're making me crazy" and should instead describe one's own state only without blame: "*I* feel crazy."

At a larger meeting in the school's library, the same parent highlighted for the group how Bailey discouraged "external rewards" such as prizes for good behavior: "Material rewards often backfire. Children learn to expect 'the goods' for being good, and to seek approval rather than wisdom" (Bailey 2000, 58). Conscious Discipline emphasized instead the natural consequences that ensued from different choices children might make (198–199). "I've been guilty of the food thing," she said, recalling having told her son, since there was no dessert in the house that night anyway, "you won't have any dessert *tomorrow* if you don't sit down and finish" the task he was supposed to be completing. "I probably shouldn't have done that," the facilitator worried. "That is probably a bit of a stretch to think of that as natural consequences."

These semipublic discussions provide small windows into the disciplinary challenges parents faced at home and how they struggled to master skills they believed would benefit their children. More implicitly, all this reflected fundamental sensibilities about what the tasks of child socialization entailed and what it meant for a child to be a separate-yet-related, semiautonomous-if-not-yet-matured agent. Anthropologist Diane Hoffman (2013, 229) explains how such approaches bespeak deeper cultural assumptions and tensions; they reveal "culturally situated notions of power, selfhood, and emotional control." She describes as "child-centered" those child-rearing approaches that focus on children's developmental needs, that seek to respect the child as a separate individual, and that operationalize this through the provision of *choice* to children. Among mothers Hoffman interviewed, whom she characterizes as economically privileged white Americans, and in the child development literature power struggles are treated as inevitable because "the need to exert control or experience one's personal power is naturalized as a developmental imperative linked to the emergence of an autonomous, independent self" (231). Hoffman acknowledges that providing choices to children is still ultimately a means of exercising adult control, however; ambivalence about adult control versus children's independence indicates "unresolved cultural tensions over the power of the emotions to undermine relationships, and uncertainty over how to harness them for the social good" (241; see also Hoffman 2009).

Hometown parents were not unique, then, in their concern to help develop inner discipline without squashing a child's independence and to provide empathy and care without overstepping boundaries between the adult's and the child's separate selves. Similar issues are at stake when the notion of *self-regulation* is raised. In popular usage and scholarly literature, self-regulation generally refers to a skill that can be acquired by individuals, though it also can be understood as contextual and interactive, that is, as a product of the interplay among individuals and social contexts to produce certain behavioral outcomes (McClelland et al. 2015). "The theoretical concept of self-regulation refers to taking in information, weighing choices and consequences, and making adaptive choice(s) to attain a particular goal" (McClelland et al. 2015, 7–8), but which information is treated as relevant and how "goals" are defined vary across disciplines, referring to the abilities to practice delayed gratification and impulse control (developmental psychology), to engage for the required period of time in specific school tasks (educational psychology), or to apply attention and working memory to accomplish complex tasks (neuropsychology) (8). "Self-regulation" and "self-control" are often used interchangeably, though in some literature "self-regulation" can refer specifically to an ability that is more internalized and flexible than a mere capacity to control one's behaviors in accordance with the immediate expectations of a caregiver (12).

The rising normativity of "self-regulation" as a goal for young children in the United States is evidenced by the adoption of this theme by Sesame Workshop, home of the long-running *Sesame Street* children's television program. According to the show's website, a 2013 initiative focusing on the character of Cookie Monster was designed to teach families about self-regulation, defined here as

> a set of critical skills for preschoolers [that] affects children socially, behaviorally and academically. In fact, self-regulation is often a better predictor of a child's academic success in reading and math than a child's IQ. . . . Unfortunately, children often begin kindergarten without important skills, such as being able to follow directions, stay on task with focused attention and regulate their own emotions using concrete strategies. In fact, kindergarten teachers view self-regulation as being more essential for school readiness than academic skills, such as counting or recognizing letters. Skills, such as regulating emotions, controlling and resisting impulses and exerting self-control are essential for social-emotional competence and academic success.[4]

The famously greedy Cookie Monster—a lovable, furry blue creature who had shoved his mouth full of crumbly cookies for decades—was now associated with the tag line "Me want it, but me wait" (Mustich 2013).[5] Though "self-regulation" applies to behavior in general, it has made its way into conversations about eating in particular: for example, researchers in the *Journal of Obesity* argued that "children's deficits in the ability to self-regulate their own behavior have been linked to rapid weight gain and obesity in middle childhood" (Frankel et al. 2012, 9).

In popular discourse, "self-regulation" can apply to the situation in which a child has absorbed parental expectations and learned to defer gratification adequately to discipline his own impulses, which is seen as a sign of emergent maturity. In an essay in the *New York Times*, one commentator discussed limiting children's screen time:

> It's easier said than done, but if you commit to the expectation that they will self-regulate per your rules, they'll get it (at least the older one). . . . I should say that I've eased up for my 13-year-old, who saved up for his own iPad, which he is required to use for school. No games or videos during the week . . . but I don't mind him reading articles and essentially wandering the Internet looking for interesting stuff during his free time in much the same way I do. . . . After years of parent-regulation, he's ready for some self-regulation. We'll continue to relax limits as he gets older. I hope we'll be able to do the same for the other children, but that's going to be child-dependent. (Dell'Antonia 2014b)

I heard similar principles applied to expectations of bodily and vocal restraint in the cafeteria, as when one visibly frustrated teacher announced to the school's fifth graders, "I am going to ask you to self-regulate today, because we can't have as much noise as yesterday." (At the end of the period, the teacher called one student up to the front of the room to lead her peers in a relaxation exercise.)

Some parents at Hometown had incorporated this language into their parenting practice. Interviewee Wendy, a married white/Caucasian mother of two and university instructor in her early forties, spoke of her daughter's conscientiousness in limiting her own consumption of desserts.

> W: [My daughter] is very good at self-regulating, like she'll even say . . . um, like if I'll say "It's a beautiful day, let's go to [the local ice cream

shop] and get some ice cream," she'll say, "oh but Mommy we already had cupcakes at school because it was somebody's birthday" and she won't want it.

JP: Wow.

W: She'll be like—yeah, and you know sometimes she's with me—"Oh honey, it's okay, everything's okay in moderation!" [laughs]

While praising her child, Wendy implied that her daughter's ability to self-limit was surprising for a child her age (six years at that time) and perhaps even showed a level of food awareness that slightly concerned Wendy by virtue of its unexpected seriousness.

In short, parents' worries about food were situated within broader ones about self-control, how to teach it, and how not to *over*teach it. In fact, in addition to teaching self-control and moderation to kids, parents were working to regulate themselves: to find balance as the right type of parents, exercising the correct kind or degree of power/discipline through food. In this sense, they were concerned not only about their children but about the modulation of their own personae. Their aspirations often were expressed in the negative, such as through talk about "helicoptering" and other figures of careful parenting gone wrong.

Helicoptering versus Benign Neglect

In my conversations with parents at Hometown about food—and, I began to notice, in my own social circles outside the research—I heard people speak of "helicopter parents" or of "hovering," sometimes in reference to distastefully overconcerned parents and sometimes, rather self-consciously, about oneself. For example, one Hometown mother who claimed that her own children ate very well—that they ate all kinds of nutritious foods without complaint—added that she would not be a "helicopter mom" about it; that wasn't her style. Kids, she believed, would eat if you didn't freak out about it or give them too many choices. Here, helicoptering seemed linked both with excessive parental anxiety and with the notion of catering to children's complaints. Claudia, a married white administrator at Hometown who also had a middle schooler there, spoke of how some children she had observed at the school— third, fourth, and fifth graders—were making their own lunches, and judging from what was in them ("Pringles, maybe nuts or a cheese stick. Where's the sandwich?"), she believed that their parents were short on time. "They are probably not taking the time to look in the lunch box." She observed that "I would never let my child . . . *I guess I'm just a hovering mother, but . . .*" (emphasis added). Even as she indicated she would never let her own children leave for school with such inadequate lunches—such a thing would not get under her radar—she expressed doubt or perhaps simply mitigated and softened her own claim to superiority by saying, "I guess I'm just a hovering mother."

Indeed, sometimes people at Hometown (and in my other social networks) mentioned "helicoptering" to express self-consciousness about their own parenting boundaries, as when a former graduate student of mine explained to me that she would not let her young children stay without her with relatives overseas because she was a helicopter mother. It could express deeper self-examination, too, as it did for Vera, a white Hispanic Hometown mother whose high schooler had been figuring out his own food intolerances and had communicated to her that he felt she was hovering; she said she had heard this and learned to step back a bit from the process of regulating his food choices. She acknowledged, "I think it's sort of my way of, um, shoving myself into his life, you know," a behavior that she had decided bespoke her own need to be needed by her child. The child, about fourteen years old at the time, willingly had gone on an elimination diet to remedy gastric symptoms that had turned out to be connected to food sensitivities. He was now feeling better and gradually adding foods back into his diet. She said she was letting up on her monitoring and hovering, though her tone suggested that this was not necessarily easy.

I attended an evening orientation session for parents whose children soon would be entering the middle school. One theme of discussion was the expectation that parents would see their children getting more independence there than they had in elementary school; for example, students would be expected to stay on top of their own assignments, with less "handholding" from parents. A middle school father who had been recruited to speak to the group offered that he "was a hand-holder by nature" and that this had been an adjustment for him. As the session continued, the conversation moved to Conscious Discipline and other topics, then back to the father, who volunteered, "I'm kind of a helicopter parent." He had worried about talk he had heard to the effect that teachers had little control over students here, and he had felt that mixing incoming sixth graders with older eighth graders was scary. He feared that his daughter would get lost, and that as a parent he would have little voice. Most of his fears had been unfounded, he said, though indeed the environment required more independence from children. As one example, he offered that kids were given the chance to miss deadlines; they were not ridden by their teachers along the way. (Later, the principal assured visitors that "people at this school are *amazingly* passionate about teaching your kids. *Amazingly*.")

Across these examples, "helicopter" and "hovering" were words that indexed uncertainty about the proper degree of attention and intervention in children's lives, whether it concerned a child's diet or her homework. This was not just a local preoccupation, but part of a national and perhaps global debate about parenting anxiety, not infrequently triggered by the topic of children's food. In 2014, a British press published a picture book (subsequently featured in the *New York Times*) titled *Q Is for Quinoa: A Modern Parent's ABC*. In addition to suggesting that trendily healthful quinoa was central to a modern style of parenting, the book playfully intermingled terms related to food with those evoking anxious pathology—its entries for the letter "o," for example, juxtaposed the words "organic" and "OCD" (obsessive-compulsive disorder)—as well as representing many classed rituals of parental consumer initiation: "cloth diapers," "IVF" (in vitro fertilization), "IKEA," and "over-scheduling" (Rickett and Wilson 2014). During the same year, *New York Times* columnist Mark Oppenheimer (2014) critiqued American attitudes toward the regulation of children's eating by way of commenting on recent controversy over chocolate milk being served in school lunches. "As a parent, I think that it's time to declare a period of benign neglect when it comes to food. Today, too many Americans make a virtue, even a fetish, of monitoring what goes into our children's mouths. Rather than raising our children to consume in moderation—whether food, drink, drugs or screen time—we forbid them pleasures that adults take for granted." Calls to practice benign neglect or simply moderation have been framed as pleas to stop the "madness" (Warner 2005) of child-rearing approaches that not only strain parents but may be more harmful than beneficial to children themselves. It is implicit in such discussions that overattention is practiced by parents with the resources of time and money to do so; for meanwhile, publicity about childhood obesity and diabetes continues to highlight what would appear to be other Americans' woeful underattention to, or undereducation about, proper nutrition.

Calls like Oppenheimer's for parental moderation in the realm of children's food should not be understood as a softening of attention or lowering of expectations placed on parents. This is, rather, a tense truce between conflicting imperatives of middle- and upper-middle-class adult personhood. These discourses highlight the challenges parents face in working out how their own, rather self-conscious progressivism should translate into daily, resource-intensive choices for their children; and they point to deep contradictions in contemporary, middle-class forms of American individualism (Kusserow 2004) whereby parents labor to present and understand themselves both as conscientious, well-informed monitors of their children's well-being and as laid-back, unneurotic, and open-minded.[6] Parents tended to be concerned to be attentive and engaged—to be closely involved with their children and to monitor their behavior, consumption, and health (both physical and emotional)—but also feared that overattention, overmonitoring, and overconstraint would harm their children and reveal a negative kind of persona for themselves as adults.

In this sense, insistence on moderation actually was quite affectively charged, as parents sought both to regulate and monitor their children's eating sufficiently and to deflect the personal qualities of "control" and "anxiety" away from their own personae. Thus in talking about feeding their children, parents also unwittingly articulated models of desirable self and relationship. People referred to notions of "moderation," and while—to me, and perhaps to many readers for whom these discourses will also seem familiar and reasonable—that can sound like a measured kind of self-awareness on the part of earnest parents, it is *also* indicative of a particular ideal of middle-class selfhood, whereby one should be "engaged" and actively protecting a child from what is available out there in an industrial food economy, yet meanwhile mindfully calm (as opposed to anxious) and respectful of a child's separate personhood. Calls for moderation in children's food are also, then, concerns about the boundaries of the self and about the adult experience of walking a tightrope to maintain such boundaries while still shielding and guiding a child.

Though my observations arise from a distinctly progressive, highly educated class niche in urban Atlanta, dramas of helicoptering and hovering as parental dysfunction take place on a national and international stage. Wiktionary defines "helicopter parent" as "a parent who pays an inordinate amount of attention to their children and often makes decisions, particularly educational ones, normally the province of the student."[7] In self-conscious opposition to the notion of helicoptering is "free range parenting," a philosophy popularized by writer and blogger Lenore Skenazy. In Skenazy's rendering, "helicopter parent" is "a sort of disparaging term for parents who believe their child is so vulnerable—to injury, to teasing, to disease and disappointment—that they have to sort of hover (like a helicopter) over the child, ready to swoop in if anything remotely 'bad' happens."[8] To call parental supervision "hovering" is to suggest that it is excessively nervous and unrelenting, the failing of a parent who should be allowing her child more space free from supervision. What is communicated is that while parents should not let potential risks escape their notice, they also must not be overvigilant nor protect their children from engaging with any risks at all. Critiques of helicopter parenting, with its implication of a whirring, watchful parental immediacy, denigrate parents "for their failure to 'let go,' which would enable their children both to experience the joys and freedoms of childhood and to develop their own resources for dealing with risk," even as the media continue to inform them of a "bewildering range of risks to their child" that they should be able to "anticipate and manage" (Bristow 2014, 214).[9]

Pamela Druckerman, author of the popular parenting book *Bringing Up Bébé: One American Mother Discovers the Wisdom of French Parenting* (2014b), observed that the excesses of helicoptering extend beyond the United States to middle classes around the world:

> I used to think that only Americans and Brits did helicopter parenting. In fact, it's now a global trend. Middle-class Brazilians, Chileans, Germans, Poles, Israelis, Russians and others have adopted versions of it too. The guilt-ridden, sacrificial mother—fretting that she's overdoing it, or not doing enough—has become a global icon . . . the economists Matthias

Doepke and Fabrizio Zilibotti say intensive parenting springs from rising inequality, because parents know there's a bigger payoff for people with lots of education and skills. . . . Hyper-parenting is also driven by science. The latest toddler brain studies reach parents in Bogotá and Berlin too. And people around the world are breeding later in life, when they're richer and more grateful, so the whole parenting experience becomes hallowed.[10]

My point is not to argue that a harmful form of "hyper-parenting" is taking over the world, though scholars have made powerful cases for the intensivity and "hallowedness" of parenting in the United States today (Hays 1996; Katz 2008; Zelizer 1994), and this study too supports the idea that some U.S. parents are highly involved in monitoring certain aspects of their children's lives. My intent rather is to show how intensivity is being struggled with—both encouraged and disavowed—in communities such as Hometown's as well as in some of the country's most authoritative media outlets.

In a coffee shop in Southeast Atlanta, I positioned my digital voice recorder to capture my conversation about children's food with a mother of two children who attended the charter school. Wendy hedged as she sat in her armchair that she was concerned about how what she was about to say was going to sound. Continuing, though, she told me that among parents she had observed in this school community, some were "very, um, like, I don't want to say that like—to me almost an extreme level of concern about everything that goes into their child's body. And my motto is more, you know, everything is okay in moderation, you know, and I don't want to—I mean I try to steer my kids to make healthy choices and I think my husband and I both eat pretty healthy so I think that speaks for itself, um—but I don't want them to have any kind of quirks or anything." "Or anxieties, yeah," I offered, echoing what she seemed to be getting at. "I don't want them to have food anxiety, you know," she continued. "I just want them to make good choices." She went on to speak of her daughter's surprising ability to self-regulate, mentioned above.

Rather than simply accepting at face value that adults like Wendy, while perhaps nutrition conscious, have not "gone overboard" like "some" parents and are self-aware about their attempts to balance a number of different concerns they have for their children's well-being, what if we step back a bit further to ask instead what it means, or what kind of work it does, that these adults so often employ self-deprecation, distancing, and softening strategies to present a certain low-keyness—even as they narrate their own careful attention to food and particularly to their children's food? In this neighborhood in which many explicitly valued "diversity" as an enriching aspect of community life and of a child's education, I heard parents both expressing concern about lower quality foods to which their own children might be exposed at school and, at the same time, striving to separate themselves from the appearance of overcontrol and to express acceptance toward those who made choices with which they disagreed.

While most of the parents with whom I conversed in this school community were able to describe for me at length the thought processes behind the choices they made and rules they set for their children's food consumption (whether that meant limiting sugar or insisting that children eat the same meal as their parents each evening), they also were likely to temper these depictions by assuring me that they were "moderate," "not too rigid," or "not freaking out" about it. Guiding children toward autonomously making "good choices" about food seemed to be something parents felt far less ambivalent about than they did about the notion of actively controlling and limiting their children's eating, especially as children grew older (Patico 2013). In this way, children's food summoned adult ambivalences about issues of control versus autonomy, regulation versus laissez-faire, and sameness versus difference.

Control as Attractive and Unattractive

A married white mother, Sheila, when describing her own preference to buy organic foods when possible, qualified that she was "not a total crazy person about it you know, I'm sort of like everything in moderation as long as we eat good. You know, I have a garden." A similar wish was expressed from different angles. Rather detailed descriptions of rigorous attention to what their family members consumed often could be tempered with acknowledgments that one's own choices might be seen as problematic by other parents. While chatting with married working mother Faye after a parents' Health and Wellness Committee meeting,

I asked if she'd be willing to be interviewed. She instantly agreed but warned me that her family was "wacky." When I said that sounded intriguing, she explained that "we are stricter than most, though we do let some things through." Later, as Faye detailed her practices, which emphasized meat broths and fats and included "nothing instant," she referred to herself as "manic and obsessive about the [choice of] fats." She said she would love to be able to promote her views on nutrition in the school community but felt it would be viewed as "extremism."

Faye spoke of understanding that not all families had the budget or priorities to eat the way her family did; hers was a two-income professional family, and she was able to come home from work in the late afternoon to prepare home-cooked meals every night. She said she had come to terms with the fact that upon occasion, other parents at the school would bring in things like Froot Loops for the snack her child's entire class would enjoy. "I've accepted that there's some things I can't control and as long as 80 percent of the time I feel like [he is] eating something healthy I will let the rest of that go. It's just gonna happen. You know, it's reality. I don't want him living a life thinking that everything is a no."

I heard similar sentiments in parents' depictions of their own or others' efforts at control as being futile or counterproductive, perhaps even detrimental. Diane (originally from Europe, and who worked a professional job part-time while her husband Robert was in a lucrative technology field) said that parenting was "a very good exercise in learning how to not have any control over anything, you know? You just—do what you do." Robert agreed, arguing that "as much as anything, as long as they understand—I think you've got to teach 'em how to look after themselves and make the choices." Later they offered that when you force kids to finish their food, it becomes a power issue and they didn't, as parents, make their children sit and eat. "Yeah, yeah," Robert said, "we don't beat her into submission." Control was opposed to the provision of choices, and overzealous pursuit of control was mocked.

As we chatted after dinner at Faye's house, she said that on nights like tonight, the children might take seconds (as they had), but she and her husband Adam did not require them to finish what they had in their plates (indeed, neither child had finished). The meal had been home-made chili made with "hidden" pureed carrots (Faye explained that she also sometimes hid a bit of liver in recipes, though "you can't go crazy with it" and expect the children to eat it) and a quinoa corn bread baked with bacon grease. I had watched her chop, puree, and cook with aplomb after greeting me warmly at the door, slightly harried: traffic had been worse than usual so dinner would run a bit late. At the table, Faye had reminded her son that "I made your favorite thing!"—chili—to which he replied that there were other things he liked better, such as pizza, and ultimately settled on the conclusion that this chili was his *fourth* favorite thing. As we talked later, Adam offered that the children were sometimes cunning; one would say something was "too spicy" when it was not spicy, having learned that this was an acceptable reason for a child to reject a food. I asked what happened when the kids did not like something; did their parents make something else for them? No; Adam elaborated that he thought "going down that road is a mistake" because then the children would understand that they had some control over what the family might do, which was not the message he wanted to give them. "That's an interesting point," mused Faye, as though she had not thought about it that way before. She acknowledged that she did accommodate them somewhat, such as offering a piece of fruit to replace something they did not like. "But they're good eaters."

Robert and Diane spoke about hormones in animal products and that to avoid them, they typically bought CSA (community supported agriculture) meats; but they noted that since there were still things you could not control, the issue of unwanted elements still came up: "snacks, sleepovers." Yet what the children had on a more daily basis shaped their palates, Diane believed. Robert went on to complain that there was a lot of control (that is, oversight) over the pharmaceutical industry but not over the food chain; Monsanto could do whatever it wanted, and by the time you found out it was a bad, you were a few generations down the line! This concern highlighted how "control" was not just abstract nor simply a control being exercised *over* children, but a control being wrested *from* other potentially nefarious influences.[11] Barry, a white father who did much of the cooking for his two-lawyer household, said the question was "how do you kind of control the torrent of stuff that's coming at them. You can't stop it all but you can try to direct it." You could not throw up your hands, he said, even though it was difficult to control even for yourself, "so you have to be able to say: okay, well, we're going to limit this, we're going to not do this, we're going to stop this, you know. I know you really, really want that but . . . even if you got it, it wouldn't satisfy because you'd just be on to next thing." The tasks of teaching children moderation and of pushing back an overwhelming onslaught of "stuff" were two sides of the same parental effort to maintain a modicum of control.

Again though, parents often framed this control gingerly, questioning and reassessing their own decisions and approaches. Robin, a Caucasian professional nutritionist, offered that she did not feel that she really controlled what her kindergartener ate "but I do say, 'hey, think about this. You shouldn't have chocolate milk and a juice [in the cafeteria]. That's a lot of sugar—not the best choices.'" She said that she was not very picky about the foods he chose at school because she cooked at home and felt that the one school meal, if less than ideal, would not be a significant problem. Later, she spoke of having loosened her limits on dessert recently: she had decided a dessert a day was alright for her son. "I mean, that's not a big deal. So, but as long as it's teaching him control. Like you can't have this huge bowl of ice cream. It's just, you know, just portion it out." The challenge was to carve out areas of control while ceding it (to some extent), especially at school and in the broader world. The child should be enabled to make some choices, but needed to be instructed in self-control and about "*best* choices" (especially when it came to sugar).

To some, children should be given the opportunity to make "bad" choices in order to learn to make "good" choices independently. This opinion came up, for example, in the controversy that surrounded a vending machine in the middle school lunchroom. Because it contained processed, caloric items such as a packaged honey bun (the honey bun seemed to be the most iconically offensive of the offerings there, which also include Doritos, Cheez-Its, Minute Maid lemonade, Gatorade, and Lorna Doone cookies), some parents and teachers had lobbied to have it removed. Married white teacher Tina reflected that parents at Hometown talked about the importance of children making independent decisions in the course of their educations, so it seemed ironic to her that they wanted to limit children's access to the vending machine. Instead of banning the machine, shouldn't they talk with their children about their own family's food practices and about making good decisions? She observed as well that when students moved from the elementary to the middle grades—which meant access to the vending machine—it was a rite of passage, "the most exciting thing ever." It was exciting for students not just because they got to buy certain items, but because of the very act of independent buying: bringing their money to school and using it was part of the experience of being a "big kid," moving into a context where things were less regimented and controlled than in elementary school. By the time they hit middle school, Tina added, "We are training them to make good choices. But to do that, you have to *give* them choices," such as whether and how to use the vending machine. She presented the vending machine, then, as an age-appropriate opportunity for students to practice exercising their own judgment and self-discipline.

Noelle, an African American mother who worked from home, was one of those who "would like to see the vending machine completely gone . . . it's just that whole dynamic of introduction at school, of what we're introducing them to." Yet when it came to chocolate milk being served in the cafeteria, to which some parents objected, Noelle took a different tack, one more similar to Tina's:

> I think [chocolate milk] should be there because I think at this school and what we stand for at this school is making choices and independent learning and sitting back and letting them work through something. They need to have options to make decisions on their own and to make the right decisions, otherwise when you get out in the real world, there's not—you know, the Mercedes dealership is not going to be closed. You can get any car you want, you understand what I'm saying? Like your concept of what you want in the world is all there available to you, you can make a decision and you know, if you make the decision [to go the Mercedes dealership] and get a car, you know it's going to be more expensive so you need to—I just think the judgment comes into play. You know, making those options and having to make those choices.

Noelle's implication was that if a child was kept from making her own choices in early adolescence, that same child might become an adult who had not learned the skills needed to self-limit independently and to defer gratification when it was strategic to do so (Patico 2013).

Thus contestation around issues such as whether there should be a vending machine and whether chocolate milk should be sold in the lunchroom was not only about the specific foods offered but also about the extent to which children should be trusted to make their own choices, on what terms. Was it preferable for parents and administrators to set up students for "success" (and protect their health in the shorter term) by limiting their array of choices to only "good" ones? Or was it crucial, especially by middle school, to let children make more of these decisions themselves—even if there was potential for many "unwise" decisions—in the name of training their capacities for independent self-management? How meaningful and risky should the choices offered to children be? What kind or degree of control was really desirable?

Giving the opportunity to make choices could be wielded as a parental management tool, as Amanda, a white university administrative professional, recognized when she spoke about negotiating conflicts with her middle-school-aged son. She had realized if she didn't appease a demand from her son, he stopped pushing back. "It's really just about the adapting and wanting to feel like he has some kind of control over the situation, and I also find that if I give him some choices—even if they're not choices he loves—that works better than not giving him any choices at all." She acknowledged too that she and her son faced similar challenges at times: when he wiped out the supply of Girl Scout cookies in the house and would not confess to having done so, his mother laughed, "I don't have a lot of self-control with Girl Scout cookies either, right, so I want to be human about it." Amanda sought to manage and guide her son's behavior through the provision of options even as she could relate to the "humanity" of having a weak spot for cookies, which seemed to imply too that she felt she should not be overly punishing when she considered his choices less than ideal.

Like Amanda, Karen expressed concern not to be too unyielding or harsh when it came to regulating her children's eating. She was a Black mother whose professional activity involved supporting her husband's fine arts business. After describing her efforts to educate her two daughters about why fast food was bad for them and to limit the sugar in their diets, Karen told me that her family usually ordered out Chinese food or wings (chicken wings prepared with a spicy sauce) on Friday nights. Since those nights involved the indulgence of eating fried foods, she explained, they tried to avoid them the rest of the week; fried foods were a treat, not an everyday experience. Karen was ambivalent, however, about limiting and surveilling her children's eating. She recalled that recently her daughter had put some chicken fingers and French fries in the oven to heat up for herself. Quietly observing how much her daughter would choose to prepare and to eat, Karen had said to herself, "Okay, I'm just going to monitor this"—her facial expression while telling this story suggesting a surreptitious, pseudo-casual side glance toward her daughter—rather than stepping in to tell her what was acceptable. When she saw that her daughter had consumed only a few pieces of the chicken and fries, Karen was reassured. "I try not to be a Nazi about it," said Karen of her efforts to manage and modulate the family's diet.

Tina similarly used Nazism as a metaphor for talking about the fact that school policies designed to ensure healthy eating by children could be taken too far. The school's well policy required that when parents brought in cupcakes for birthdays, they also needed to provide a "healthy choice" such as fruit, so that any child whose parents did not want to allow them to eat cupcakes would have an alternative snack and could still be included in the celebration. When her own son's birthday came around, Tina explained that she had offered cupcakes and, as the "healthy option," strawberry shortcake. "Okay, it's a little cakey," she allowed, "but it had strawberries, and I put a little whipped cream on it. I don't want it to be a Nazi state because birthdays are still important."

In expressing concern not to become "Nazis" toward their own children and students, adults showed how, while accepting that monitoring and limiting were parts of their jobs as parents, they were also acutely cautious about not carrying out these tasks too harshly. It seemed that nutritionally "healthy choices" could be in conflict with children's capacity for choice and for pleasure, and adults did not always take clear sides on which objective was more important. They implied that adults' best efforts to ensure healthy eating could become harmful to their children, inasmuch as they might stymie their freedom, self-determination, and enjoyment. They did not necessarily argue for Oppenheimer's "benign neglect," but they signaled awareness of some of the same concerns.

As we have seen, the choices parents made on these issues not only affected their children but also were part of their own public personae in the school and broader community. More than a year after our initial coffee shop interview, I was at Wendy's home for a weeknight dinner with her husband and two elementary-aged children. After a meal of chicken, green salad, and corn on the cob, as we were clearing the table, her husband asked what my final product would be—or, Wendy inserted, perhaps he was really asking what my research question was. (Though she knew the topic of my study, she was asking a more pointed, academic question.) I explained that one of my interests was in how these food issues are connected with class—how people judged and perceived class identities through food; and that furthermore, as the project went on, I had become interested increasingly in issues of independence versus control and how these general issues of child socialization came out through food. Both parents nodded, and Wendy affirmed, "I can really see how those things about parenting style come out through food."

Continuing, Wendy said that "parents make snap judgments based on food," admitting that she did, too. As an example, she said that her family had gone to a neighborhood festival the day before and had stopped to get food on the way. Normally they would have done Subway [a submarine sandwich franchise] sandwiches and gotten something like a ham and cheese on wheat there. But "things happened" and they showed up with greasy pizza instead. And, she said, she observed other families with their hummus and grapes and things, and she felt self-conscious, feeling an impulse to justify their food by saying, "I was in a hurry!" Her husband chimed in to remind her, "Hey, it was Neighborhood Pizza, so that's supporting a local business!" He seemed to be neither entirely serious nor mocking in this defense, but rather savvily pointing out that there were multiple ways that this game could be played, that is, different ways in which people in this community found value and spun "correctness."

Wendy said that she felt that some people wore their Whole Foods, organic, and gluten-free foods "like a badge of honor," while some went too far in the "other direction." Looking to her husband for affirmation, Wendy concluded that they had "always been about moderation." She contrasted this approach to that of a relative of hers who was "literally up in the faces" of her children trying to get them to eat certain foods; Wendy thought this stressed out the children and would lead them to have "issues" with food as they grew up. When I asked about any changes Wendy had seen in her two children's eating habits in the time since we had last spoken, she spoke a bit about each child and said that they were becoming a bit more open to experimenting by trying new foods. I asked whether this had changed their rules at all, such as any rules about what the children must eat or finish, but this didn't seem to be the case. Her spouse offered, "They are good eaters in general. They're hungry. You saw what they ate and they will be back in a little while asking for an apple." Wendy told me that they, the parents, never took a stance of "you must eat it." If there was something a child wouldn't eat, they would offer a "healthy substitute. If you don't like it, eat carrots. I don't think we've ever forced them to eat anything they don't like. Also, we try not to have stuff in the house we don't want them to eat." (Indeed, earlier that evening, when Wendy had put a bag of baby carrots on the dinner table, she had explained that her seven-year-old daughter would probably not eat the green salad that was there for everyone else, but could have the choice to pick carrots instead. When she really hated what was for dinner, they would give her a yogurt.)

But Wendy, still thinking about my question about rules, pondered, "Maybe we adjust a little, offer them more things, try to convince them a little more since they are more rational. But you hear stories of kids sitting at the table for two hours." She reiterated that basically her children were good eaters and "we trust them" if they really don't like something. "I'm just not cooking two meals," she qualified, which was something she had watched her sister do. As for many parents, it seemed important to Wendy that she not attempt to control or limit her children's eating with excessive stringency or rigidity—even as she drew the line at accommodating children's tastes too generously by preparing separate meals just for them.

The Beleaguered American Individual

Models of the self tend to seem natural and self-explanatory from an insider perspective, which can make it difficult to gain critical purchase. Anthropologists have done so by employing cross-cultural comparisons. In one notable ethnography Dorinne Kondo (1990), a Japanese American who conducted anthropological fieldwork on labor, gender, and conceptions of selfhood in Tokyo, contrasted what she learned about Japanese ways of thinking about the self with the American ones she had grown up with more intimately. Kondo defined the Western model of self as one that was bounded, coherent, and consistent through time (see also Giddens 1991), and she contrasted this with the one she observed in 1980s Tokyo, where "persons seemed to be constituted in and through social relations and obligations to others. . . . Relationally defined selves in Japan—selves inextricable from context—thus mount a radical challenge to our own assumptions about fixed, essentialist identities and provide possibilities for a consideration of cultural difference and a radical critique of 'the whole subject' in contemporary Western culture" (22, 33). In other words, Kondo both denaturalized the idea of an essential, coherent, individualized self, which many Americans take for granted, and argued that in some cultural contexts (such as Japan) the misleading ideology of "the whole subject" is not even in play.

Anthropologist Amy Borovoy (2001) drew related comparisons in a very specific context: that of Japanese support groups for the families of alcoholics. These groups had adopted a U.S. ideology of the harms of "codependency." This framework assumes that poor emotional boundaries between family members and excessive responsibility for one another's behaviors and feelings are signs of dysfunction and often part of the familial context of addiction. In Japan, reactions to these ideas were mixed because relationships that might be identified as "codependent" in American therapeutic settings here were treated as rather normative examples of filial obligation and desirable interdependency.

> In the context of dominant American ideologies that fetishize individual rights and view social participation as a threat to self-development, there is little language for conceptualizing the necessary compromises in self-determination that sociality entails. . . . In contrast, Japanese postwar cultural cosmologies describe a wide range of asymmetrical hierarchical relations as benevolent and mutualistic, making it difficult to draw a sharp line between those relationships that are "for one's own benefit" and those that veer into exploitation, systematic forms of inequality, or violations of dignity. (Borovoy 2001, 23)

Again, cultural context shapes what people see as natural, functional, and healthy in self-identity and interpersonal relationships. As compared with these recent Japanese contexts, the "Western" model relies on a notion of an individual self with clear emotional boundaries as both natural and normative (cf. Carsten 2012). As we have noted, this conceptualization of the self has a deep history connected with European intellectual, institutional, and spiritual life (Mauss 1938/1985; Lutz 1988); in its most contemporary version, it tends to emphasize the responsibility of individuals to maintain those boundaries through rigorous practices of self-management.

That being said, what we might call "American individualism"—or with a more contemporary slant, "neoliberal selfhood"—can be practiced and understood in a variety of ways. A simplistic, unitary view of "Western individualism" as the opposite of "sociocentric" models can create a "reverse Orientalism . . . in which the Western self is often flattened into a supposedly uniform and rather generic individualism" (Kusserow 2004, 20; see also Carsten 2012). To avoid this, we can attend to how this individualism shifts over time, is contradicted by other currents, varies from context to context, and is expressed in a range of highly practical and sometimes implicit ways—such as in Conscious Discipline workshops and in school debates about honey buns and vending machines.

This is also why it makes sense to consider practices and discourses that would seem to bear little relation to children's food but that, upon closer observation, do take part in related notions of self and self-management: for example, the realm of romance. To sociologist Anthony Giddens (1991), the modern (Western) self is a reflexive project of self-narration that requires, among other things, a "pure relationship" that helps to fill in one's self-narrative. This is a romantic partnership perceived to depend on disinterested feeling and compatibility as opposed to financial considerations, kin expectations, or "traditional" social structures (see also Carrier 1999 on modern friendship). Anthropologist Julienne Obadia (2016, 2018) observed an updated version of this idea in polyamorous couples (committed romantic partners who agree to have a nonexclusive relationship). Though considered unconventional by many, polyamorous relationships draw on ideologies and strategies that are similar to those that currently reign in other arenas, namely professional labor. For while these relationships require labor-intensive emotional effort that is felt to be satisfying by practitioners, they also draw on "the impersonal management techniques of neoliberal capitalism for inspiration and assistance" (Obadia 2016). "They valorize choosing, self-sovereign individuals, who come together to enable one another's development as choosing, self-sovereign individuals, pathologizing distributions of responsibility, desire, and personhood itself that are not neatly contained within each individual, and insisting that feelings of mutual inhabitation are not valid, and are products of anxiety to be named and known through self-examination and communication" (Obadia 2016). In concrete terms, such values are enacted and validated through specific strategies that highlight both autonomy and (carefully framed) relatedness. The practice of polyamory, as observed by Obadia, involved strategies such as the creation of written contracts between the two primary members of the relationship. These articulated their understandings, intentional boundaries, and aspirations for the partnership. Meanwhile, in a Conscious Discipline parent group at one member's house, we had glasses of Trader Joe's red wine while white married mother Rebecca explained that her own family had a formal contract whereby if a child didn't ask permission to use the iPad, the device was taken away for a week. "It's in the contract. The kids don't fight it," she explained, suggesting that part of the attraction of this method was the avoidance of conflict through the understanding that children have already agreed to the family's rules—have even put it in writing—which frames it as a matter of their own choice and commitment.

Rebecca's family also had posted its "guiding principles" on a wall in the open living room / kitchen area. The leading principle concerned the family members supporting one another in taking care of their bodies and minds to achieve peace. Rebecca told our small group that it was embarrassing because sometimes people would come in and see the framed statements and comment, "Oh, you've got. . . ." The tone in which Rebecca echoed them seemed to suggest that people found it quaint or silly. "But we need it so we don't forget," she said of her family.[12]

The polyamorist's anxiety to keep her own personhood distinct from her partner's, like the American therapist's concern to identify and transform codependency, might seem at first unrelated to the self-examination of the progressive parent who worries about the school vending machine, wonders whether he has offered the "right" choices to his child, composes a family mission statement, or questions whether she is "wacky," a "Nazi," a "helicopter parent," or an appropriately protective one. Yet all these concerns share common themes. Social theorist Eva Illouz (2008) argues that the "emotional style" of contemporary capitalism demands "the *suspension of one's emotional entanglements in a social relationship.* . . . The emotional control of the type propounded by the therapeutic persuasion is at once the mark of a *disengaged self* (busy with self-mastery and control) and of a *sociable self*—bracketing emotions for the sake of entering into relations with others" (104). The themes play out variously, in contexts with specific dynamics and concerns, but the notes struck—notes of tenuous balance between relatedness and autonomy, enmeshment and independence, involvement and coolness—resonate across contexts.

Conclusion

In the realm of children's food, middle-class Atlanta parents were combatting a seemingly "mainstream" acceptance of sugary, packaged, and other lower quality foods even as they deployed strategies that echoed corporate management and that were dependent on ideas of the bounded, contractually defined individual. In her work on intensive mothering, sociologist Sharon Hays (1996) described labor-intensive parenting practices as a counter to commercialization; this style of mothering was a means of affirming that not all spheres of life were commercialized, and it brought along with it ideas about the sacredness of childhood and of parenting (see also Zelizer 1994). Yet these very realms of intimacy, market wariness, and effortful personal care also are engaged using practical models and implicit ideologies that share much, perhaps more and more, with capitalistic models of possessive individualism in which the individual is understood as the unique owner of his or her body, self, and capacities.

Contemporary food movements—from vegetarianism to locavorism ("eat local") to fad diets—focus on individual change and consumer choice rather than systemic policy interventions (Lavin 2013; Allen and Guthman 2006). In this sense, they both critique consumerism and the "food industrial complex" *and* reproduce logics of neoliberalism that go hand in hand with today's consumer and labor markets, which ask individuals to be self-regulating and which privilege consumerism as a (limited) realm of choice and power. As political theorist Chad Lavin (2013, 5, 150) puts it,

The tools and practices of dietary regulation help to produce the very kind of self-reliant and entrepreneurial subjects needed by a capitalist economy.

Concerns about this powerlessness are channeled in to manageable, metabolic programs for individual control. Consumer activity is elevated to political action, control of one's body compensates for control over one's life.

My conversations with parents at Hometown were not explicitly oriented toward political action, and the degree and emphasis of their food concerns varied (for example, whether they leaned toward vegetarianism or emphasized cage-free and organically raised local meats; whether they shopped for organic milk and eggs or kept chickens and goats in their own back yards; whether they limited fat content or welcomed fats as long as they were minimally processed; whether they refused packaged snack foods or just sought to keep them a minimum; whether Goldfish crackers were wholesome enough since they were not sugary or were suspect as high-carbohydrate processed food; and so on). Yet the broader context of their practices and ideas concerning food and child socialization reflected deeper and shared preoccupations with the boundaries between themselves and their children. Striking the right (or *a* right) balance between protection and letting go seemed to be a rather tenuous and difficult task, but it was one parents generally took on themselves without question.

In the face of such stress, it is not surprising that parents such as Rebecca attended workshops such as "Mindpeace for Moms," which, according to an emailed flyer, promised mothers a nonjudgmental environment in which to pursue their own "sacred journey" by cultivating "the capacity to connect, speak truthfully, and take bold action to create a life rich with love, purpose, meaning, and contribution." Similar to Conscious Discipline and the principles of mindfulness advocated at Hometown, emphasis on one's *own* individual and authentic story coexists with the mission to "connect" with other, presumably unique and respected individuals, including their children.

Forms of stress and ways of coping with that stress varied, of course, and Carmen, a married African American staff member at the school and a mother whose children attended a different charter school in Atlanta, highlighted this: she was busy finishing a degree and found she often took her two girls to McDonald's ("Pick it up and eat it in the car on the way home . . . nice and healthy . . .") to eat on weeknights "because we're running out of time" after work and after-school activities. She perceived Hometown parents as particularly health-conscious, and when I asked what she thought about some of their common concerns (sugar, high-fructose corn syrup, pesticides, and the like), she answered, "I think those are all wonderful concerns to have and if you can figure out a way to work them into your lifestyle, that's great, but I don't know very many people who can work them into their lifestyle." To Carmen, the ability to do so or not was patterned by race: "A lot [of] white people . . . can probably try to figure it out, but I don't know any Black people who do all that." Yet as we shall see, many nutritional concerns were shared by white and African American parents I interviewed, in ways that suggested class to be the more salient factor in divergent food styles at Hometown. Still, Carmen's comment spoke to the ways in which such material and emotional repertoires helped define both race and class as these identifications were lived and perceived.

For many at Hometown, providing choices, lending skills of emotional regulation, and being "human" about problems concerning Girl Scout cookies were all ways in which parents sought to walk very careful lines with their children. The specter of the helicopter parent reminded them that it was all too easy to be judged for one's best efforts to guide and protect a child, even as too little attention was also unacceptable and dangerous. "They are probably not taking the time to look in the lunch box. . . . I would never let my child . . . I guess I'm just a hovering mother." The ambivalence expressed in such statements is part of an urban, middle-class American understanding of the boundaries of the self, which are policed rather anxiously as parents attempt to avoid becoming helicopters but also accept the responsibility of protecting their children from the onslaught of poor-quality foods they might consume otherwise.

3

"He Doesn't Like Anything Healthy!"

Constructions of Childhood

Among my many activities at Hometown Charter, I co-taught an enrichment course on food and culture for middle schoolers. A theme that recurred in our classroom conversations was the idea that certain foods, while marked as "junk" or as "unhealthy," were also collectively felt to be appropriate and important at certain times: for example, when used to mark festive occasions such as birthdays, holidays, or rites of passage. Meanwhile, students and their parents both spoke about children as particularly partial to the appeals of sweets, packaged chips, and other "unhealthy" foods. Thus it was with some intentionality and self-awareness that I brought in donuts for the students in my class to enjoy at our last meeting, close to the end of the school year in 2015. They were visibly and audibly pleased. One student remarked, "I thought you would bring something like carrot sticks . . . healthy food." When I said that I hoped they would enjoy them, another student piped up, "Of course we will! We're kids!"

Adults at Hometown were caught between concerns to regulate their children's food consumption and not to overcontrol their children. Recall one mother who, while serious about feeding her children very healthy food, also worried that if they did not have enough opportunities to eat less nutritionally optimal items such as birthday cake, they would not remember their childhoods as full and happy—especially given her own illness and the shadow it cast. We have seen the conflict and ambivalence that were in play when parents both encouraged kids to eat in "healthy" ways *and* worried about overenforcing those rules because of their hesitation to limit the autonomy and personhood of the child. In this chapter, we look more closely at how Hometown adults linked certain kinds of food and eating habits with childhood itself. Further, this chapter explores children's own perspectives on the meanings of childhood as constructed through food. In classrooms and lunch-rooms, I heard children explore ways of talking about food and nutrition that closely mirrored adults'; I also heard them rather self-consciously take on stances that sometimes opposed adults' in their goals but mir-rored them in certain assumptions. For both adults and children often acknowledged that as compared with adults, children had bigger ap-petites for sugar and junk and less self-control to limit themselves from indulging those appetites. "*Of course we will! We're kids!*"

But the idea that "of course" children like sugary treats such as do-nuts merits consideration. To many American (and, undoubtedly, other) readers, this will sound entirely commonsensical and familiar: yes, of course, kids do like sugary treats. Yet we cannot uncritically assume that children naturally, inherently, or unproblematically *are* how adults in our society tend to describe them. The tastes and habits adults ob-serve in children are shaped by cultural norms and commodity markets. Moreover, adults' perceptions of children are filtered through their own histories and goals. We will examine both how childhood is imagined by adults through food and how incorporating children's own reflections and actions shifts the picture.

Including the voices of children in anthropological research entails rec-ognizing children as competent social agents and potential co-researchers, even as the ethical dilemmas and interpretive complexities of ethnogra-phy may be especially weighty when working with children (James 2007; Bluebond-Langner and Korbin 2007; Valentine 1999). It can be tempt-ing to cast the perspectives of children as voices of "authenticity and in-nocence." Yet as in any ethnographic account, individuals' utterances are chosen and wielded by the ethnographer to particular analytical ends (James 2007, 261, 263, 265). Nor are those voices precultural, even if adults at times represent children as the inverse of all adults are supposed to be, learn, and master. Children's perspectives may be "silenced by images of childhood that cling to the more traditional, developmental discourse of children's incompetence, rather than competence, as social actors," and such discourses themselves impact the experiences of children at home and at school (James 2007, 266). For all of these reasons, as we listen to adults talk about what children are like and even as we hear children themselves chime in on these matters, it is important to take into account the interdependent social contexts from which they both speak.

University institutional review boards are especially concerned to protect vulnerable populations such as children, prisoners, illegal migrants, or the mentally ill—those who may have less capacity for meaningful consent, greater structural vulnerabilities within institutions, or greater risk of psychological harm or legal ramifications—from any potentially detrimental outcomes of scientific research. While my ethnography was unlikely to be harmful or particularly intrusive to any child (or adult) at Hometown, I was aware while planning my study and submitting my IRB protocol that schools are in a position to guard the privacy and well-being of their students and that any requests for direct enrollment of children as interviewees could require a good deal of trouble and paperwork for administrators, possibly causing more consternation than was merited by my research needs. Mindful of the fact that my leading goal in the research was to investigate adults' ways of thinking about children and their food—while also wanting to place their narratives in their organic and interactive social contexts as far as possible—I put together a plan that focused mainly on adults (interviewing, attendance at parent meetings, and so on) but that also included opportunities to observe informally teachers, parents, and students in community with one another in the ongoing social life of the school. Hometown administrators and teachers were generous about allowing me to observe and participate in campus life in various ways, such as attending school events and observing classes.

I was also eager to make myself useful to the community given their generosity in hosting me. After some conversation with school administrators, it was decided that they would benefit from daily help in the cafeteria during the third, fourth, and fifth grade lunch periods (serving children aged roughly eight to eleven), when fewer teachers were on official duty to supervise than in the younger grades' lunches and the additional help would be welcome. My two research assistants and I divided up the five days of the week, so that barring illness one of us was always there to help out. While I did not initiate conversations with students during these lunch periods nor record any identifiable information about individual children, I learned a great deal by being present for the lunchtime routine. I also heard and was engaged by students in conversations about food at times, and some of those conversations are recounted in this chapter, again without any identifiable details given about the students. One of my assistants also helped out with Hometown's middle school after-school program.

When a middle-grades enrichment class (serving students aged roughly eleven to fourteen) was offered that accompanied the building of a new vegetable garden on the school grounds, I attended many of the class meetings. Students participated in helping to plant the garden behind the school and learned about the crops as well as issues in food politics such as the potential dangers of genetic modification. Toward the end of the term, I ended up assisting the instructor by facilitating group conversations about nutrition and the social meanings of food when extra course content was needed. Through subsequent conversations with the class teacher and principal, we decided that it would be mutually beneficial for me to play a bigger role and to plan a new class on food in the following term.

The course—co-led by the new school chef and me—would not focus on the garden but rather would engage the children in an examination of the role of food in their own lives at school and at home (my job) as well as getting them into the kitchen and familiarizing them with the processes by which meals were produced at school (the chef's task). I created an amendment to my IRB protocol that allowed me to record observations and collect written assignments from those students from whom I had received both a parental consent form and a child assent form. Nine of the sixteen or seventeen students in the group, which included girls and boys, Black and white, from the sixth through eighth grades, ultimately submitted both of those forms. (An additional four submitted child assent forms but no parental consent forms, so I did not collect their materials. I did not administer a demographic survey for any of the students; thus any racial/ethnic identifications made are my estimations.)

This chapter recounts some broad observations from our work together as a group and includes specific spoken and written contributions from several among the nine students who opted in to the study. I valued the input of students not because they represented the authentic voices of childhood in some pure state, but rather because they were positioned social actors of the community with their own interpretations to be considered (James 2007; Bluebond-Langner and Korbin 2007; Thomas and O'Kane 1998; Metcalfe et al. 2008). Thus I approach children not as raw, unfinished adults but rather as people actively mastering and playing with adult norms around food as well as engaging in their own, somewhat distinct and more peer-driven food practices.

The scene of the school lunchroom provides a context for listening to the ways that adults reasoned about what children wanted and needed as well as the ways that children navigated food cultures. While we will examine, among other issues, some of the pressures faced by the school in creating school lunch menus that pleased staff, parents, and children, this discussion does not point to specific correctives to the social justice issues raised by scholars of school lunch politics such as Janet Poppendieck (2010) and Julie Guthman (e.g., Allen and Guthman 2006). Rather, its focus is on how risk society's food cultures shape not only culinary tastes, not only our experiences and assumptions about which foods are easy or hard to like, but also our perceptions of children and how their tastes and abilities differ from adults'. In other words, the point is not to question whether most kids at Hometown really like donuts, but rather to examine how childhood as a category is constructed and reinforced through such conversations. Ultimately, "the child" as constructed through food at Hometown also teaches us about the meanings of adulthood in this community—and how universalizing statements about "children" implicitly incorporate assumptions and judgments about class and other forms of social difference.

From the Sacred Child to the Selective Child

Elinor Ochs, Clotilde Pontecorvo, and Alessandra Fasulo (1996) furnish an excellent starting point for denaturalizing the presumed connections between children and specific ways of eating in the United States. These linguistic anthropologists analyzed dinnertime conversations among U.S. and Italian families, and they found distinct differences. When the middle-class Californian families in their study talked about food, they focused on nutritional contents and invoked moral reasoning to explain why children should eat the foods parents wanted them to eat. Adults and children were often in conflict at the dinner table, with children expressing opposition to adults' preferences. Adults expected that children would like dessert but dislike many savory foods (while adults were understood to enjoy both), and dessert was held out as a reward for the conscientious eating of one's dinner. Generational differences were "unwittingly promoted through cautionary comments of parents that anticipate[d] the possibility that a child may not enjoy a particular food" (Ochs, Pontecorvo, and Fasulo 1996, 35). Whereas the Americans tended to consider children's tastes as inherently distinct from adults' as a group, the Italian families by contrast paid more positive attention to the role of pleasure in directing one's food choices, and they encouraged children to express a diverse set of tastes as part of their growing, unique personalities. Each population had distinct pedagogical goals and distinct assumptions about who children were vis-à-vis adults.

More broadly, the category of childhood and the meanings attached to it have been linked to fundamental shifts in capitalist economies. Sociologist Viviana Zelizer (1994, 8–9) has examined how the growth of an industrial economy, with its splitting of economic production away from the home, came along with increasing value placed on family members—particularly women and children—no longer as laborers, but as emotional actors and assets. Men earned a "family wage" while women were hailed as caregivers in the "cult of true womanhood" (9). With the passage of child labor laws and other cultural shifts from the 1870s to the 1930s, children became economically "worthless" and emotionally "priceless." Falling birth and mortality rates also contributed to this revaluing of children, which was evidenced in phenomena such as outrage over child deaths caused by streetcars, payments to parents for the wrongful death of a child, and the rising desirability and cost of child adoptions. Moreover, childhood became "sacralized": in an increasingly commercialized environment, childhood was consigned to a noncommercial, nonproductive, yet precious existence; education and play were appropriate there, but economically productive labor was not (11). These shifts were gradual, contested, and class-inflected, but they progressively took place across the United States (209).

Sociologist of childhood Daniel Cook (2004) has examined the rise of the child consumer, particularly as seen in the clothing industry circa 1917 to 1962. He notes that in consumer markets of the time, the definition of the "child" and "childhood" increasingly involved "extending to children the status of more or less full persons, a status most concretely realized when children gain recognition and adjudication as legitimate, individualized, self-contained consumers" (Cook 2004, 3). Not only were children the targets of direct marketing using popular culture characters, but children themselves were posited as "subjects with desire": that is, individuals with the wherewithal to want things and to have those desires and needs treated as legitimate (3, 12). To Cook, childhood indeed held sentimental value as described by Zelizer, but in twentieth-century consumerism this value became less a "bulwark against the market" than a "portal between children and merchants"—for example, through the marketing of "beneficial" children's goods to mothers (11). Americans' imagination of childhood innocence, preciousness, and authenticity not only marked off their children as nonlaborers, then, but also worked to frame and extend children's agency as consumers with desires to be served.

The targeted marketing of convenience foods to children has been on the rise since the 1970s, often promoting the purchase of foods that parents like those at Hometown consider to be junk foods. As we saw earlier, brands such as Annie's cater to concerned parents with convenience foods such as macaroni and cheese mixes that are marked as healthier than more mainstream brands of similar items. The construction of "children's food" cannot be reduced to a marketing scheme, however, but is part of a larger symbolic framework through which food marks life stages and the rhythms of everyday life. Scholars of children's food observe that these items often have meaning precisely through their opposition to regular family meals and to the preferences of adults generally, so that they work to demarcate children as separate from, and inferior to, adults (James 1998; Curtis, James, and Ellis 2010). "In highly commercialized food cultures, 'children's foods' and 'children' define one another, reflecting one another's presumed qualities—particularly their inadequacies—vis-à-vis adult rationality and aesthetics" (Patico and Lozada 2016, 202). Yet children are also actively involved in this process: sociologist Allison James (1998) has shown how items such as the inexpensive, mass-produced candies called "kets" in Britain reveal how children use foods to create their own worlds that are experienced as separate from and oppositional to adults'. James found that children, by consuming items that resembled inedible objects, were brightly colored, and did not fit into the familial scheme of meals, in effect confused adult categories and "create[d] for themselves considerable room for movement within the limits imposed upon them by adult society" (395).

Marketing campaigns often, in turn, frame foods targeted to children as fun and "anti-adult" in their sensibilities (Pomeranz, Lobstein, and Brownell 2009).

These marketing campaigns appeal to and augment categories that exist in the mundane perceptive frameworks of everyday life. At Hometown, I noticed that even when describing the idiosyncrasies of their own children, parents often used a more general category of the "typical child" to play against. Thus when parents described their children as either "normal for their age" or unusual compared to other children, they implicitly invoked the category of childhood at large. Kristin, a married mother of two who identified as "Caucasian (European) and Chicano" and who worked as an independent consultant, explained that she wished her seven-year-old son ate more vegetables, though there were some things he would eat predictably, if not eagerly—such as a few spinach leaves or some avocado ("which I know is not technically a vegetable," Kristin laughed)—so that she would put a token amount of that plus some fruit on the side of his dinner plate while the adults ate bigger servings of raw vegetables. As for his general tastes, "I would describe him as normal for his age. [laughs] But I would think he tends to like things that are pretty typical, or that I've seen to be typical at that age. Quesadillas, grilled cheese, mac and cheese, things that—eggs. His favorite, favorite thing, like I said, is breakfast for lunch or dinner. That's his number one."

Jane, a married Caucasian psychotherapist, noted that her five-year-old son had been angry when none of the other kids at school tried the "really yummy okra" that she had brought in for their class snack. "He was like, my mom made this and it's so good, like we love this." She had brought the class snack for her older daughter just a few days ago and "we ran out of sugar so we had to make sugar-free, kinda hippie banana bread muffins. And my daughter said nobody liked them, which—I really wasn't surprised. But I was like, well, you know . . . what are you gonna do?" She said her kids were "foodies" and that her family did not "do kid food." Not "doing kid food" seemed to be a positive thing, especially as she characterized her children as "foodies," which carried a class inflection of knowledge and cultural capital as well as active interest in cuisine.

By contrast, Rita, an African American Hometown staff member and mother, told me a bit about her own son's awareness of healthy eating, and instead of taking credit for it she talked about the influence of Hometown. By her own telling, Rita's family (which included her husband, their kindergartener, and their two teenage/young adult children) had been influenced by the health-conscious environment that prevailed at this school, which her youngest child also attended. Recently, she had become accustomed to seeing cut carrots, mini cupcakes, and juice boxes or water at cookouts and children's birthday parties, rather than the sodas and hot wings that had been expected party fare in her previous communities. Unlike most of the households in my study, Rita's qualified for reduced-price lunch. In addition to working at Hometown, she held a part-time job at a local grocery store. She said that she mainly bought the store brand of everything, particularly meats. As described earlier, when probing in an interview with Rita about her grocery shopping habits, I asked whether she was concerned about things like high-fructose corn syrup, chemical additives, and antibiotics in meat—issues other parents had brought up. In response, she addressed the issue of food safety more broadly, saying that she always saw the list of recalled foods at the store. "And lately I have been 'cause the five-year-old [her son] did a task in the after-school program about healthy eating so now he's into like recognizing sugar, which is kind of a weird kid. [laughs] 'You can't fry fish anymore, you can't fry chicken anymore.' So he's into that, yeah . . . 'Oh you can't buy sugar.'" Rita thus redirected my question about food additives to general trends in healthy eating, and she found that her child's growing attention to these matters was unexpected; it made him a "weird kid." It seemed to be positive to her, but it was still counter to expectation.

Overall, there was loose consensus around the idea that children preferred sugary, packaged, mildly flavored, and starchy foods, even if specific children diverged from expectations. There was also conviction that children preferred familiar foods, as when one third grade teacher told me that the students were not excited about the day's lunch, whose main course was a chicken drumstick. I commented that I thought it looked pretty good, and she agreed that the food was good in this cafeteria. But, she thought, if they had not had chicken in that form at home, they did not like it. Her own son had told her, "I'll eat whatever they've got in the cafeteria, as long as it's not that chicken!" Another teacher with a child at the school had a similar story about her own son: he liked chicken but that particular drumstick he just would not do. "For this week I'm okay," she processed, "except Friday which is turkey burger. He doesn't like that. He likes it when I make it, but not here." One father told me at the school's fund-raising run about his notably picky third grader. When I told him about my research, he said, "You should talk to my son; he's a whole project unto himself. He's a picky eater . . . he'll eat bagels, cereal, did I say bagels? . . . White rice . . . vanilla yogurt. . . ." Lately the boy had gotten a taste for steak, which his parents were happy about. The father said that this son had always been hyper-cautious about foods that way. Yet, he noted, the boy was an athlete and healthy, so "it seems to work for him." "So you don't force him to eat anything?" I asked. "No, we don't. It would be a battle every day."

Parents dealt with specific, individual children and their requests, balancing instruction with accommodation. The preference for children to participate in familial food cultures sometimes ceded to making room for children to be "normal" and to avoiding daily "battles," suggesting that parents did not necessarily see it as within their power to shift children's preferences, at least at this stage of their lives. Yet parents' general commentaries about child feeding indicated that teaching children to modulate and constrain their own desires was a big part of what parenting was all about, since "normal" children's tastes were not really considered desirable. In the meantime, invoking a general characterization of "kids" and their food issues helped adults to normalize conflicts as to be expected and made a child's exemplary nutritional awareness or broader palate a surprise or point of special pride. The issue of "what kids like" and how parents and administrators should indulge or combat those desires became especially salient in discussions about the school lunch program at Hometown.

School Lunch: Debating What Children Need and Want and How to Give It to Them

The National School Lunch Program was founded in the 1940s, but it had precedent in the Americanization movements of the early twentieth century and their efforts to teach newcomers middle-class tastes and habits (Levine 2008, 5–6). As the Lunch Program evolved, debates arose concerning how school lunches could help to alleviate poverty as well as how to balance local and federal expense against children's nutritional needs (Levine 2008; Patico and Lozada 2016). In the twenty-first century, contestation has surrounded school lunches as well as classroom birthday celebrations and vending machines due to concern that schools are contributing to, rather than helping to ameliorate, childhood obesity through the sale or provision of sugary and high-fat snack foods to students (Crooks 2003). The debates have only intensified since the passage of the Obama administration's Healthy, Hunger-Free Kids Act in 2010, which triggered new guidelines for caloric content, sodium content, and other aspects of menus (Confessore 2014).

These changes generated appeals from school administrators and corporate lobbyists who needed to figure out how to institute them without financial losses (due to increased costs) and putative food waste (via students' thrown-away lunches) (Confessore 2014; see also Dell'Antonia 2014a; Siegel 2014; Szinn 2016). The *New York Times* reported in 2010 that conservative commentators such as Glenn Beck were railing against the Obama administration's push for regulation of fattening foods, saying that its "choice architects" believed "you're incapable of making decisions" and that "left to your own devices . . . you're going to be a big fat fatty" (Warner 2010). During the same year, Sarah Palin tweeted about visiting a Pennsylvania school with "dozens and dozens of cookies" in tow to "intro kids 2 beauty of laissez-faire" at a fund-raising event (Warner 2010). Decisions about whether to prioritize the protection of children's health or their autonomy and "choice" clearly touch political nerves in the United States: as journalist Judith Warner observes, Palin's media event was meant to suggest that schools' attempts to limit high-sugar foods were "an assault on the American way of life. On freedom and simple pleasures. On wholesome childhood delights and, of course, the integrity of the family" (Warner 2010).

The valuing of choice and autonomy can become particularly thorny in contexts such as public schools, which are, after all, state institutions charged with the instruction, socialization, and management of children. Sociologist Janet Poppendieck (2010) examined the web of regulations and financial pressures that, combined with assumptions about children's food preferences, led school cafeterias in the United States to offer what they do. Among other factors, Poppendieck highlighted that many cafeteria managers apply a "kids-are-customers model": the notion that school planners must serve children's preferences even when they are considered unsatisfactory in their nutritional content, which Poppendieck calls "an abdication of adult authority and responsibility" (272). Indeed, national media outlets highlighted in the 2000s how schools to varying extents attempted to provide foods considered healthful for children—both before and after the tightening federal guidelines of 2010—but also considered questions of cost and of "customer" demand in planning their menus (e.g., Hewitt 2001; Schulte 2002; Rosenberg 2003; Hallett 2003). Staff underscored that children needed to have choices and that when given choices, "of course they go to the ones that are not so healthy" (Reinolds 2005).

It was in the context of these debates and the implementation of stepped-up federal regulations that I encountered Hometown's lunch program, which itself was in a transitional moment. My most intensive year of research, 2014, straddled two school years. During the first (2013–2014), an outside catering company was providing school lunch service, serving several other schools simultaneously. Comparing to my own memories and stereotypes about school food—and more specifically, to the food I had occasionally seen on my children's plates in a different school district close by—most of what the catering service served looked fairly appealing to me. I recall an entrée of whole chicken drumsticks that I perceived as particularly appetizing and wholesome (counter to some children's reactions as described above). Certain items seemed more prefabricated and processed, but there also was a salad bar for a time. Yet I also learned that Hometown's administration was not entirely pleased with the service and that their current contract was soon to be concluded, leaving the door open for change in the 2014–2015 school year.

There were many complexities involved in planning school meal service. Most of these were introduced by the USDA regulations that needed to be followed given the school's participation in the National School Lunch Program and the funding and oversight these carried. During the 2014–2015 school year, 18 percent of the student body at Hometown received free or reduced lunch: 12.5 percent in the elementary grades and 28.1 percent in the middle grades. The disparity appeared to reflect income differences in the immediate neighborhoods of each campus as well as ongoing gentrification of the area as younger, wealthier families moving in presumably made free and school lunches less and less needed (though the issue is rather more complicated, as we will see). The percentage of students qualifying for free or reduced lunch at Hometown was on the decline, and administrators anticipated that within a few years they would no longer receive the same level of government funding. This could give them more freedom in the planning of their food service, particularly if they eventually chose to opt out of the National School Lunch Program entirely.[1]

At an August PTA meeting, the school's executive director acknowledged that in the previous four years the percentage of students at Hometown getting free or reduced lunch had declined from 40 percent to under 20 percent, and he attributed this to "who was applying" to the school (admission was by lottery); he also felt that the school could improve its outreach efforts to fight "stereotypes of what a charter school is," since the demographics of the surrounding public schools were not the same as Hometown's. In other words, the school could maintain its economic diversity if more of the lower-income families who lived in the area saw Hometown as the right option for them. When a board member requested that he say more about free or reduced lunch for those who were unfamiliar with its significance, he explained to the audience that the government measures socioeconomic diversity through rates of free or reduced lunch, where schools with 35 percent and above qualified as Title I schools and garnered additional funds. As another administrator explained to me, the school had been grandfathered into Title I for the current year, but the suggestion was that that status would be lost soon if the demographic trends of the school did not reverse.[2]

The USDA provided target calorie counts for school meals as well as guidelines for nutritional content by food groups. For example, the 2012 regulations differentiated between fruits and vegetables and set weekly requirements for different categories of vegetables (dark green, red/orange, starchy, and so on). There were minimums and weekly ranges set for grains, which now needed to be all whole grains; daily minimums and weekly ranges were given for meat or meat alternatives as well.[3] School cafeterias needed to be able to meet these criteria week in and week out, and on a budget. Only fat-free and 1 percent low-fat milk was allowed, though flavored (such as chocolate) milk was also allowed, per USDA regulations;[4] and as Tina, a white married Hometown administrator, pointed out in an evening parents' Health and Wellness Committee meeting, the USDA required that every lunch served be accompanied by a milk unless the parent had delivered a doctor's note that documented an allergy. Even lactose-intolerant children needed to be provided with lactose-free milk. Tina noted that many students threw their milks away, leading to thousands of dollars wasted, and that she had to bug students to remember to take their milks in the lunch line.

Mothers in the committee group rued the fact that chocolate milk was being offered in the lunchroom, even if it was fat-free. "Because sugar is *so* much better than fat," one attendee noted sarcastically, shaking her head with exasperation. The members laughed. "It's a processed food. They're forcing processed food on our kids." Tina noted in the meeting that parents often had complaints about aspects of the food service while not understanding how the school was constrained by USDA regulations. "We know a lot of people are asking questions like, how can tomato on a pizza count as a vegetable? It doesn't sound right when you say it, but it's one of those things that it is beyond our control." In an interview later, Tina told me that parents wanted to debate the milk issue with her. They hoped to be able to write a note to say their child did not like it and have them excused from purchasing it; but even in the case of allergy or intolerance, the school was required to offer an alternative milk product (soy or lactose-free). "They want to argue the point, but they don't realize that they are arguing it to the wrong person." In the committee meeting she said that "we need to educate people about" these regulatory issues and that she had started a blog on the school's website for that purpose.

I spoke with Tina one day in her office, which was lined with large books and binders that contained regulations and recipes gathered from long hours she had spent at USDA workshops she had been required to attend. One of the guidelines that bothered her most was the requirement that everyone in the middle school receive the same standard serving; she found that middle schoolers were wildly variable in body size, so that the serving was large for some while for others it simply was not nearly enough. She noted that there were already so many guidelines about serving whole grains and a range of vegetable groups without too many starchy vegetables served in a week, and then the calorie count on top of that. "I feel like we don't need this [portion control] on top of everything else. It would be nice to have the flexibility on this. Some schools may need to have a hard and fast policy, but it's frustrating when it doesn't make sense for this population or this kid right here." She reiterated that parents in the community took issue with details such as the kind of milk served, but they did not see the challenges faced with the regulations, including stringent limits on portion sizes: "So you know it's like, I'll be mad at her because she's serving chocolate milk, but I won't help her out by saying you only give my kid two chicken tenders! You know?" Tina noted, too, that the federal nutritional guidelines required higher spending but "they are giving us eleven cents more per meal. Really? Because it costs us thirty to fifty cents more to do that. And they want you to be excited about it."

In the 2013–2014 school year, Tina also had had specific dissatisfactions with the school's current food service and talked about changes she hoped to see when they changed providers. She emphasized the importance of familiarity in identifying foods that would be desirable to children, while also arguing for variety:

> I don't know, [I'd like to see] hamburgers with real hamburger, and I think we're hoping that the food becomes a little bit more recognizable or a little bit more . . . taster-friendly, that that would increase kids that are actually purchasing the lunches. That hamburgers actually look like hamburgers, taste like hamburgers, or . . . I guess things that are more recognizable, like you know, Salisbury steak or meatloaf. And it's done in turkey [by the current food service]. It looks different and so then the kids are a little skeptical of it. So we definitely want to start looking into broadening our menu rotation, because right now it's five weeks but it really is chicken, turkey, chicken, turkey, you know.

She acknowledged that some of her own preferences as an eater played into her wish list for the cafeteria, observing that the current chef seemed to use dark meat chicken a lot, which she did not like and which she assumed many children also did not like. She argued for what was "taster-friendly" as well as "regular": "Yeah, we could have regular french fries. That would be awesome, instead of sweet potato fries. I like them, but the kids aren't really all that into it. I'm saying we could keep them, but just think, we could have regular french fries. [whispers] It would be awesome!" A salad bar had recently been established; it was offered briefly for elementary grades but, I was told by the chef, had eventually proved less popular and overly expensive. It lasted longer at the middle school, though there was some contention around it since, in addition to salad greens and other chopped vegetables, it had rotating items such as pasta salads and typically included Goldfish crackers as one of the toppings. Some students would opt to pile their plates with Goldfish and mandarin orange sections and call it a lunch; staff would monitor to try to ensure that this did not happen and that students walked away with plates that were more well-rounded. (When the middle school salad bar was shut down, the chef told me by way of explanation that the students had "had a chance to be young adults about it" but had not done so; I am not certain whether this had to do with their food choices or with other behaviors.) Tina said that it would be desirable "to really start using the salad bar, to really look at how to do that, how to do it well, you know? It's really popular in the beginning, but what makes it fall off? Is it because kids want different options? Okay well, what different options do you want? Is it feasible to get those things on the salad bar?" She noted that strategies such as offering all white meat were "a cost point," but went on to say, "You know if you want more people to buy the lunches so that you have the money to use, you're going to have to make a change somewhere."

Indeed, she ultimately emphasized the need to appeal to children as consumers: "Just really making it more like . . . it's a . . . it's a destination restaurant down at the end of the hall that they—'Yeah, I'm going to lunch and I'm going to buy lunch today.'" Perhaps for this reason, Tina considered that someone geared more toward commercial than institutional food contexts would serve the school well.

> The candidate [for new chef] I think would be somebody who is interested in trying new things. We definitely don't want someone who is from the cafeteria world—uh, public school. I think we're looking more along the lines of someone who has actually been to culinary school or is a working chef either for like a Whole Foods [an upscale national grocery chain featuring organic foods] or you know, someone who has the knowledge of . . . organic and a variety of different things to choose from—ethnicities, everything—however is still very much aware that these are

kids and this isn't where you should practice your, you know, anchovy dah dah dah dah dah.

Many Hometown adults' interest in organic and healthful foods would be met in this fashion, though Tina called attention to the specificities of children by remarking that they could not be expected to welcome an upscale chef's pitches to more acquired tastes with dishes such as "anchovy dah dah dah dah dah." Still, she did incorporate the goal of edifying children through food.

> While you want food to be comfortable and yummy . . . maybe doing something a little bit different—you know at this school we do so much that's cross-curricular, this is something that we could . . . we could talk about spotlighting, you know, African food or—and nothing too crazy, but—just looking at where these kids—you know, they're studying Australia in sixth grade. Okay, well, what do they eat down there? I mean, vegemite I heard is really nasty so I don't think I'd have them eat that, but what other local—do they fix something and they just do it differently, you know? Those are things that I think we're ready to take a hit on, to be able to pursue as opposed to staying kind of stagnant and where we are.

At the PTA meeting mentioned earlier, Hometown's director articulated goals for Hometown's in-house food program—which by that time had just been initiated with the hiring of a new chef—and he highlighted it as an educational, not just nutritional, program, in which students learned about the role of food in their lives and about the production of food. The goal, he said, was to "set an example for other schools."

School lunches were significant to administrators, then, as means not only to nourish students—a task that in itself was not necessarily easy, in the face of limited public funds and overwhelming government regulations—but also to effect progressive change that might prove to be influential beyond Hometown's walls. However, as school leaders considered how to achieve this, they did not think of children's consumption and their tastes only as things to be shaped by educators; rather, they relied on ideas about what foods children already liked and could be expected to try, further revealing how childhood as a category of being was constructed through debates about food.

A New Approach at Hometown

In the summer of 2014, the school had ended its contract with its existing service and hired a new chef, an individual who would be an employee of the school, not a contractor. I spoke with Claudia, a married white school administrator involved with school lunch at Hometown, about the transition. Their previous chef had been serving a total of six or seven schools, she pointed out, whereas the new person would be devoted to their elementary and middle school. His background was in cooking at a high-end restaurant in Atlanta, and he would have a lot to learn about federal regulations governing school lunches, she allowed. He would have to go to multiple required trainings over the summer to learn about the guidelines and administrative practices. She laughed that she thought she had scared him by warning him in a recent conversation that "you're basically not going to be able to cook with salt," since the newest regulations coming down the pipeline concerned limiting sodium. "Last year it was [replacing processed grains with whole] grains; this year it is sodium." She hoped that the menus might differ between the elementary and middle schoolers since their palates were somewhat different: elementary schoolers "just want grilled cheese, something simple like that."

The new chef, Carl, seemed to satisfy parents and staff by striking a reasonable—even impressive—balance of what could be called foodie sensibilities and children's sensibilities (as adults perceived them, but to some extent as evidenced by students' willing consumption of his dishes). Early in the chef's tenure, the school newsletter featured his thoughts on the changes he was introducing at Hometown. His writing not only illustrated his personal views, but—as he was quite well received by the school community—also bespoke the dominant norms and values of many parents and staff.

> I'm excited to bring as much locally grown and raised produce, meat, fish, and dairy as we can into the food the school serves. Supporting local food has long been important to me, and I find that the quality shines when one is able to have something really fresh. Among students and the community at large, I'm hoping to develop an appreciation for good food and how it gets to us by making delicious meals and eventually ex-

ploring ways to use my kitchen as part of the education and curriculum at the school. I'm looking forward to the gardens on both campuses and learning how to best use them in the service of breakfast and lunch on a daily basis. The restaurants that have been most inspirational to me in my career so far are those with a tangible connection to where they source their food. . . .

Our program is still getting off the ground, but the response has been very positive and our students, parents and teachers are all enthusiastic about having a well-made, fresh and nutritious meal program. We've supported a handful of local farms and purveyors, and I'm always looking for more opportunities to incorporate GA [Georgia] grown meat and produce. We bought a whole, fresh, pastured lamb from [a regional family farm] for our shepherd's pie in October. We featured produce from the wonderful [local] Farmer's Market for vegetable plates in September and October.

Carl, a white married father whose own child now attended the school, highlighted the importance of freshness, local (small-scale) production, and the notion of awareness and "connection to" one's food. In my own observation, parents did indeed respond positively to these efforts and the meals they produced. In response to the blog, Hometown mothers posted warmly laudatory comments, such as, "I would have eaten the watermelon and tomato salad! Thank you so much for the work you do and for taking a chance on us!" Another comment read, "You and your team are wonders in motion! Planning, chopping, scouring, scurrying and putting out delicious, thoughtful food. It is a pleasure to see such a successful program develop. Thanks for your dedication and such a forthcoming article. And also, pot pie and PICKLED BEETS today. . . . swoon." White married mother Diane, who worked close by to the school, commented—when I told her that I had noticed that she often stopped in for lunch with her daughter—that this really was the cheapest, best place to eat lunch in the neighborhood (adults paid about five dollars for the lunch, while students' rates were lower).

I had to agree with her, despite the fact that there were a handful of popular neighborhood restaurants and coffee shops within walking distance. In the previous school year, when helping out in the lunchroom, I would occasionally partake of the meal on offer to the children, but most often I brought my own lunch with me from home. In fall 2014, I quickly realized that eating the school lunch was a more appealing option. The offerings that Carl was able to produce far exceeded my expectations for a school lunchroom. I was surprised to see meals such as spring rolls with shrimp and basil or individual shepherd's pies, all made from scratch, served to the children. Menus were thoughtfully coherent, often representing particular cuisines (from Thai to U.S. Southern), complete from entrée to side dishes. Perhaps my favorite meal was a poached salmon that was, to my taste, perfectly done, extremely simple, and utterly delicious. I marveled at the fact that Carl could do this so well on such a scale and working across two different lunchrooms. Reflecting on the challenges of catering to a crowd, I remember thinking to myself while savoring the poached salmon that I would have been impressed and pleased had I been served food this good at a catered wedding (or indeed at an upscale restaurant). Though he was on a budget and experimenting (he sometimes realized certain items were too time-consuming and crossed them off the list for future menus), Carl seemed to be making it all work.

He did acknowledge in his blog entry that doing all this while following government regulations had been challenging: "Being the chef at an elementary and middle school has not been without its challenges as well. The greatest of these so far has been wading into the ocean of regulation that I was not subject to before coming to school nutrition. We've had to put the new meal pattern into practice and make changes on the fly to ensure that our almost entirely from-scratch food is compliant." Like Tina, he pointed out the gap between the upscale food tastes that might appeal to many of these children's parents and the tastes of these children themselves:

> Of course there are also big differences between feeding a relatively sophisticated midtown Atlanta clientele and kindergarten and first graders. While I knew that I wouldn't be serving any more grilled octopus, curing my own trout roe for caviar, or finishing scallop crudo with lemon oil and sugar snap pea jus, getting myself to really think about food like a grade school student has sometimes been a challenge. I have a daughter in kindergarten at Hometown, and cooking for her at home has certainly helped, but dishes that I thought would be a hit were anything but. On

our first farmer's market veg plate, I had purchased some beautiful tomatoes and watermelons. I decided to make a very simple salad with the
two of them and shaved parmesan cheese. I reckoned that everyone loves
watermelon, and while this is true, my students weren't interested in trying this combination.

Sometimes he thought he knew what might be "child-friendly," but he
couldn't always predict it. In one of my many conversations with him,
he noted that he had introduced sesame noodles one day and had not
been sure what to expect. Students from the fourth grade up seemed to
enjoy them, Carl said, but the younger kids were not at all interested.
He had expected that the young children would say, "Oh! Noodles!," but
they did not. Another day he had served miso soup along with brown
rice and a cucumber salad. The reaction to the miso soup was mostly
positive, he reported; he had seen that a lot of children at the elementary
school seemed to be familiar with it. "I got more 'what's thats' at the
middle school," he said. I offered that this said something interesting
about the constituencies of the two schools, since one might expect that
the older they got, the more they would know something like that. "Yes,
but this school [the elementary campus] is overall much more well off
than the middle school," replied Carl.

His point seemed well taken, but our conversation also raised the
question of how the themes of maturation and class sophistication and
taste can be intermingled subtly, as when Tina had mentioned the benefit of a Whole Foods chef—which spoke to Hometown's parents' and
staff's interest in foods marked as healthy, high-quality, and expensive—
but warned that children qua children would not be interested in anything so rarefied as an "anchovy dah dah dah dah dah." Children were
expected to participate in their parents' food ideals and practices only
provisionally and within certain bounds, and staff recognized as well
that not all families participated equally in the same nutritional and restaurant cultures, so that children were variably exposed to and absorbing the food norms discussed earlier. One Hometown teacher shared
her opinion that children here were, on the whole, less nutritionally
conscious than the students she had gotten to know at a local (private)
Waldorf School, where she said you would never see processed and
prefabricated lunch items like Cheez Whiz and Lunchables (which did

appear in some lunches at Hometown). "And if you did, it would be a stigma. The kids would be like, 'Oh, shit!'"

The implicit assumption—or hope—seemed to be that children were gradually or ideally moving toward tastes that would be embraced by their parents; but consideration was still given to the opinionated, if not entirely sensible or sophisticated, consumers children appeared to be in the present day. In the enrichment class for middle schoolers that I co-taught with Carl, he gave a demonstration of how xanthan gum works as a food additive. His talking point was that while he may try to avoid food additives in general, some of them did have very useful properties. He showed students how xanthan gum was used to thicken the teriyaki sauce that he was serving in the cafeteria that day. After the class, in conversation with me, he remarked that a benefit was that the xanthan gum added thickness without added sugar, and he wanted the kids to be able to say, "Yum, that tastes like the teriyaki sauce I had at the mall." He mentioned a particular elementary student who was new to the school and had expressed distress about the food being served. We both knew that she had complained loudly and made faces about his food; she had described it to me as *naaasty* on more than one occasion, though she seemed to gradually warm up to his offerings that fall. A child like this one needed to be able to make that connection of familiarity, Carl explained; the sauce had to "read" as the teriyaki sauce she already knew.

One day, I heard a third grader coming through the lunch line on a day pizza was being served. He commented knowingly to the staff member on the line: "I know that comes from Pizza Hut." The staff member replied with a smile, "I'll take that as a compliment." This lunchroom decidedly was *not* serving mall fast food, but to some extent adults felt bound to address children's established consumer tastes in order to make school lunches work.

"That's Not a Thing!" Children's Food Judgments

Elementary students at Hometown talked a lot about food in the lunchroom. They expressed opinions about their own food and others', including mine. One boy saw my salad bar plate and asked, "How can you eat beets with cucumbers? That's gross!" Another day a boy peeked into my lunch from home and asked, "Is that sweet potato? I love sweet potato!" I told him I also had kale, broccoli, and tofu. A girl sitting next to him piped up, "You have tofu!? I love tofu!" Once while I was on lunch duty a fourth grade girl raised her hand to say, "This food is hurting my stomach but I'm still hungry. It doesn't taste real . . . it doesn't taste like real meat." Someone else complained that his milk seemed to be past its expiration date. On the day when Acadian redfish was served, students complained about its smell until a teacher told one who was asking for a clothespin for her nose to "stop being dramatic."

Many children brought their lunches to school with them. My assistants and I noticed that some children seemed to pack the lunches on their own. We knew this because a few of them commented on it; in other cases we found ourselves assuming that to be the case simply because the lunch (for example, one that consisted solely of packaged items such as potato chips and a granola bar) did not fit the standard profile of a "good" lunch here at the school. Others brought standard sandwiches and fruit, tubed yogurts, or thermoses full of soup or other home leftovers. Some children had metal lunch kits with individual, small compartments filled with different items. I observed one such lunch kit that held sliced cucumbers, some spinach leaves, strawberries, Goldfish crackers, and a small pile of chocolate chips. Sometimes I saw little clusters of pepperoni or cheese sticks in those kits, and small packs of crunchy seaweed were popular in some classes.

Children who were getting school lunch on any given day were called to the lunch line by homeroom class to have their trays filled. Most of these students, most days, chose the hot lunch option, while a few opted for the salad bar. In the latter case, a staff member would help them by listening to their choices—salad greens, cucumber, bits of egg, cheese— and heaping them onto the plate with as little mess as possible. I often stood at the lunch line and helped hand down trays to students, get them cutlery, and remind them to take their milk. Children commented on the food as it was being served or asked questions about what it was. Sometimes these were complaints, but often the children's questions were driven by interest and curiosity, since Carl experimented with meals that were not always familiar to the children.

One day, the main course was pasta with meat sauce; vegetarians had an option of pasta with pesto sauce and scoops of ricotta cheese. A number of children asked about the ricotta cheese; what was it? One child ventured that it might be ice cream. When shrimp basil rolls were served, a child asked, "Is this like sushi?" When a frittata was featured, children poked at it at their tables, one asking whether it was quiche. Carl told me about how he had noticed that children at Hometown were often highly aware about food, as when one boy showed his knowledge of world cuisines when he mistook the hush puppies (a U.S. Southern classic made of cornmeal) he had been served for the Middle Eastern fried chickpea dish falafel (which, Carl noted, was on the menu for the following month). Carl continued that a girl had asked for an extra meatball yesterday, though he had answered that he could not give it to her since they needed to serve set portions; her friend had said, "She needs three because she's Italian," and the first had added, "I think I might also be from Greece, because I love olives." Children were asking questions, drawing comparisons, and coming up with ways to categorize foods and eaters as they moved through the school lunch line.

This exploratory practice continued as children moved from the lunch line into the lunchroom, where they at round tables in a set seating arrangement. When I first started spending time in the lunchroom, an announcement had been made in some grades about why I was on campus, and their awareness that I was conducting research about food might have explained why I was sometimes the target of random food questions that interested them. In a fifth grade lunch period, a girl raised her hand. I walk over to her table to see what she needed (often students were asking to go to the bathroom or for help with a difficult-to-open thermos or food package), and when I arrived she asked me, "Can you define red meat for me?" I hesitated a moment, and she added, "Is pork red meat?" I told her that pork was not really considered red meat, although it seemed to me some people might include it when they say they are not eating red meat because they mainly mean that they do not eat meats that are not poultry, which they might eat. "What's red?" she probed. "Cow?" Yes, I responded, that's the main one; but there are other red meats, like deer (venison) and lamb. "I love lamb!" another girl at the table chimed in. The first girl turned to the one next to her and said triumphantly, "See? There is no such thing as 'brown meat'!" Another day, a girl asked me whether fish was meat; she and her tablemates were debating whether a vegetarian could eat fish. She offered that she ate some meat, so she was "sort of a half vegetarian," to which a girl at the table cried, "You can't eat meat and be a vegetarian, and you can't be a half vegetarian, that's not a thing!"

In one notable case, I observed a boy using the familiar category of the "treat" to complain about Carl's menus. While passing through the lunch line one day, he stated to Carl indignantly, "You're making pizza a treat." The next boy in line overheard and wrinkled up his face, echoing incredulously, "*Pizza*? A treat?" Carl, attempting to understand the nature of the first boy's comment, probed, "You mean by not having it very often?" (Pizza was served about once a month.) The boy affirmed that this was what he had meant.

The elementary school students with whom I spent time in the lunchroom also, at moments, played to their awareness that the connection between childhood and transgressive eating was both undesirable to adults and expected. One fourth grader asked a teacher whether soda was allowed in school, as he watched a boy a few seats away having a can of Sprite with his lunch. The teacher and I agreed that we did not think there was a rule about this. "At least it doesn't have caffeine," the teacher added, remarking that if it did contain caffeine, she would guess it was not (or should not be) allowed. "It has plenty of sugar, though," she noted. The boy drinking the Sprite—he also had a Rice Krispie treat in front of him—grinned. "Yeah," said the first, "but he knows how to handle it." The teacher and I laughed in surprise at the comment; in my interpretation, it was as though the boy was referring to imbibing alcohol or some other powerful substance, as though being able to "handle it" spoke to the other boy's strength, cool, or manliness. In a middle school health class, on a day when they had been enjoying treats brought in by another student for the class project, I heard a girl squeal and then say, "I think it's the sugar!" A fifth grader approached me on a day when birthday cupcakes were being served to announce pointedly, "I'm really not supposed to eat sugar," before hopping off to tell a teacher the same thing.

In-class work provided imaginative chances for children to express nutritional knowledge and to reflect back things that they had learned from school, parents, and the consumer environment. All middle schoolers took a class called "Fit for Life," whose curriculum included a unit on nutrition as well as others on personal health issues such as physical fitness and handling stress. In addition to being given concrete material about different nutrients and how they supported bodily health, students were engaged by assignments that asked them to bring in a special dish from home and to speak to its nutritional components; or they worked in groups to come up with restaurant menus, to bring in some of their foods to share with the class, and to provide assessments of how it was or was not healthy and why. Other students could then "buy" their samples using play money, and there was a competition to see whose dishes were most popular. Some of the students really got into this, coming up with inventive names for their "restaurants" and describing their menu items with some flourish. Some recurrent choices the groups offered included familiar savory dishes such as chili and macaroni and cheese as well as sweets like brownies, cupcakes, and chocolate chip cookies. Others brought bean and turkey quesadillas, wonton soup, salads, or fruit smoothies. Dishes were described as "baked to perfection" or "infussed [sic] with cheese," and genres such as "bar food" were invoked as themes.

Across these contexts, children were applying their understandings of categories that were used to define food groups or styles of eating, aware that there were normative and stylized, adult ways to define these that they were trying to exhibit, to master, or perhaps to transgress or to wield to their own purposes. Students also, at times, arbitrated what was "healthy" or not and exercised these judgments upon one another. One of my recurring duties was to help students make their way through the salad bar. The idea was that they would be likely to make a mess or to take too much of one food without a bit of assistance, though they were given fairly free choice about what to get. One day, a boy asked for some lettuce on his plate, and when I served him some, he then asked if he could have less. (There were also items such as grated cheese, sunflower seeds, and raisins, and some children made meals of these alone.) At this, the girl next to him in line proclaimed, "He doesn't like anything healthy," to which he replied indignantly, "That's not true." The first student had taken upon herself the task of judging the inadequacy of her schoolmate's food choices; meanwhile, the second seemed to take it seriously inasmuch as he was stung by it and refuted it.

A similar but more dramatic encounter played out during one fourth grade lunch. A boy called me over to tell me something, and when I stopped in front of him, he pointed to the girl next to him and said,

"She is judging my food and it's uncomfortable." I was not sure how to mediate this situation; judging from the girl's expression, she seemed indignant in her own right and perhaps embarrassed. How should I intervene as one of the adults in charge, given that I had no intention of delivering a lesson on (my own opinions about) optimal eating or proper meal etiquette to either child? I was also aware that the school's ethos promoted relationship-building and personal responsibility; I wanted to facilitate some kind of harmonious outcome for the children, but I did not want to make either child feel unheard or unable to express their tastes, opinions, or feelings. Moreover, the child who had called me over was African American and the girl he had accused was white, and I did not know to what extent their racial identities felt salient to them in this conversation. In the moment, I could think of no other way to start than to ask for more detail. "She did?" I queried. "What did she say?" The boy picked up a bag of French fries in front of him and said that the girl had told him that this was not healthy food and that he would get fat. Measuring my words carefully, I told him, looking to the girl as well, "Well . . . we all do different things with food. You've told her you didn't appreciate it, and she has said what she wanted you to know, so how about we just drop it now and you each do your own thing?"

This seemed to be an acceptable resolution to the two of them, though I do not know what conversation may have transpired after I walked away from the table, nor how I might have been able to inspire a livelier exchange between them without seeming to take either student's side. More important to this discussion is that we have observed how children were not just the target of teachers' and parents' interventions around food. Rather, as we shall see further, children were acquiring food knowledge actively and experimenting with casting judgments and locating one another socially through food.

Thinking Critically with Students about Food in Their Social Worlds

In the class I co-taught, I found that middle schoolers were readily able to generate food knowledge about the way things were categorized in their own world. I talked with them about anthropology as a field and ethnography as a methodology, as well as specifically inviting them to think critically about their own food cultures. My goal was not to get them to critique their own practices or to rethink their own eating, but rather for them to consider in new ways how culture shaped categories and meanings that were often so taken for granted. How did *they* understand what was "good" and "bad" food? What kinds of interactions did they have with their parents or peers through food? What kind of social information was embedded within food choices and food talk? I approached them similarly as I would my university students: posing questions and drawing their attention to certain topics, but also encouraging them to provide material and insights from their own experiences to create their own collective analysis.

In one exercise, I had them brainstorm about the foods that they considered to be "good" and "bad" ones nutritionally, and we mapped their responses on the board; what ended up on the board was a set of meanings closely resembling those expressed by Hometown parents. Good included vegetables, grains, fruit, fresh, moderation, "real," unprocessed. Bad included fast food, processed, greasy, candy, anything excessive, artificial, "most of food sold at CVS [a national drugstore chain]," packaged, canned, not fresh, chemicals, pesticides, bleaches, and Takis, the bright red, super spicy chips that were so popular for trading in the lunchroom. Some foods were recognized as ambiguous in the sense that they were acceptable in moderation or that they contained both desirable components (such as protein) and undesirable ones (such as sugar or fat).

I used academic texts to try to provide children with new angles of vision on their own tastes and preoccupations and how those were historically situated and less timeless than one might think. In one lesson, I lectured on Sidney Mintz's *Sweetness and Power* (1986) to explain how sugar was embedded within colonial histories and had uses (such as medicinal or sculptural) other than as a sweetener before it became a global consumer commodity. I described to them Allison James's (1998) analysis of "kets" in Britain to get them thinking about which foods served similar purposes in their lives. (The closest parallel for these students may have been Takis.) In one unexpected conversation, the group generated the observation that adults must discipline themselves not to eat too many sweets, whereas children are constrained by adults, and that a child seen walking around the school eating candy was far more socially expected and acceptable, or in other words given far more moral leeway, than an adult doing so would be given. I was struck by their implicit recognition (alongside their deep internalization of "good" and "bad" food categories) that a link between "bad" foods and childhood—and thus a lack of tolerance for "bad" foods in adulthood—was socially constructed in contexts such as their school.

I asked the students to do two ethnographic mini-projects. I saw this as an opportunity to have them tell me about their worlds in a more developed and attentive way. I also viewed this as a chance for middle schoolers to gain new skills in qualitative research, analysis, and writing. All students completed the assignments as part of their work in the enrichment class, but only those with the completed forms could be gathered for my research. I returned the writings to students with comments, but they were not graded. In one assignment, I instructed students to interview their own parents about food practices and beliefs. To prepare for the interview, I asked them to consider issues such as the following: What do you think some of your parents key beliefs about food are? What do you want to learn more about in terms of your parents' food concerns? What conflicts do you have with parents about food? Each student was to come up with their own list of interview questions, and I sat down with each to talk with them one-on-one about what they wanted to learn from the interview and what good questions to get at those issues might be. We held mock interviews in class to prepare them for the task, such as practicing how to ask probing follow-up questions. Students were interested to find out the logic behind some of their parents' rules and preferences (Why is dessert or sugary food allowed at certain times but not others? What is wrong with snacking?). Ultimately, each child interviewed a parent and turned in a write-up with the results, but their write-ups tended to be quite brief, with one-sentence answers from their parents to each question.

Richer were the students' write-ups of another project, in which I asked them to conduct participant observation in the lunchroom. They were to notice what people were actually doing during one lunch period. The overall themes that emerged included their fellow students' behaviors, which tended to be fairly loud, and how people stood in line (occasionally cutting, especially if something desirable seemed to be in short supply on the lunch line). Food trading was a ripe topic: students recounted how people traded things from their own lunches or some-times brought in bags of candy or gum specifically for giving out or trading. In an in-class debrief discussion, student Leah commented that when someone gave her something like gum, she did not think they would be friends or that she liked the other more—consciously—but maybe subconsciously, she acknowledged, it did make her think better of the other student.[5]

The lunchroom project also led to group discussions about the social contours of their middle school worlds. The students noted that girls and boys ate lunch differently, which led to a lively discussion about how girls and boys related to food differently, in their experience over-all: for example, boys tended to eat more quickly and urgently—they "needed to eat," were messier, and ate junkier, less healthy foods; girls were slower, neater, pickier, and more health-conscious, as well as con-scious of their appearances. Segregation of seating arrangements by gender and friend groups was noticeable to them. Leah mentioned that some people might think they have cliques, but in actuality she did not think anyone intended to be exclusive or to say, "We don't want you sit-ting here. It's just about where people feel comfortable." Another student mentioned racial segregation in lunchroom seating, and Leah (who was white) intervened, "That doesn't mean you're racist." I pointed out to the class that they were observing culture in action: in lunch seating, as with many other phenomena, there was no explicit rule about it and no one was saying they wanted it to be that way, but it still happened and was something that they collectively chose to do.

In his essay, student Mac offered that seating groups in the lunchroom were based on race, gender, or "home life." During our class discussion I asked what he meant by "home life," and Mac explained that some kids were from wealthy families, for example, and it was about what they did at home, the things they liked to do, and so on. I asked him whether he was talking about socioeconomic background, or was he trying to get at something more subtle? "What is that?" Mac asked in response to my question about socioeconomic background. "I mean like your class—wealthy, or middle class, or poorer." Mac said he had not necessarily meant that; he was pointing more generally to the things one was used to or liked to do. For example, people who played sports sat together. In his essay, he had noted that "I think our school cafeteria is not as diverse as we believe, as people normally sit with people they know." Another student, Lana, commented in her essay, "Something I found interesting was how instead of them being trades or good entertainment, people keep their place. So I think that was what really was going on during lunch, not simply just trying to get better food."

Below I render two student essays in their entirety. I chose these two because they are particularly detailed and astute in their observations. There is commonality between them—they both evoke the noisy social context of the lunchroom quite nicely—as well as divergences. For example, they both position themselves explicitly toward my assignment, but they strike very different attitudes in doing so. Essay 1 was submitted by Corbin, a white sixth grade boy; Essay 2 was the work of Crystal, an African American/Black, seventh grade girl. I have retained spelling and grammar as in their original essays.

Essay 1: Corbin

SUMMARY

This summary will explain and show what happens at the different tables during 6th Grade lunch. This will tell you what they do and what they prefer to eat. The tables are numbered so I will explain what tables the numbers correspond to.

The first table I will discuss is table 1. This is the one that is closest to the salad bar. This table is the "unhealthy" table for me because I saw chocolate, snacks and unhealthy drinks. There weren't many school bought lunches (only like 3 or 4) but many home lunches. This comes to the conclusion that most of the unhealthy things came from home.

The next is table 2. This is located closest to the milk container. I noticed that this is almost opposite from table 1. There was a lot of talking at this table, along with more school bought foods than table 1. There were still snacks, which is a similarity between the two. To counteract the snacks there were some grainy foods such as pasta and rice that were at this table. Fruit was present as well, concluding that this table was just a bit more healthy than the first table.

Table 3 is quite interesting. It is closest to the poster on the wall of pick of the day/the backdoor. People here find card games interesting, so they play them while eating their food. Another thing is that they again have cafeteria food (quite a bit of it) and many lunchboxes or home lunch. I noticed that many people had water bottles present along with their lunch. To balance the unhealthy foods they have fruits.

The next tables are joined together so I do not need to point out what tables they are. There are 3 tables however I mainly saw 2 sections. The first section I will talk about is section 1. These are the 2 tables closest to the main doors. Here I again saw the pattern of home lunch and school lunch. Unhealthy foods were present along with much talking. There were many people who were getting up out of their seats, which was quite strange in my opinion. The biggest part of this section was the competition. There was competition for food or another thing that was important to more than one person.

The final paragraph is the second section for the joined tables. The last table in the trio. This one was the most interesting for it had the most "excitement" to it. There was fighting, yelling and trading at this table. Competition completes the cycle for this table. The cycle is this: Someone says that they have this great object and they are willing to **trade** it, starting **competition**. In this moment people start to **yell** and **fight** over the thing that is being traded. The cycle is complete. Someone would eventually get the precious item and then throwing food begins for some other person tries to catch the object if it is thrown to the winning person. The other people sitting at the table then start to fight and yell yet again and the competition starts all over again. This is what I personally saw at this table. There can be much more however I may not have caught it.

In conclusion these tables vary from each other in many different ways and they are similar in many ways as well. I hope you eventually use this work to help you with your studies and that it can help you in later life or soon. Thank you for teaching me about food in the class and it has meant a lot to me for I am also concerned with food in certain cases as well. Thank you for reading. This observations have come from the 6th Grade at Hometown Charter School just to remind you. Again thank you for making me observe in my cafeteria so I could learn more about my fellow Grade members.

Essay 2: Crystal

Lunchroom Observation Essay

I observed different things that I wouldn't have payed attention to if I was just having a normal lunch. I noticed how people liked what was for lunch. What we had was barbeque chicken as the main dish in our lunch. Yes it was very good. People were licking their fingers. I also noticed that people were having a lot of fun. They were singing loudly and in a funny voice. People would group themselves with people they talk to usually, and those people are their friends. They sit next to people they like. Most were big to medium sized groups and some were small. I saw that a person was making fun of a friend in a playful way. I observed what people ate. I noticed that people buy extra milk because they like the chocolate milk from the lunch line so much. I saw a person eating a sandwich. I saw another person bring funions, and another with cookies. Some people had the regular school lunch, some people had the salad, and some people brought their own lunch. People had oranges and chips, too. I believe that every seventh grader at school that day was in the lunchroom because no one could go into the teachers' room for lunch. When I was observing, people were asking what I was doing. Of course they would because most of the people in the lunchroom were not in my [food and culture] class. They were confused about what I was doing. I asked them if they cared if I observed them. No one cared if I did. I just told them to act as they normally would. So they looked at me and talked to me. They went back to what they were doing and I just observed them. I saw someone accidentally pushed down when her and her friends were playing with each other. They just laughed about. Not much drama happens in the lunchroom everyday. I could show what had happened in the past though, you would be laughing. It wasn't dramatic, but it was funny. Anyways people would tell jokes and play around. They would eat while talking to their friends. People would ask for food or steal it from one another. I saw a person give away the food that he/she didn't want. Even though I didn't see it, I bet that someone or people stole food or a beverage that they thought was good because this happens a lot. If they did, than those people would have hidden it away. I saw someone asking people if they wanted there oranges. People like certain things on their plate. I know from other lunches that people don't usually have everything on their plate because they don't particularly like it or want that food. I didn't really notice how much someone ate. I think from my remembrance from looking that not everybody ate everything on their plate. The teachers get to have the sweet tea and the students don't. I noticed the signs and items in the lunchroom that makes it a lunchroom. The signs had different foods from different countries. I also saw how their were fake cans of food and other fake foods to represent the lunchroom. Another item that represents the lunchroom that people seem to enjoy is the sign that tells us what's for lunch. It always has an interesting background to it done by the school's art teacher. Things that I didn't write down that make the lunchroom the lunchroom are the utensils, the kitchen, the microwave, the chefs, and of course the food and drinks. These are things that make the lunchroom a lunchroom. I observed that people use the microwave, but I'm not sure if a lot of people pay attention to it being right there. I didn't notice when they put it up and when I did, I thought it was only for teachers. It is for students also. I saw someone throw a milk carton at someone else. I saw how a teacher were lecturing two people when they got in trouble. The lunchroom is a loud place, too especially if every seventh grader was in there. At the end of lunch, we got in trouble and one of the seventh grade teachers was standing on the table scolding us in a calm manner about our behavior. We have been scolded before that same week.

I didn't really learn anything. I reviewed that this is how younger people act. I realized that adults probably would act in a calmer and better behaved way than middle schoolers. I know that people hang with the people they like and know. These are there relationships. I bet that there conversations were about gossip and about who they know. It probably was about sports and jokes. Others could have been talking about weird, random stuff that they were doing. It also could have been about youtube videos and tv shows. There could be a lot that people talked about at lunch. The teachers could have been talking about their students' achievements or behaviors. They could have been talking about assignments or other things in the school. Who knows?

Well these are the things that I observed in the lunchroom. I hope they were useful. It was fun journaling about what happens in a lunchroom.

These essays are notable for the firsthand, participants' view they offer of the social scene of children's commensality at school. Corbin displays nutritional beliefs through his observation that the children seemed to be grouped at different tables according to their relatively "healthy" or "unhealthy" eating habits, while Crystal offers descriptions of the physical environment (such as signage) as well as how items such as sweet tea served to segregate adults and children. Both students highlight the high-energy nature of middle school lunchtime as their peers exchanged, stole, or threw foods from person to person, activities that in and of themselves set apart youth from authority figures ("I realized that adults probably would act in a calmer and better behaved way than middle schoolers").

Rather than treating these observations as transparent representations of children's worlds, however, it is important to situate the accounts in terms of the politics of the school and classroom, that is, "to accompany those statements with accounts of how what they say is played out with attention to the social and cultural constraints in operation at that time" (Bluebond-Langner and Korbin 2007, 243). For example, students were required to complete the assignment as part of their work in the class, but their written products were somewhat varied in length and attentiveness. Corbin and Crystal were among those who seemed to take the task quite seriously, whether because they were conscientious toward their school work generally, felt obliged to contribute to my research since they had opted in to it officially, or were actually interested in the topic. All of these may have been at play, and the students' essays suggest that they inhabited the project somewhat differently, with Corbin stating, "thank you for making me observe . . . so I could learn more about my fellow Grade members" and Crystal indicating, "I didn't really learn anything. I reviewed that this is how younger people act," but "it was fun."

Overall, these middle schoolers displayed (and perhaps gained an increased awareness of) social divisions within their school community, among their peers and households; they also, perhaps, were more attuned than their elementary school counterparts would have been to social issues that were salient but sensitive for group discussion, such as race. While they were highly engaged by activities such as the redistribution of spicy chips and candy at school, they also were able to reproduce in their own voices nutritional ideologies that closely mirrored those of the Hometown parents I interviewed. Children worked with one another but also in tandem with adult-led guidelines and within an institutional context to explore and reinforce food norms and perceptions of social difference. In fact, I had created in this class, rather inadvertently, one more context in which the children schooled one another in what the complex expectations for eating were for both youth and adults, even as I had hoped to help denaturalize those categories and to expand their awareness of the social politics of food in their lives. I may have done both.

As sociologist of childhood Daniel Cook (2004, 14) highlights, children's agency and subjectivity are variously but inevitably embedded within adult-created structures and institutions that shape what we hear from them:

> Every decision to act or not act in the name of a child—whether made by a person, like a parent, or an institution, like a school—is a political act in that it fixes on the child an identity which calls forth and favors certain kinds of responses. When, for instance, a parent discourages a child from viewing a particular type of television program because it promotes values contrary to those that the family wishes to encourage, that parent (perhaps unwittingly) invokes a construct of a child who is able to be influenced by such media but who cannot make that determination on its own. In the same vein, if a parent gives a child an allowance to be spent at will, then that parent is applying a model of the person as one who can and should make purchase decisions on its own.

For Cook, these scenarios represent two divergent but coexistent approaches to the agency of children. Adults may portray children variously as those who cannot be trusted to make decisions for the benefit of their own well-being and/or as individuals who indeed can or who should be actively apprenticed toward doing so. Either way, children's "voices" are "always already mediated through adults and organizations" given their structural positions within institutions and as a result of adults' framings of their capabilities and competencies (Cook 2004, 15). I cannot, simply by virtue of engaging students in direct conversations about food, transcend those social and institutional contexts to allow us a "direct" or "authentic" child's voice. As Crystal's and Corbin's essays remind us, children's own analyses take form in conversation with adults' and to some extent in frames (like my essay assignment) set up by adults. Even so, listening to Hometown's children reminds us once more that they are not simply pliant or resistant when it comes to their parents' wishes for their eating. Rather, they are building toward internalization of parents' and school authorities' norms *and* enacting some of the expectations of immoderation that they already know are attached to them as children.

Conclusion

How do constructions of childhood shape the ways in which children—individually, at large, and in socially differentiated groups—are assumed and encouraged to eat, and to desire? Zelizer and Cook pointed out nineteenth- and twentieth-century processes whereby the "child" as such became more separate from the category of "adult" or "person," gaining a sacralized and nonlaboring—yet increasingly consumerist—position. How is that category evolving today? How are the meanings of childhood and the value of children being produced in our school lunchrooms and beyond, and to what ends?

Certainly the process of growing to like (or at least to eat) more "difficult" and wholesome foods has become part of what it means to transition from childhood to adulthood in the United States. Recall Rebecca, a highly involved, white, married Hometown parent. When I asked her about a contested vending machine in the middle school, she explained her opposition to it by explaining that children, as a group, were not equipped to handle this situation. "I just don't think kids are able to make wise choices, if you put that kind of stuff in front of them with a healthy option, they're gonna choose the junk, they're just drawn to salt, they're drawn to probably packaging, they're drawn to the color you know, whatever, it's just not—it's just setting them up for failure. There's no, they're not going to make wise choices most of the time." Rebecca did acknowledge that some children seemed to be making good choices at the snack bar, so that maybe if there were some healthy choices in the vending machine, they could do so there too. But part of the operative concept of the child was that children had definite tastes and that these tastes in many ways challenged parents' goal to have them eating nutritionally useful foods. At the Health and Wellness meeting mentioned earlier, married working mother Faye was concerned about processed foods and wondered whether bread items really needed to be included in class-wide snacks. "Do we need to give them a bread as their snack when they eat it anyway? Anything you put in front of a kid that has a bread item, they'll eat it. They love bread." In other words, it was up to parents to present children with the things that were *not* so easy to like. Children also were described in terms of their comfort with the familiar and the expected, which sometimes translated into seeing children as mainstream consumers of foods that their parents and teachers found subpar, unhealthy, or uninteresting—which is not necessarily to say that the speakers did not enjoy eating any of these foods themselves, only that these items were placed lower in a hierarchy of explicitly valued foods. A few children were praised as "foodies" and ahead of the game, but most were thought to lean toward the lesser category of "kids' food."

Still, adults balanced directing children's tastes with acknowledgment that those tastes were in some ways legitimate and should be met. As anthropologist Joylin Namie (2011, 406–407) has argued, what is seen as "junk food" certainly can reflect poorly on parents who let their children have it, but "not allowing your child to indulge marks you as a mother who does not care about your child's happiness. Acquiescence and denial are equally problematic." Foods like Takis or sweet, sticky, packaged honey buns that children could elect to eat outside the view of their parents were anxiety-provoking to some adults in this community; but adults also worked with an idea that children could be *expected* to like treats and to not be able to control themselves with these—and that to some degree, providing space for those childhood ways was the right thing to do. Concerns to protect children from their own immoderation *and* to allow them (at least bits of) that unchecked pleasure seeking were entangled and interdependent with one another, part of an ongoing dilemma and contradiction. Furthermore, when children were understood as powerful consumers, as in the school lunchroom, adults sometimes felt bound to cater to those tastes, whether it was strictly to the nutritional benefit of individual students or not, because they had to make the economic venture work. Thus individual adults and institutions got caught between multiple, potentially contradictory ways of framing the agency (or lack thereof) of children to make valid decisions about eating.

Of course, actual children exceeded those constructions of childhood as well as being shaped by them, playing with and to them. Children's own tastes were expressed and construed in a range of ways. When the student told me, "Of course we will! We're kids!," she was affirming the cultural belief that kids inherently gravitate to desserts and banking on the understanding that some allowance is given for children to enact this desire without feeling that they violate their roles as children or as good students. When they enact a lack of moderation or love for sugar, they are in some ways fulfilling expectations, even as they fuel the flames of adult concern.

All of this shows how talk about children's food sets up children's desires and eating as both continually problematic and unsurprising. Even as adults devote considerable energy toward monitoring what children eat, childhood provides a kind of protected realm where the embrace of pleasure and immoderation is considered if not normative, then at least inevitable and to some degree permissible. Childhood is marked as a problematic space representing a lack of self-control but also as a space where the requirements of adulthood need not (or cannot) yet be fully enforced. This is not to say that adults themselves necessarily or consistently eat (only) what have been deemed "good" foods; recall white parent Amanda, who acknowledged that she shared with her son a weakness for Girl Scout cookies, which encouraged her to want to be "human" and tolerant toward his food transgressions. Still, as we have seen, adult maturity is defined in part by the ability to practice appropriate self-constraint in food consumption, such that children are by definition understood to be only minimally capable of their own self-regulation. This creates childhood as a space under extreme scrutiny, but it also means that childhood pleasure is in some ways defended, even valued. That is, children are at least partially excused from immoderations that might be more bothersome or harshly judged in adults, as my students pointed out—or that might be differently perceived when they are cast not as inevitable matters of maturation (or lack thereof) but as a more shameful lack of education or as dimensions of class difference or racial identity.

Might it be useful to think of the immoderate child not as a natural fact but as a kind of "Noble Savage" model that provides a meaningful contrast to (some) adults' more obligatory sophistication and restraint? Statements such as "Elementary schoolers just want grilled cheese" or "Of course we will! We're kids!" are not self-evident statements about what it means to be a half-cooked, less socialized human being; rather, they speak to how childhood is being narratively and materially constructed in the United States, even if the naturalness of such statements seems consistently (though not uniformly) affirmed in our lunch lines and dining rooms. By extension, they also speak to what it means to be an adult in the context of fast-paced consumerism, individual responsibility for personal risk, and intense food moralization. As we have seen throughout this book so far, parenting itself is a space under continual scrutiny, not least because adults are "responsibilized" for both their own self-management and, to a great extent, their children's (Maher, Fraser, and Wright 2010, 235). Is childhood so meaningful, at least in part, because it provides both a threat and an imaginative alternative to the responsibility and self-discipline expected from adults—particularly among Hometown's middle-class, urban professionals? And what social conditions do statements about "children" at large also tend to elide or to background?

Anthropologist Elizabeth Chin's (2001) ethnographic study of African American girls in low-income New Haven speaks back to media discourses about African American youths' "lack of self-control" and impractical consumerism. Chin found practicality and self-restraint in her child collaborators that did not meet the stereotypes, and she contended that "children's lack of self-control or values are often blamed for [consumer practices seen as irrational and greedy], without a recognition of the significant pressures at work in children's lives" such as marketing, poverty, and racism (67). My research context at Hometown was markedly distinct from Chin's, but I harken to her account for the reminder that while a child's "lack of self-control" (or love for foods that some adults see as unhealthy or low-quality) can be naturalized and defused as a relatively expected aspect of childhood, these judgments are also, inevitably, part of larger social conversations and, as we will see, can readily become entangled with only partially acknowledged matters of structural inequality.

For, of course, gaining self-control and "foodie" tastes is not only a matter of growing up. Rather, these traits are perceived and measured with yardsticks that are reflective of one's resources, experiences, and class-inflected aesthetics. In some moments Hometowners are circumspectly aware that other families' finances, schedules, and life conditions shape which foods and feeding strategies are attainable and appealing to them, but that understanding is not foregrounded in the many conversations in which the "child" appears as a relatively natural and universal category.

4

Honoring the Cheese Puffs

Class, Community, and Engaged Parenthood

One afternoon Rita, an African American administrator at Hometown, had planned to make fruit smoothies with the children who attended the middle school after-school program. Yet finding that the blenders had not been left out for her by the cafeteria staff, she put that project off for the following week and opted to make Rice Krispie treats instead. Taking their name from the popular puffed rice cereal Rice Krispies, these snacks are a sticky amalgamation of melted marshmallows, melted butter, and puffed rice cereal that are mixed together while warm, spread into a pan, and allowed to cool into a sheet that is then cut into portion-sized bars. When Rita ended up running late on her way back from an appointment with her own child that afternoon, my research assistant and I found ourselves gathering the ingredients she had left there and looking around doubtfully for mixing vessels to begin the project, as students were complaining that they were hungry and wanted to get the treat before their parents picked them up. Thankfully, Rita soon returned and found from behind her desk a suitable bowl for mixing the butter and marshmallows.

After microwaving the marshmallows and butter in the school's lunchroom, we glopped mounds of it onto each child's plate along with some rice cereal, allowing each of them to mix up an individual portion to eat. Most of them came back for seconds. A student was sent down the hall with a plate for the school principal, who in turn walked in a few minutes later to joke about how wired she was by the sugar. One boy's father arrived to pick him up; this man was a white lawyer and an avid home cook who disapproved, I knew, of the vending machine in the school because it contained sugary items and encouraged not only nutritionally unsound but also, in his view, potentially addictive behaviors. Seeing the Rice Krispie treats that afternoon, he quipped edgily, "I figured something like this was going on." He explained that his son had called asking to be picked up at a particular time (presumably not so early as to miss the treats), and now the request had become decipherable.

Rice Krispie treats triggered edginess in others as well. One school administrator grimaced when she heard about students having made them at school and what the process entailed. A married Mexican American university professor and parent emailed her son's teacher to complain when she learned that his after-school enrichment class had prepared a similar cereal treat. "Here I'm paying $80 for you to teach my son about bad eating. You have their attention. This is a moment to teach them about healthy eating, and how it can be fun and good, and you're giving them this crap?" Afterward, however, she reflected that she was not sure that she should have sent the email while she was upset.

Indeed, while some parents worried or complained about subpar foods being served at school or by other parents, questions of tact and inclusion were often at the forefront of their attention as well. When I was planning my research at Hometown in 2011, an initial step was to meet with the then principal of the elementary school to discuss my project. In this first meeting, Barbara offered that there was a kind of dichotomy that split parents at Hometown: there were the "green freaks" and "healthy food freaks" or "granola parents," on one hand; on the other, there were those who brought in huge cupcakes with blue frosting from a local grocery store chain. "And they're excited. And the kids love them." These were perhaps the same parents who would bring in big jugs of commercial cheese puffs when it was their turn to provide class snacks. Barbara, a white career educator, noted that she personally liked the cheese puffs, but she said the school encouraged parents to bring healthier snacks such as fruit, cheese, and crackers.

When I asked whether there had been any complaints from parents about classroom snacks such as the cheese puffs, Barbara explained that she thought adults who might otherwise object tried to "honor the cheese puffs for the children's sake." Further, she noted that the blue cupcakes seemed to be met more with indifference than with resistance. She believed that the divergent food choices were connected with "socioeconomics," and she named both relative household finances and parents' education (or lack thereof) as part of that differentiation. She suggested that the role of the school was to educate people about what was good for their children without offending them. She had had only one parent really raise a fuss, she observed, and it had been an African American parent who had wanted her child to eat only the snack that she had brought from home. The school had had to reassure the mother that it would be on top of making sure the class snacks were appropriately nutritious.

What did it mean to "honor the cheese puffs for the children's sake"? I understood Barbara to suggest that adults in the community sometimes placed the feelings of children (and parents?) above nutrition; perhaps they declined to criticize "unhealthy" food decisions in order to help children save face when their parents brought in foods that were not considered acceptable choices to many others at Hometown. There were noticeable differences in food choices among parents as well as between parents and staff at times, and these could lead to conflict, concern, and emotional upset. Yet many Hometowners valued social, racial, and economic difference—they explicitly sought to draw it to Hometown and to nurture it—even as they also experienced discomfort over their own children's potential consumption of foods that did not align with their aesthetics or nurture their sense of their own children's safety. Such food-conscious parents were typically well-educated, progressive, and often (but not exclusively) white; and while they expressed support for racial and class inclusion, they also worried about less educated, less well-off, or less committed parents offering their children unhealthy foods. That is, concern for their children's healthy food intake at times seemed to counter their left-leaning values.

In short, empathy (and the efforts of parents to be circumspect about the circumstances of parents with whom they disagreed) was in conflict with anxiety (especially through fears of one's own child being harmed by foods chosen for them by other adults). Food was often discussed in moralizing tones that avoided any explicit racist or classist sentiment, yet did allow for some expressions of discomfort about (and judgment of) parents who did not seem to get it right enough. Ultimately, many Hometowners' sensibilities about food bespoke their wishes to prioritize the inclusion in their community of those they considered unlike themselves; yet they spoke implicitly, too, about the comforts of cultural homogeneity. In this way, the politics of children's food challenged, dramatized, and, in certain ways, fed, shadowed, or elided dynamics of social inequality.

We will see, too, how parents spoke of the atmosphere at the school and its surrounding neighborhood as one that was highly positive, valued precisely because of its present sense of "community" and "engagement." This engagement included volunteering at school and being tuned in to food issues. The mother mentioned above complained about her son's off-the-rails after-school cooking lesson: "I gave them a whole list of foods that they can make that are healthy and fun. . . . And [the teacher was] all, 'We'll take it into consideration some of these ideas that you have.' So I'm like, 'I'll come in and do one if you want me to,' 'cause I just think it's a moment that kids can learn about food. It should be an educational moment." Many parents at Hometown believed that actively participating in the life of the school was a good and important practice, and some of them had the flexibility to do so on a regular basis. Such flexibility was inevitably related to people's economic resources and household divisions of labor, but it often was framed not as a question of money, jobs, or class but rather in terms of the affective frames of caring, being involved, and not "checking out" on children.

If some parents managed to "honor the cheese puffs," the goal of this chapter is to honor the same parents' and administrators' express intentions toward inclusion and awareness of economic disparities and social injustice even as we also examine how, given that adults felt charged with the protection of their children from the excesses and toxins of an industrial food system, the same differences felt threatening. Indeed, the consumer economy pits these concerns against one another; and while at Hometown the conflict remained largely implicit, it is an important one to examine if we are to understand how food anxieties shape and are shaped by perceptions of social difference on the ground. Middle-class parents' protective consumer labor—analyzed at the end of this chapter as a form of "conspicuous production"—indexed their relative privilege, but it was also fueled by fear and ambivalence.

Grappling with "Diversity"

At a parent coffee in the fall of 2012, Hometown's director, Scott Burke-head, reminded parents that the school was part of a consortium of schools that emphasized diversity. "Not because you can get different colored faces on your brochures," clarified Scott, a white educator, "but because we know—research has shown us—that having people from different backgrounds in the classroom has some amazing educational and social benefits." At his state of the school address a few years later, in 2014, when the parent-teacher association (PTA) was beginning to discuss changes to the school's eligibility zones, he prefaced the discussion by stating, "Diversity is a central part of who we are as a school." Scott went on to explain that the school wanted to be open and welcoming but also to challenge its students to be informed citizens and that to do that, "you have to work with people who are different from you." In a blog entry the same year, he responded to recent publications and media debates that had suggested that "progressive" education might be appropriate for middle-class students but not for poorer ones. Strongly disagreeing, he explained that progressive education provided experiences such as "collaboration, social-emotional learning, perspective taking, and chances for reflection and revision" that fostered "engagement," which he described as a proven way to increase chances for social mobility for students of lower socioeconomic statuses. Thus Hometown's administration framed diversity as beneficial to all in the school community: both the economically poorer students who seemed to represent "diversity" and the middle-class students who appeared as the unmarked category and (to some) the more expected audience for "progressive" educational strategies.

Yet during my research in 2012–2015, diversity was a growing concern at Hometown. The school's population did not mirror the economic or racial demographics of the surrounding urban area very well: the school was whiter and more affluent. In a school blog, Scott explained that the middle school campus still held Title I funding but probably would not for much longer, while the elementary school had a free or reduced lunch (FRL) rate of just 15 percent, which was far below the 35 percent that qualified a school for Title I. Scott acknowledged that many attributed these trends to the area's general gentrification. A married white mother with a background in real estate, longtime Hometown parent Sheila, described the process this way.

> The school actually I think helped the neighborhood. People heard about the school and they wanted to move here so their kids could go there and so it did bring people in for sure. . . . The only problem now is because there's a limit as to how many kids they can take and when families don't get in, that's becoming a problem because a lot of the families, they don't want to send their kids to Englewood [the local public elementary school] and then they send them to [a charter school a bit further away] and as soon as there's a slot open they pull them out and put them at Hometown and so it's become this thing now. And also because the demographics are changing in the area—I feel like we base the charter on being a diverse school and that is obviously changing, and it's going to even get worse, less diverse over the years, so that's the big question right now.

There was good housing stock that people had come from more affluent neighborhoods to purchase relatively cheaply, Sheila said, and "now they've got kids at the school. It's a positive change to the neighborhood, it's just that being a charter school and the way they do it, I don't know what's going to happen in the future, unless they rezone." In fact, rezoning was on the agenda, as we shall see. Yet as Scott pointed out in a state of the school address to the PTA in 2014, the demographics at Hometown were quite different from those at other public schools in the immediate vicinity. In the last four years, he said, the FRL rate had gone from 40 percent to under 20 percent; and since these demographics did not match other schools in the same area (at another event, a Hometown board member reported that the FRL rate at Englewood was 75 percent), the explanation had to lie in who was applying for entry and stereotypes in the larger community about what a charter school represented. In other words, there was "diversity" in the neighborhood that was not being attracted to the school, and Scott believed that there was more that could be done in terms of outreach to those groups.

It bears repeating that in terms of the official efforts of the school, FRL rates were the available measure of "diversity." Racial diversity was named at times as important to the school, but as Scott acknowledged in a PTA address, only socioeconomic diversity could be considered by the school legally for the purpose of admissions zoning. According to figures I collected from Hometown staff circa 2013, its elementary student body consisted of about 30 percent African Americans and 57 percent Caucasians; the ratio was roughly flipped in the middle school grades (50 percent African American versus 33 percent Caucasian). There were about 10 to 11 percent identified as multiracial at both levels. Comparing these numbers to those of a few years previous, the proportion of African Americans was dropping and was continuing to drop: I learned from the elementary school's principal that in fall 2014, there were only a handful of Black children out of more than seventy kindergarteners. Trends toward reduced numbers of FRL students and African American students undoubtedly were linked; notably, the local elementary school, Englewood, which had been mentioned for its much higher FRL rate, was also a majority African American school.

Yet it is far from the case that race and income can be treated interchangeably. Of fifty-two adults who were interviewed formally for this book, nine were African American/Black. Three of these never completed my income survey, but among the other six, self-reported annual incomes ranged from $12,000 (the individual income of a young teaching assistant who lived with her parent) to over $90,000 (the household income of a married teacher). For comparison, responses of the group overall ranged from $12,000 (the lowest white household income reported was $14,000) up to an estimated household income of $340,000. Still, the $12,000 to $90,000 spread among African Americans is significant. Moreover, the income figures do not speak directly to other factors related to class identity and cultural upbringing: for example, all of the African American interviewees were college-educated, two of these (Noelle and Lila) at Atlanta's well-known historically Black colleges. There were a few food narratives—such as Rita's and Carmen's, described below—that diverged noticeably from those of most white parents with whom I spoke at Hometown, while others, such as Lila's and Noelle's, struck notes highly similar to many white Hometowners'.

In short, "diversity" was a prized value for many at Hometown, and race was a present element of conversations about diversity. In the United States at large and certainly in Atlanta, experiences of race and of class are linked inextricably due to the long-term legacies of slavery and racism, which include persistent forms of structural violence. Still, it would be a mistake to assume that race mapped cleanly onto socio-economic disparities or food cultures at Hometown, either in perception or in reality. Nor does the conventional primacy of race in American conversations about diversity and social conflict guarantee that race is always *the* spoken or unspoken bias that underlies people's discomforts with social difference. When it came to children's food, the socioeconomic diversity that confronted Hometown parents in the material, viscerally impactful form of untrusted foods seemed more fraught than the politics of race as such, even if they were often wrapped up together.

"Not in a Vanilla, Monotonous Suburb": The Politics and Aesthetics of Hometown

I often asked people what it was that had brought them to this neighborhood or to this school in the first place. For some, they had enrolled their children in the school because they already lived close by. Others had moved to this neighborhood specifically for the school. People talked about the neighborhood's central location, which included its easy accessibility to major highways. The area is part of Atlanta proper and is considered "intown," as Atlantans phrase it—that is, close to downtown and inside the highway that rings inner Atlanta, separating it physically and symbolically from what is considered to be suburban Atlanta. Hometowners also talked about its relative affordability, its walkability, and its general vibe as compared to other neighborhoods in which they had previously been residents. For example, married working mother Faye described having lived in the Highlands, a higher rent neighborhood known for its popular restaurants and shops, before moving close to Hometown in 2005. She explained how she had decided on this move:

> I wasn't that conscious about the schools back then, but I knew I liked the lifestyle of the area. I liked that it was kinda laid back, and you still had . . . still close to stuff . . . close to the highway . . . easy accessible. And frankly the Highlands was out of our price point, and so this neighborhood fit everything we needed. So it was a good fit. At first I wasn't convinced we would be here this long, and then the more . . . the longer we stayed. We feel like we are outgrowing our house, [but] we are like, "We are not mov-

ing." We are not leaving our street. We are really entrenched. We are not planning on going anywhere anytime soon.

Similarly, Margot, a married woman in her late thirties who identified as white and Caucasian and had worked previously as an architect, recounted that she previously lived in an area slightly farther away from central Atlanta. When she and her husband started a family, however, the house they were in became too small. They found that Hometown's neighborhood balanced good schools with space and affordability, in a walkable setting that she described as similar to what they had experienced during six months living in France. To white married mother Lynn, the area was notable indeed for its walkability: "All of our friends are within walking distance. Our world is within walking distance. It's really nice. . . . It's magic. I mean, the community at school. You know the first day of school all the kids are excited, but so are the all the grown-ups. You know we're all so glad to see each other. Talking about your summer and feels like you're comin' home. That's the magic part. . . . It's pretty unusual. It's what we had in a tiny town." Walkability not only was a convenience, then, but was linked with a sense of small-town life and community.

Jane, a Caucasian married psychotherapist, explained that her family had been renting in the more established, affluent (still "intown") Atlanta neighborhood of Morningside, but they had applied to Hometown and decided to move when her daughter got in. She described the difference between the two neighborhoods as "night and day . . . it's like tomatoes and pineapple," and when I asked her to elaborate, she explained, "It is a community. So there's that, and it's very intentional. And you know, just the school. All of the value systems that they promote is what draws like-minded people into that environment. Which fits with us. And so, you know, people noticed that we were the new family. People reached out to us. People connected with us. People are really super friendly, engaging. It's smaller. It's more connected. Yeah, we drank the Kool-Aid [laughs]." In saying they had drunk "the Kool-Aid," Jane implied that there was a brain-washing aspect to her own enthusiasm, since this phrase refers to the Jonestown mass suicide event of 1978. This was a self-deprecating acknowledgment that she and others had really "bought in" to the idea that this place was special in ways others might find cultish.

In fact, the trope of "community" came up time and time again as people spoke about what they valued in this neighborhood and in the school. Fran, a married Caucasian health professional, said that she had been looking at the school for years before she even had children, and that she was attracted to it by "the community of the school. I really love the constructivist model. I really love the teaching the children problem solving, conflict resolution and now self-regulation." Another white married woman who worked from home as a graphic designer said that her family had been considering Catholic school until she remembered her own childhood and how much she had hated all the rules. They got into Hometown, decided to try it, and found they "absolutely loved it." "We love the community aspect of the school, that not only are the parents excited about the school, but the kids are excited about their own school." Amanda, a white university professional, said her child was going through some significant adjustments in his home life and had benefited from the individualized attention he had gotten at Hometown. "They feel very much like a family. The community involvement is huge."

Thus, to many, a densely urban environment actually felt more "small town" than the suburban neighborhoods some residents might have considered as alternatives. Sheila talked about a northern suburb of Atlanta with which she was familiar, Roswell, and how it differed from the Hometown area:

> All I can think of is how much fast food people eat, processed food, not as much fresh food. Not many people have gardens or chickens in their yard. Here you've got, how many families have chickens and gardens, and there you've got these real cookie cutter neighborhoods where if you had a garden they would fine you. My cousin was like, "I want tomatoes, but I have to hide them, they'll get cited." Their yards have to look a certain way or the homeowners' association will put a lien on your house. I mean they get crazy, so they don't encourage it out there. Here, it's like my whole front yard. I tore up all the grass and put vegetables you know, it's like you can walk by the house and see tomatoes and all kinds of things growing right in the front yard. . . . I don't have to worry about anybody complaining [that] my tomatoes are too high or something's too high. . . . We're just glad you don't have cars up on cinder blocks, you know what I mean, we're fine with the garden.

Circling back to the topic of food, Sheila explained that she and her friends here went to local restaurants instead of fast-food chains, as a rule. Likewise, an Italian/Jewish married academic said that people who, like her, appreciated local establishments and "something that vaguely resembles regular food" were just "the kind of people the neighborhood attracts."

These lifestyle choices were contrasted favorably to ones like those in the suburbs: lifeways associated not with poverty or Blackness but with bland prosperity and whiteness. On the website of a parent group in one of the neighborhoods immediate to Hometown, a local resident and mother of an infant talked about how wonderful it was to have a supportive parent group with meet-ups close by.

> Having my mother-in-law here has brought to light some obvious differences in our baby raising. I'm thankful for living in Hometown and not in a vanilla, monotonous, distant suburb. Seems like the Baby Boomers really made bringing-up-baby more isolating by moving to the middle of no where [*sic*]. Not only did they not have the Internet (and sharing) but some of them never left the house with a baby (like my mother-in-law). The city is back (!!!) and has brought with it the strongest sense of community. It surely takes a village to raise a child.

White married mother Rebecca compared Hometown to another school for which her family previously had been districted, which was reputed to be a good public elementary school (just outside Atlanta, though still "inside the perimeter" or "ITP"). "I felt like everybody was pretty much the same, although they were from different nationalities. There wasn't a lot of economic diversity or anything like that. It was a gated community kind of feeling to me, and it made me feel uncomfortable." Living in a neighborhood that had economic diversity, that was not overly sanitized or manicured, and that was also actively sociable and close-knit in a way they found or assumed the suburbs not to be clearly was valued and appreciated by many at Hometown.

And yet some speakers acknowledged that maintaining all of this in one neighborhood also meant that they had found a comforting sameness in many of their neighbors. As Fran, a white, married at-home mom and previously a technical writer, put it when I asked about whether she thought other families in the neighborhood favored less processed and organic foods much as she did, "In general there is a higher concentration of like-minded people that live around here." Indeed, small-town intimacy seemed to depend upon a great sense of affinity among households and individuals. A new school staff member, a married white man, said that his family had moved to this neighborhood before their child was born and "really loved it": "It's beautiful and all of our neighbors have chickens and, you know, there's all this stuff and it seems like, um, it's just a really interesting place with interesting people who all, you know, kind have similar ideals to me." Renee, a white at-home mother and former academic, said that she felt she had found "her people" at this school after talking with other parents about the "role of scientific thought." These were the intellectual, adult conversations she had been missing since leaving academia. She had noticed, too, that a few Hometown families had, like her, moved over from a small, private, "alternative hippie school" that her daughter had attended in the area previously.

Not all adults in the area, of course, shared the same needs and priorities. A staff member had visited a close-by, lower income housing complex to do outreach for the school, and its residents had told her that one reason why they did not enter the lottery for Hometown was its lack of bussing. Walkability obviously was not prime for all members of the greater community, perhaps especially those whose work schedules made walking young children to school every day less feasible. Indeed, Lynn acknowledged there were now fewer children at Hometown on FRL, and by way of explanation she said that she thought it was difficult for some parents, such as single mothers, to fit its model, which included required volunteer hours. She also attributed the demographic shift to a kind of cultural inertia: "I think it's easier if you just do what you know and unless they're knocking on your door saying, 'Come be with us,' then it's just easier to drop the kid off. There are people we see walk, you have to get the school bus at 6:20, you know, and the mother can get to work at 7 or 8 you know. I think it's a hard school to go to if you're a full-time working parent, and let's be honest—we all gravitate towards that which is similar." Lynn described feeling very close to other families at Hometown and feeling blessed by that, but she also rued that "we [don't] do so good on the diversity thing."

Rita gave a glimpse of community experience from another perspective. An employee at Hometown, Rita herself enjoyed sharing a closeness and informality with her students and their families, though it was not what she had grown up with. She resided not in the immediate Hometown neighborhood but in another neighborhood still close by, and she lived amid many of her students. This resulted in a neighborliness that her husband believed crossed lines of expected propriety:

> Growing up you never lived in a neighborhood with your teacher or your school person, you know. I would, for a kid, get out a book, like, "Oh, come by my house and pick it up." And you know, parents like, "Okay, I'll come by your house after work." And come over to the house, like—their parents in your house. Well, they live two houses down. [laughs] You know, or in the morning, kids need rides to school, they come over to my house and wait for me. And my husband is so, "[This is] not how it's supposed to happen. People shouldn't know where you live." I was like, "Well, we live in the same neighborhood."

Rita described how the differences extended to other parenting practices as well, and how members of her extended family had actively resisted these new practices or criticized her for adopting them.

> [Hometown is] a different environment than what I grew up in. I grew up in the housing projects and then when I moved into a home, the environment was totally different. So, for me and especially for my oldest two kids, it was the learning curve for me. And then when [my younger son]—my friends changed 'cause of my work, you know, going out and having a playdate like a mom. My oldest two kids, they didn't have playdates. . . . So, and then the people I'm around changed, so, yeah. Yeah, 'cause, you know, growing up in the housing projects everybody got a beating [laughs], you know, and then for me it's like, "No, I don't wanna beat my kids." 'Cause my [inaudible], "You know you're not from the hood anymore." I'm like, "I know." [laughs] Yeah, well, even 'cause when I took my oldest son to counseling, well, he was going basically out of the growth thing, figuring out who he wanted to be and my [sister?] was picking at me, saying, "Can you believe she is paying a therapist?" "Oh, you're—you're doing what?" "Yeah, we're having family counseling." And

they're like, "Are you serious?" . . . I have four older step-brothers and they all like, "well, what did the therapist say this time?" "They told him to keep a journal." And just—[laughs] "A journal, Rita? Everybody's writing their feelings down in a journal!" And I'm like, "Yes, that's what she said to do and we're learning about each other's feelings." . . . So yeah, it was a different thing for me, yeah, yeah.

Though Rita described herself as willingly on a learning curve, the mockery she received from discomfited family members serves as a reminder that not all families living in the surrounding area would find the Hometown milieu—with its emphasis on social-emotional learning and intimate community—to be comfortable or welcoming.

Meanwhile, some white parents acknowledged racial tensions and expressed empathy for Black parents who might understandably feel excluded at Hometown. Simultaneously, they considered how "diversity" came in multiple forms. When I spoke with Rebecca about issues of class diversity at Hometown, she expressed her awareness of race as a factor of exclusion, even if an unintended one:

> I think the Black parents are concerned, the Black parents who are involved I think are concerned, yeah, one in particular, she's like: "I don't feel like I fit in when I go to some of these things," 'cause—and I don't know why—you know, we go to the social events and even like the non-social events, the academic events that are hosted by the school like reading night, and you don't get turnout from the Black community that's part of our school. So we're going to the auction [a school fund-raising event] and I'm going to be keenly aware of the color of the crowd, and it's my theory that we just are not, for some reason, we just are not relating to that aspect of our community very well.

Amanda spoke about how her white son had African American friends at school. He had compared experiences with them and gained opportunities to reflect on racial and class differences, from the foods people ate to their financial ability to participate in extracurricular activities. Yet she observed, as had Rebecca, that among parents there was less engagement across racial groups.

Everybody is so afraid that it always feels uncomfortable to talk about it, right, but we need to . . . I don't know, I just know I look around and I feel like not all the volunteers are white but a lot of them are and a lot of the leaders are and I have to ask myself . . . if I was . . . the minority walking in and I saw that it was all the majority, would I want to volunteer with that group? You know . . . so that's just something I worry about, in terms of us really embracing what and who we say we are as a school.

Both women acknowledged, too, that race and even socioeconomic differences were not the only relevant forms of difference. Neither of them lived in the neighborhoods immediate to the school, and they had felt it had been more difficult to feel welcome, at least initially, among parents at Hometown. As Amanda explained it, "Even though it's a highly engaged community because most of them do live in the neighborhood, especially at the elementary campus . . . they've all kind of known each other so they have their routines that include each other, and they don't mean to be cliquey, but you're just not part of their routine." Amanda also noted that she was part of a same-sex couple and "we're not the only ones . . . I feel like there's kind of a really large acceptance for kind of general difference."

A similar point was echoed by Lila, an African American teacher at Hometown and single mother whose own son had recently transferred there from another Atlanta charter school. She highlighted that there were different *kinds* of diversity at the two schools; she estimated that this school (perhaps specifically the elementary school, where she worked) had about 80 percent Caucasians, while the previous school had been 80 percent African American. Meanwhile, her son had asked recently why there were so many kids with gay parents at Hometown. The question had taken her by surprise, but she welcomed it and explained to me that he would not have had the opportunity to ask this question at his old school, where gay parents were present but perhaps less so and certainly less visible. She said she had explained to him that "every family's different." "Even our family's different than the people across the street and don't think that because you have two parents in the household that it's better. Please don't ever believe that. I say it because they have three kids across the street, they have two parents in the house and they've never been on an airplane. You go on an airplane easily twice, three times a year. . . . So within diversity, no, it's not just about color, it's about everything." Race represented one aspect of social identity of which Hometowners were certainly aware, but it did not stand alone as the defining aspect of meaningful difference in the community. Rather, it stood alongside class and sexuality, among other aspects of life experience.

Still, one white Hometown administrator spoke to the implicit, yet perhaps powerful, role of race in shaping white families' decisions to send their children to the school. She had observed that many parents at Hometown thought of it as their neighborhood school; she had to remind them that Englewood was the neighborhood public school, while Hometown was set apart by its pedagogical approach. She said that there was a misconception that charter meant "private" and served as a means of school segregation; and while this was not the intent of the school, she wondered whether some parents at Hometown sought that segregation. She felt that these attitudes were in evidence at times, even if people would not come out and say it. Parents would come in and ask, "Why are the kids sitting on the floor?" The administrator rehearsed the answer to me: "Because that's how we do it here." She went on, "They don't know; they just know they don't want their kids to go *there.*" She believed the "not that" reaction was more about race than people would admit.

This was all coming to a head in the context of the fact that the school's charter was coming up for renewal and that its eligibility zoning would need to be reexamined. Originally two separate schools, the elementary and middle campuses had different zone boundaries but would now—upon renewing the charter in 2016—be required to share the same policies. Both schools used a lottery to determine admission. Each had a first priority zone; if not all spots were filled by applicants in this zone, a lottery was opened for students in a second, wider zone; and if slots were still available after that lottery, students from throughout the Atlanta Public School system became eligible. Currently, the elementary school gave top priority to the two immediate neighborhoods in which the school campuses were located, with the second tier of eligibility defined by a slightly larger administrative zone; meanwhile, the middle school campus defined that same, broader administrative area as its first zone. When the school's charter was renewed in 2016, it would be required to have one uniform zoning system.

At an evening PTA meeting to discuss the rezoning project, a Hometown board member, a white woman of forty or so with long brown hair, stated that "we need to not let [the process of figuring out a new zoning policy] tear us apart." She explained to an audience of about thirty parents in attendance that night that the school could choose to draw the zoning lines by radius, by administrative district, or by neighborhood. She continued that "we have political cover" for drawing lines by neighborhood; "other neighborhoods have done that." She acknowledged that there were competing factors: there were the two immediate neighborhoods whose communities had founded the school and "there should be some protection for that." On the other hand, she noted, was the question of diversity. "We're at 12 percent free and reduced lunch now, which is really low. All the other schools around are 75 to 85 percent." Recognizing that "there is diversity in that zone [the immediate neighborhoods] that we're not attracting," she stated that there was also the option of pulling further away school districts into the priority zone, and she ran through a number of variations, noting along the way which of the neighborhoods proposed for inclusion were walkable to Hometown. The possibilities ranged from keeping the zone limited to the two immediate neighborhoods (she noted that 50 percent of the children in those neighborhoods currently attended Hometown) to adding multiple new neighborhoods that would nearly double the pool of students included in the lottery priority zone.

As we have seen, many of my interlocutors were concerned to nurture economic and racial diversity at the school. Yet at least a few parents were more worried and resistant. In a question-and-answer session at one of the PTA meetings on zoning, a mother stated, "We live in Atlanta and we can see diversity all around us [as we drive through the city]; why do we have to bring it to our school?" She said that years ago the FRL rate had been 50 percent, and it since had gone down while fund-raising had gone up. "We should be happy about what we've created here." Similar concerns may have occupied the parents whom my research assistant Jessie Burnette observed at an informational session, where what she described in her field notes as an "overwhelmingly white and majority female" group of about fifteen people responded to school leaders' statements about the charter renewal and zoning explorations. These parents indicated that they were concerned about the impact of zoning changes that, as Jessie rendered their view, could lead to an influx of "poor, possibly homeless, and possibly attention-needy kids." The effort to maintain a not "vanilla, monotonous" but also comfortingly familiar and like-minded environment was contested, then, and rich with conflict and contradiction.

Perceiving Class and Race through Children's Food

As we saw earlier, many Hometown parents presented themselves as both careful to monitor their children's food intake and eager to avoid appearing overly judgmental of others' choices. They sometimes highlighted economic disparities they knew to exist in their broader community and the ways these informed food choices they themselves considered less than ideal. Likewise, some interviewees noted what they viewed as the excesses of some adults in the community who overemphasized the importance of "correct" healthy eating. Wendy, a married white university instructor, addressed both ends of the spectrum when comparing Hometown to another charter school her child had attended previously, in particular recalling a school event that had been held at a park:

> People had brought like huge, from Publix [a major grocery store chain], cupcakes with icing. . . . That green or that blue, like it's not a natural color icing. It's like, "What is that?" It's kind of creepy, but you know it's cupcakes and cookies, predominantly sweets. The one at Hometown, you know there were a few sweets on the table, but people had brought fresh fruit chopped up, they had brought grapes, they had brought the white cheddar Pirate's Booty [a brand of puffed grain snack]. So to me part of it is also socioeconomic status. You know the Pirate's Booty is very expensive compared to the big bag of Doritos [tortilla chips] or whatever, and the moms—I have no proof of this, but I think there's more stay-at-home moms at Hometown that have more time to bake cookies and chop up that fruit, so I definitely saw a difference in the food choices that were laid out for the kids. You know, I mean that's a good example, but then you notice sometimes just little comments that parents would make about,

"Oh well, like, we're vegetarians" or "We only eat local food," more of that—like local, organic. I'm not saying that's bad in any way, I think it's great. I just think it's almost like an obsession. [laughs]

Wendy believed that some of these local parents wore their Whole Foods, organic, and gluten-free foods "like a badge of honor," while other people went too far in the other direction by eating unhealthily. Looking at her husband for confirmation, she concluded that they themselves had always been about "moderation."

In my interview with Pam, a Caucasian, white, non-Hispanic former lawyer and married mother of two, she explained that she was worried about sugar as something insidious that snuck into people's diets, but less so about fats. She drew a distinction among fatty foods, assessing butter (which she cooked with) more favorably than fatty fast foods ("I'm not going to take them to McDonald's . . . you know, that's just not something that we choose to do"). But Pam also acknowledged how the concern with food itself could go too far:

> I try to be thoughtful about it, but I don't know . . . sometimes I worry about my lines, where I'm coming down on things, but I mean at some point, you just have to make your peace with it because it can really consume you, you know, and I don't want to be *that* parent either . . . who is always talking to their kids about food. ALL. THE. TIME. You know? [JP: Do you see that . . . do you observe that a lot in the community?] Oh yeah. [laughs] You know, I mean and it's fine . . . but I mean, I just feel like . . . you know, maybe the one time I've had that person, they were talking to their kid about food. Maybe that was the one time during the day that they were, you know . . . so I'm being sort of facetious when I say that, but I mean there seems to be a lot of talk about food in our society and even kind of in this area. I mean we've got a farmers' market and everybody's very proud of that.

When we discussed the practice whereby individual families were asked to bring in a week of classroom snacks for their child's entire class at the elementary school, Pam talked about her own struggle to balance nutritional standards with understanding of the financial constraints of others. "I think for some families it's really hard to provide twenty-five more snacks every day for a week so . . . but then you know sometimes I walk into the room and I see the cheese ball thing and I'm just like, ugh! But I don't make a big deal of it you know, because . . . my kids need to learn to live in the real world anyway. They need to make choices and . . . it's okay . . . I know some people who would have a heart attack over that." Likewise a married working mother who had been active in a parent committee focused on Health and Wellness and had, along with a Hometown administrator, drawn up guidelines for parents about what to send for snacks, spoke of being careful not to judge those who had financial constraints that limited what they might bring for snacks, even as it was important to her to give them a nudge in the right direction.

> I knew from the start that I didn't want to be a food Nazi and accepted that there are people here from different backgrounds . . . different economic backgrounds too. Not everybody can afford—. . . . A box of cereal is a lot cheaper than bringing fruit for the class. I didn't want to make a parent feel badly for doing that. It was meant to be encouraging. Instead of saying, "don't bring this." There's nothing in there, in the snack guidelines that says do not bring this. It says, "Hey, just think about what's on the label." You know, start reading the label, and if you are cool with what's on the label, then bring it. I was really trying to be subtle without being really pushy about it, but my snack guidelines got confused with some of the teachers' snack guidelines. I was like, "No, those aren't my guidelines!" Some of the teachers were [requesting] like only organic, homemade. "If you are going to bring meat, we want both a complex carbohydrate and a protein." They were trying to combine stuff . . . so they were asking parents to bring two things in for a day. It was like, wow! I just felt really uncomfortable with paying . . . in a public school . . . you are already signing up for a week. Giving the financial situations here, you just can't assume that everybody can afford to spend two hundred dollars that week on snacks for the class. I'm hoping that message got through. I always try to tell people, "Oh no no." . . . It comes up every once in a while, and I'm like, "No no no . . . that wasn't me."

While this mother's discussion suggested that improving the overall quality of school snacks was important to her, she also was highly concerned not to appear as an insensitive "food Nazi" dictating what others could do. She "didn't want to make a parent feel badly" for bringing in an inexpensive item that did not meet her own standards for healthfulness. In some moments, it seemed as though the most acceptable form of judgment lay in criticism of those who were themselves perceived as overly judgmental, overly restricted, or overly invested in eating the "right" foods and in displaying this to others.

Yet the language of tolerance sometimes wore thinner, too, as parents commiserated about food events that had provoked discomfort. At an evening Health and Wellness meeting with other parents, one of the participants talked with a side group about "teaching people that Cheetos for snack is not a good idea." Another (who, notably, also had talked about the sensitivity she had tried to practice in creating class snack guidelines for the school) vividly recounted how she had discovered that her son had been given Froot Loops for class snack one day. He had been trying to describe to her a food previously unfamiliar to him or at least whose name he could not remember, and he apparently had been very excited about it. "They were circles, and they were purple and red," this mother recalled her son telling her, which prompted her reply to him, "Was it Froot Loops?" "Yes! It was Froot Loops!" She noted that the Froot Loops, a colorful, sugary breakfast cereal, actually had been mixed with pretzels, which she allowed was "creative." She and the two other mothers with whom she had been conferring went on to discuss Welch's fruit snacks. "It's candy, really." "We had those in our Halloween bowl but it's not—" "Not a daily snack." It seemed to me that there was a kind of bonding and reassurance to be found in sharing these standards and the worry that swirled when the standards were abrogated. These women had similar sensibilities, and they had come together to air them, even as behind-the-scenes reprimands of other parents competed with explicit intentions to be politically circumspect and encouraging of all parents in the school community.

A married, white former lawyer and now stay-at-home mother told my research assistant Liz Barnett about a neighbor who had told her about a good deal she had found on meat. This interviewee sympathized with the other mother's financial situation, which was more strained than her own, yet she was troubled by imagining a situation in which she could feel compelled to give her own children that inexpensive meat.

So our next door neighbor, they have kind of a different situation. I mean, they're older, they've been in the neighborhood for like forty years. She works in the bank and he works at a hotel and they're probably not . . . they're not a high-income family and she's this great bargain shopper. And so my kids were over and I was chatting with her. But she's telling me she got six pounds of chicken for some ridiculous price. [Liz: And can you imagine what is in that meat.] Yeah, yes. [Liz: So she's even trying to do it right and be healthy.] And I would never say anything to her, and I admire her for doing it, but then I think, and to buy that for my kids. . . . [Liz: The harm, yeah.] What if I was in the position of having to do all of this, like I say, $100 or $150 a week or God forbid—like, it's a scary thought.

As this mother attempted to put herself in another's shoes, empathy (her wish to be understanding and even admiring of another mother's struggles and choices) and anxiety (her visceral discomfort in thinking about having to make the same choices herself, if circumstances had been different) competed for affective prominence.

When I asked another parent, Fran, a follow-up question about whether she remembered any instances when she had been at someone's house or at an event and registered that what was being served was not something she would choose, she replied, "Yeah, like so if we've been like over to other peoples' houses and there might be just a lot of juice or soda available to like—our kids are just water. We just drink water and they have almond milk if they want it. . . . You know, like the pizza—get the pizza in from Little Caesar's or wherever—wherever it's five bucks, you know. And I understand that it's economical, but I'm just—I'm not gonna eat that. I don't—I would prefer that my kids don't eat that, you know?" In this example we see again how an explicit interest to take others' financial situations into account and to avoid judgment coexisted with a perhaps more visceral urge and moral imperative to avoid what were seen as threatening exposures of one's own family to harm.

Rita's story of her own experiences being confronted with unfamiliar food practices at Hometown provided a reminder, from another angle, that it was more than finances per se that determined these choices. Hometown and the communities in which she had grown up and raised her younger children were, in terms of the foods provided at birthday parties,

> totally different, totally different. Even last year some of the parties, a couple of parties only had cheese pizzas. One party—she did hot dogs, she did have hot dogs, but, you know, I don't know, I guess for me and friends of my oldest of kids, we had a buffet of food. We had chips, all kind of cookies, all kinds of candy, and all kinds of—it was different from when we had his party last year, and I was like, "I don't know, 'cause I'm inviting people from school—what can I do?" So, but, yeah. I think the Hometown environment compared to the way I grew up and parties lasting for hours and, you know, you be at a kid's party and you take home hot wings and here comes, you know, burgers and here comes—and the kids are eating literally the whole time they're at the party, so. And that wasn't the case at neither one of the parties we went to, they had a set time to eat, you know, time for kids to play, and, so. Yeah, so, it was a shock, especially last year, 'cause the first party we went to they had only cheese pizza and juice boxes. No Kool-Aid, fruit punch, no Sprite [laughs]. It was, like, juice boxes and miniature cupcakes, and I was like, "Oh, okay, this is different for me." No hot wings [laughs].

While Rita seemed to be making active efforts to conform to the standards she viewed as normative at Hometown, Carmen, an African American student teacher and married mother of two, observed differences between her own practices and those of Hometown parents as well—yet she took a more tongue-in-cheek, wry approach that foregrounded race as an explanation for lifestyle differences.

Carmen had gone back to school to become a teacher after having children. She spoke about her own family as one that rushed around between work and children's activities, eating out often at McDonald's and elsewhere. She found some families at Hometown, though not all, to be more health-conscious than that.

> C: They usually bring, they pack snacks that's—well not all of them, of course, but some of them pack healthy snacks like carrots and I call them "kibbles and bits." Twigs and, you know, mixed up trail mix, that kind of stuff. That's the kind of stuff they bring and to me,

that's much more health conscious than the potato chips and sodas and stuff. What's interesting is—not across the board but generally speaking—Caucasian children bring healthier snacks and African American children bring the junk food.

JP: Do you notice that here?

C: Mmmhmm.

JP: In the lunchroom?

C: Mmmhmm, yeah, even the snacks that they eat in class, yeah. . . .

JP: So what are some what would be kind of some of the things that you would notice like when you mentioned carrot sticks, what would be something the African American kids are bringing?

C: Chips. Like the Caucasians would bring in fresh fruit. The Black kids are bringing fruit snacks in the, you know, the little gummy snacks, and um . . . potato chips, soda, and uh . . . what else are they bringing. Oh you know, sweet stuff that you really shouldn't be bringing in and pretending that it's acceptable, so in the class [the lead teacher] teaches eating healthy snacks and I have to tell some kids "no, put that away because that is not a healthy snack." It's not even cheese, it's Cheetos . . . [and] fresh fruit versus the packaged fruit, you know what I mean? You know the little plastic thing that opens the fruit.

JP: The little, like, cup with the can.

C: The fruit can.

JP: But it's in a plastic.

C: Yeah.

JP: What do you think explains those differences? I mean . . . why do you think those differences are that way?

C: I would say habit more than anything else. I don't think it's resources. In some communities it might be resources, but I don't get the impression at this school—I don't think the white kids are richer than the Black kids.

Since I had observed that some Hometowners were concerned to avoid particular food substances such as sugar, high-fructose corn syrup, fats, and pesticides, I asked Carmen whether she had any special concerns like that or opinions about them.

C: I think those are all wonderful concerns to have and if you can figure
out a way to work them into your lifestyle, that's great, but I don't
know very many people who can work them into their lifestyle. . . .
It's lots of [making a gesture rubbing the back of her hand, then the
inside of her hand, with the fingers of the other hand].

JP: Money?

C: No, a lot of white people who can probably to figure it out, but I don't
know any Black people who do all that.

JP: Mmmhmm. . . . Why do you think . . . it's not about—

C: Income. A lot of it goes back to income, yes, because if you don't
work . . . you know, and if you're a stay-at-home mom or you work
part-time and volunteer . . . then you have more time and you have
the money to buy organic and so it does come down . . . I think it
eventually does go back to economics.

For Carmen, race stood out as the distinguishing factor. While she granted that indeed income played a role, her first impulse was to point to "lifestyle" and "habits" that varied by race.

Though she highlighted race, Carmen's sense of entrenched lifestyles spoke to Pierre Bourdieu's (1984) famous analysis of class and consumption, which illustrated through a French case study that while consumer purchases are indeed constrained or enabled by income, *tastes* are shaped by economic and educational capital in enduring, persistent ways, such that short-term changes in income are less predictive of individuals' practices than their longer-term legacies of upbringing and embodied habitus. Carmen framed this in terms of people's ability or inability to work healthy eating into their lifestyles. While she seemed to grant that "kibbles and bits" were healthier than McDonald's and chips, "I don't know any Black people who do all that." The narratives of some of my other African American interviewees suggested otherwise; it is possible that their careful attention to nutrition placed them in the minority among African American families at Hometown, but it is also possible that Carmen misperceived some of the very real divergences of income and class background that were present in the school, divergences that overlapped with categories of racial identification but not uniformly. Either way, it is instructive to know that at least some members of the Hometown community saw food differences as highly determined by race, even if my own interviews suggested that intertwined experiences of class, race, and social environment (recall Rita's story of her learning curve at Hometown) were at play in shaping food habitus.

Putting a finer point on her own inability or choice not to opt in to what she seemed to recognize as "healthier," Carmen told me about someone she had encountered who was a vegan and was incentivizing his son to finish his math homework by offering him a snack—specifically a bread stick—as a reward. Carmen thought this was comical; didn't the child know it was *just* a bread stick (and not some truly decadent treat)? "Clearly I didn't turn out to be that kind of parent," Carmen deadpanned, but "long as there's tomorrow, there's hope."

Meanwhile, as we have seen, white mothers with whom I spoke at Hometown frequently attempted to express solidarity through sympathy for the financial constraints they understood some parents in the community to encounter. They generally spoke less than Carmen did about race or even about class as persistent lifestyle (à la Bourdieu), but as we shall see, in addition to recognizing income diversity they sometimes employed moralizing discourses about parental disengagement to explain poor food choices.

"Engagement" as Moral Discourse and Material Investment

A married Mexican American university professor had an unpleasant surprise when she saw what some students at Hometown brought in their packed lunches. She allowed that she had eaten "really bad" growing up (for her this meant lots of sugar cereal, white bread, and processed foods), but she said that her own household now didn't "skimp out on food." After visiting her son at school at lunchtime, she compared his lunch to others'. "He always drinks water in his little water bottle. And I see what the other kids are eating: Capri Sun [a juice beverage], Rice Krispie treats, a Lunchable [a preboxed lunch product]. And most kids have difficult problems, which is like, 'What's up with that?' I mean, you would think that these parents who love their children would understand that that probably isn't the best thing for kids in the middle of the day, every day. But we're sold it, I mean it's sold to us, and it's convenient." Rice Krispie treats were among the items she categorized as easy and available but harmful—perhaps even responsible for kids' "difficult problems." Also worthy of note is how she emphasized that these foods were chosen because "it's sold to us and it's convenient"; she cast the choice as at least partly a matter of not enough attention or effort. Likewise, Irene, a married, Caucasian professional in the field of communications technology, remarked that when someone brought in something "weird" for class-wide snacks such as Oreo cookies, "I think a lot of the time, it's just ease and how people eat at home. I think they just don't think of nutrition. They think about people-pleasing. This is easy. They'll eat this. It's less work, less thought." Another parent explained that she believed many parents gave their children processed foods out of habit or a lack of awareness. "The snacks, the stuff, the crap . . . what's just available."

It is clear enough that, according to the broadest nutritional wisdom of our day, packaged convenience foods are indeed more convenient than home-prepped, from-scratch, previously unprocessed foods and generally considered to be poorer in nutritional content. Stepping away from the givenness of that, though, we can note how these parents discussed sugary and packaged foods as ones that were "less work, less thought," what's "sold to us," or "just available," as though these qualities were in themselves primary to the foods' undesirability. What was good for one's child would *not* be readily available or easy, they assumed; it would take intention, knowledge, and extra work.

One school administrator noted that lack of effort was a problem among some Hometown parents, and she consciously set this apart from issues of race or class. I had asked Tina whether she thought there was a broad range of what children were eating at the school, and whether that was changing as its economic diversity declined.

I think a lot of our kids, especially as they get older, like in the eighth grade or so, parents are kind of checking out on them and what they bring to lunch . . . is not even remotely close to what they should be eating. You know, dads who drop off a sack and it's like, "Oh I have to get this to her." Okay, well what's in it? And it's something he picked up at the convenience store on the way here as a snack, not as a lunch . . . because that's what the daughter wanted and you know, she lives with mom, but mom—you know, there's a whole [range] of different scenarios, but it really seems like that late seventh grade and eighth grade year—and maybe it's just the population that we've had so far and maybe it will change for next year's eighth grade—but parents that I would normally think, "Oh you would pack a good lunch for your kid"—you know, it's not about race or economics. [They are] totally checking out.

Tina chalked up (what she viewed as) poor choices to a matter of many parents' inadequate attention. Those parents simply were not tuned in (or perhaps they were tuned in to the wrong things), and Tina framed this problem as separate from household finances and any identity groupings (though she mentioned the fallout of divorce as a contributing factor)—even as she seemed to suggest that certain characteristics such as income and race may have informed her expectations about food conscientiousness more generally (since there were "parents that I would normally think, 'Oh you would pack a good lunch for your kid'"). I did not monitor what individual students brought for lunch, so I cannot judge whether Tina's assessment was more or less empirically meaningful than Carmen's, which linked differences more closely to logistical aspects of "lifestyle" and to cultural differences attributed to race. What is certain is that the notion of "checking out" held its own moral weight. Failure to provide reasonably healthy food was framed in this case not as a result of resources, of efforts to promote child independence, or even of taste, but simply as a parental lack of effort and care. Even so, as we have seen, Tina herself strove not to be a "Nazi" in her enactment and enforcement of food restrictions.

On a more general level, Hometown parents commented frequently about how close involvement of parents in the life of the school was key to its success and appeal. Their sense of small-town life and sociability aligned with the trope of *engagement*. Engagement was an explicit goal of the school; parents were expected to fulfill service hours each year, and as one administrator put it in a newsletter, "We strive to engage families and community members in our school by having open lines of communication and eliciting feedback and input into school-wide decisions. We want and expect families to take an active role in their child's education by being involved in the classroom, attending school-wide events, and maintaining communication with the teachers. Our children benefit greatly when their parents are involved and interested in the goings-on at school." Likewise, my interviewees touted "engagement" or "involvement" by parents as the central strength of the school. When Sara said that she loved the community of the school, I asked her how she would describe it. "Very active. Mm, very connected, very active. Uh, people go and commit to the school with, um, offerings such a variety of their own personal talents and bring in and contribute so much. I mean, the parents have really shaped so much of the school. The involvement is—is amazing. It's really commendable." When I asked Amanda how she would describe the community, she immediately offered, "Well, I would say heavy parent engagement. That's the big piece there." She went on to explain how her child, who had gone through recent changes in his household, had gradually become more comfortable showing affection to her and her partner through having observed other children doing it with their parents at Hometown. Though her family lived in a somewhat more distant neighborhood, she had found other Hometown parents to be generous with offers to keep her son after school or take him to baseball practice when she could not do so herself. She believed that "high parent engagement is a big piece" and that "it's a very mindful community. I think people try to be aware of each other's needs . . . try to build consensus."

Notably, the issue of engagement also came up when Hometown adults spoke about why other school options were less appealing. When married working mother Faye explained that her family would have chosen private school over the local public school if they had not gotten into Hometown, I asked her why.

I've just heard a lot from parents. We have parents here that had children there, you know . . . and it's not that it's a bad environment. There is a gifted program that I hear is really good, but they said that when they go from that to this kind of environment, and you look at the difference in parent participation, it is staggering because they were active in the school community. There you feel like a minority, if you are active. Here it is just a given, you get to know all the parents very well through the volunteer and different activities. I'm just a believer that that makes all the difference in your child's education. Not just me participating, but all of the parents taking part. Everybody has a different level that they can participate . . . but just having that interaction and involvement just makes the whole school community better.

Similarly, when I asked white, married stay-at-home father Pete about why his family had chosen Hometown, he commented positively on its constructivist approach but said,

> Really in my belief . . . if the teachers are engaged, the parents are engaged, the school's really good . . . I almost really sort of believe that any system works. I do think like schools are a bit more open like that. Just because I'm an artist and my peg fits into those little squares a little bit better but I'm not that much sold that one system's better than another. But what I am sold on is that lack of parent involvement—you know and that seems to be the big thing at Englewood. I thought those teachers were great but I thought the parents were really bad, you know . . . and I think that has some results. I don't want to be focusing on behavior with my kids, you know, I just don't.

For Pete, parental involvement—or lack thereof—was a better predictor of a school's success than its educational approach, and he implied that low parental involvement translated to behavioral problems in schools.

Meanwhile white married mother Robin, whose child was at Englewood as they waited to get into the Hometown lottery, commented that there was a core group of active parents there that did not reflect the racial demographics of the school (which was predominantly African American, the implication being that most active volunteers were white). She wondered whether holding PTA meetings at different times would help, so that parents who worked at night could also attend. She was not sure what would make a difference, but she did feel that parent involvement should not be on the backs of just a few. (Presumably, Englewood parents were less likely to attend not only evening meetings but also school-day events. I spent a few lunchtimes at Englewood to observe how its routines differed from Hometowns', and one of these was on a weekday marked on the school's menu calendar as "Family Day." To my surprise, no parents actually attended during the hours I was present. Perhaps the event was poorly advertised, but I struggled to imagine the same complete lack of turnout transpiring at Hometown. I asked Englewood cafeteria staff about this, and they agreed that while this was supposed to be Family Day they had seen no parents—though they recalled better attendance at the previous year's event and said that an appreciable number of parents had come for the school's Thanksgiving lunch, complete with turkey and dressing, that autumn.)

Noelle, a married African American mother who worked from home and was highly involved at Hometown, pointed to differences she perceived in family structure and parenting styles that seemed linked to "engagement." The Atlanta charter school one of her children attended (which was a majority African American school) did not feature as much parental involvement, she said, observing that this meant less backup for the school's lessons of "community and respect." "This community [Hometown] seems to be more family-based, of a complete family of mother, father and at [the other school] it seems to be a lot more independent. The child is focused on the education alone." At Hometown, maintaining social ties with other parents and families outside of school hours meant that "everything crosses over here." For Noelle, attentive parenting by two spouses and deep community involvement went hand in hand to support the learning of Hometown students.

The notion that parent engagement organically and independently yields benefits, and that a willingness to engage at least theoretically transcends class and race, is not specific to this community but holds sway as a normative discourse in education and public health fields. For example, the CDC's Healthy Schools program promotes parent engagement as a significant contributor to healthy school environments: "*Parent engagement in schools* is defined as parents and school staff working together to support and improve the learning, development, and health of children and adolescents. [It] is a shared responsibility in which schools and other community agencies and organizations are committed to reaching out to engage parents in meaningful ways, and parents are committed to actively supporting their children's and adolescents' learning and development."[1] The program also favors a "Whole School, Whole Community, Whole Child" approach that "emphasizes a school-wide approach rather than one that is subject- or location-specific, and it acknowledges the position of learning, health, and the school as all being a part, and reflection, of the local community."[2]

"Engagement" is not only framed as a key way that parents can de-termine outcomes but also used as a descriptor of what student suc-cess itself looks like. Student engagement can be "behavioral, emotional and cognitive," and the concept "has attracted increasing attention as representing a possible antidote to declining academic motivation and achievement" (Fredricks, Blumenfeld, and Paris 2004). "Student engage-ment research, policy, and practice are even more important in today's race-to-the top policy environment. With a priority goal of postsecond-ary completion with advanced competence, today's students must be en-gaged longer and more deeply" (Lawson and Lawson 2013). The broad acceptance and buzz-wordiness of this concept seemed confirmed when I was approached at one of Hometown's weekend fund-raising events by a candidate for local government who explained to me that her platform was, simply, "engagement."

The term often seems rather open. While it includes concrete acts such as parental volunteer hours on campus, on the whole it carries an affective weight: an engaged parent or student is attentive, involved, perhaps animated, and certainly emotionally invested in the activity at hand. Engagement is a kind of measure of positivity and can perhaps be thought of as the opposite of alienation and of being "checked out." It seems to be framed as a choice and a matter of good intention that has been carried through—as opposed to being, say, a side effect of struc-tural inequalities, logistical burdens (or lack thereof), or discomfiting social differences. "Engagement" is part and parcel of what Sharon Hays (1996) has called "intensive parenting": the increasing promotion and practice of parenting as requiring intensive resources of time, money, and emotion. It also speaks to what has been called "parental determin-ism," the reigning ideology that holds parents personally responsible, through countless mundane choices and interventions, for the ultimate physical and psychological well-being of their children, often cast as in-nately threatened (Lee 2014).

If we think of engagement as an aspect of intensive parenting, and if we recognize, with feminist theorist Kathi Weeks (2007, 239), that the lines between productive and reproductive labor (and between material and affective labor) are increasingly difficult to draw in a post-Fordist economy, we might well trouble the notion of "engagement" to consider how it functions not (only) as a manifestation of parental care but (also) as a morally valorized form of unremunerated labor in a neoliberal context, a form of personal responsibilization. In Hometown's community, practices such as urban homesteading and taking advantage of a walkable neighborhood are aesthetically valued and carry emotional weight. They evoke small-town closeness even as they are linked with progressive urbanity; they signal an attractive kind of simplicity even as they depend on resources such as free time and home ownership. They feel more like safety and protection than conspicuous consumption, though they can function as both. Likewise, parents who are not "checked out" but are "engaged" take care not to allow their children to bring junky, industrial food to school in their lunches (or worse, for the whole class to consume at snack time). The work involved in sending emails to teachers, coming in to support healthy food projects, or packing a child's lunch oneself is considered to be part of good parenting, but we can also interrogate it as a way that value was added to—and protection garnered from—the corporate and institutional entities parents did not entirely trust. In this sense, adults' efforts to create physically and emotionally healthy children, in tandem or in conflict with institutions such as public schools, constituted a kind of *conspicuous production.*

With this concept, I play off Thorstein Veblen's (1899/1994) classic notion of conspicuous *consumption,* which highlighted how consumer display—including the exhibition of leisure time through one's ability to engage in various unremunerated activities—marked social status in the turn-of-the-twentieth-century United States. Hometown adults took on roles in food production and public education that arguably are "conspicuous" à la Veblen, in the sense that they index class cultures (Bourdieu 1984; de Kramer 2016) and, to some Americans, may seem "extra" or gratuitously attentive and time-consuming. They produced alternatives to what was, from another perspective, already provided by mass consumer markets and by public institutions such as schools. Foods construed as overly industrial, cheap, and low quality unsettled these parents; likewise, activities such as gardening, cooking, and school volunteering were means many of them employed to produce value, sustenance, and substance for their children, families, and neighborhoods. These efforts should be seen as acts of production rather than simply of consumption, and we need to trouble any easy distinctions between household/reproductive and public/productive labor, inasmuch as parents were intervening to fend off the foods offered to their children by public institutions and made accessible by major corporations.

Indeed, conspicuous production co-performed and reworked the work of schools and commodity markets. Intervention to protect children from the dangers of an industrial economy and from the possible laziness, ignorance, or negligence of other social players and institutions was morally meaningful in itself, in ways not entirely accounted for by adults' concrete knowledge of nutrition. These sensibilities undoubtedly indexed socioeconomic status and reflected class cultures, but explicit talk of status or prestige often remained submerged. Conspicuous production was not so conspicuous, then, to those who performed it; rather, the language of whole foods and wholesomeness coexisted carefully with that of progressivism and social inclusivity.

One woman highlighted in a unique way how her food concerns fit into a broader ecology of labor and care. "You know when you read *Farmer Boy*," said Caucasian/white married mother Pam, who had been reading Laura Ingalls Wilder's American frontier novel with her children,

> half of that book is about the food. And—but you realize—it's because he's working all the time. And his mom is making monstrous meals to get the calories into these people that they needed to go out and do the next thing, you know? I mean, this is half that book, it's true, and it really struck me, though, that it was very much more "I'm doing this because you need this to go out and do your work," you know, whereas . . . I feel much more like when I'm making a meal it's more about . . . like I'm putting my art into it, you know . . . like when I lay a meal out on the table I've laid out kind of a, kind of part of my heart or soul, who I am, and it's much more bound up in that for everybody, I think, you know.

Pam's commentary seemed to place her own approach to feeding the family firmly apart from nutritional utility, foregrounding that her involvement in child feeding was more actively a matter of aesthetic expression, affect, and identity than of calculations of caloric need or reproduction of a labor force. She went on, though, to reflect upon it as a form of (possibly gratuitous) mental labor:

In some ways I think it's great. . . . In other ways I think that we put too much emphasis on it and it brings out a lot of stress around food and it brings out a lot of worry and it takes some of the joy of just sitting down and eating, you know. . . . And it's just kind of a waste sometimes . . . and then there's just uh . . . you don't have to enjoy every meal just eat it so you can go to the next thing, you know what I mean? There's a lot of pressure sometimes, so . . . like sometimes I wonder about all of that . . . you know sometimes I think that . . . maybe all of this is just a substitute for, you know, I just need my brain to wrap around something, you know, since I'm not doing law or in school or whatever, that sometimes this is the way . . . I . . . I cope with that kind of missing stimulation and intellectual kind of satisfaction or whatever you get. So sometimes I wonder about that in me . . . and other people.

Pam's narrative is included here not to suggest that concerns about children's food *really* represent just the floating anxieties of parents with too little mental stimulation and too much time on their hands, but to emphasize that one must *have* available time and energy to pursue "engaged" parenting and feeding, or perhaps even to see it as necessary and a good idea. Pam recognized that in her world, simply getting sustaining calories onto the table for the children was not an urgent problem. Still, food management could feel urgent in different ways, for different reasons, for her and others like her.

Ultimately, it was a mix of relative privilege (in the forms of available income, free time, and mental energy) and experiences of fear and vulnerability (including in the face of food risk) that drove "engagement." Conspicuous production built upon parents' existing cultural and economic capital and worked in turn to sustain a sense of (not entirely inclusive) "community." Yet it did not necessarily feel luxurious or optional to those who practiced it.

Conclusion

The rise of intensive motherhood has been described as a reaction to the encroachment of commoditization throughout all spheres of American life; to Hays (1996), it indicated a deep cultural ambivalence about competitive self-interest as the focus of capitalist society (see also Hoch-schild 2003; Brown 2014; Katz 2008). In this framing, time-consuming parenting practices are part of a sacralization of family life through which Americans reassure themselves that the market does not rule all. This is another valuable way to understand what we have heard from adults at Hometown: food ideologies ran against the industrial and the commodified, against what was readily provided, ready-made, or appealing to children, in favor of foods that took more work to research, to prepare, and to get children to eat—that is, which required more parental intervention and investment. The effort required was perhaps not an unavoidable evil so much as an integral element in a practice of concerted redemption.

Though some might be tempted to discount parents' attempts at non-judgment and self-deprecation as mere veils for class snobbery or racism in conversations about, for example, the horrors of Froot Loops and Rice Krispie treats, the time and affective energy they devoted to balancing all of these stances was indicative of something more distinct and fraught: perhaps something like what media and food theorist Heidi Zimmer-man (2015, 41, 43) has described, apropos of Michael Pollan's hugely popular work on food politics, as a realm where the "liberal professional middle class soul" is defined through the attempt to "carve out ethical possibility within conditions of relative privilege." Pollan's work (e.g., Pollan 2008) on food justice encourages people to think about how they can change an unjust food system, but it focuses primarily on individual expenditures of "time, labor and thought in the details of their everyday eating practices" and can be seen as "an outcome of a deeply classed struggle for ethics in neoliberal times" (Zimmerman 2015, 44, 46, 47).

At Hometown, we see ethical possibilities played out not only through choices about local food or humanely produced animal products, but also and importantly through the explicit valuing of racial and economic diversity within the community. Members argued from various perspec-tives and to various degrees about the ethics and even utility (from an educational point of view) of making sure that the people and practices that surrounded them and their children were not too affluent, too uni-formly white, too suburban, too "vanilla." They tended to view this kind of inclusion as good for the neighborhood, for their families and others' families, and perhaps, as Zimmerman would put it, for their own "middle-class souls." Anthropologist Angelina Castagna (2014, 4) has argued that in American schools "diversity" is championed primarily through a culture of "niceness" that focuses on inclusion, optimism, and assimilation but makes little real headway toward addressing sources of inequity or challenging the privileges of whiteness. This is an important insight, but it is crucial also to recognize the (potentially transformative) significance of actors' ethical stances *and* to examine closely how they are internally contradictory and conflictual.

The ethics of inclusion at Hometown was connected closely with an ethics of engagement: the idea that parents should spend considerable time not only caring for their children at home but also reaching into the school setting itself to support the school's mission through contributions of volunteer time and sometimes money. (At Hometown's fund-raising auction event, parents paid up to three thousand dollars for children's artwork, prompting a teacher to joke that she should receive a commission for having guided her class through the project and another to marvel that the amount exceeded her monthly salary and her current bank balance.) For some parents, this also meant monitoring what was happening at the school around issues such as cafeteria lunches or after-school activities and contributing their positive or negative feedback, volunteer assistance, and so on. Intensive parenting happened not only at home but at school. It was part of the glue that held together a community that felt "small-town" and "magical."

And yet, as anthropologist Neri de Kramer (2016) observed in a somewhat similar Pennsylvania community, health-conscious feeding strategies and seemingly humble "do-it-yourself" techniques depend upon time-intensive research, shopping, and cooking techniques that reflect and in turn cultivate distinct forms of cultural capital (see also Bourdieu 1984). Likewise, some of the intensive volunteering activities that helped to sustain Hometown were made possible by the fact that households had a stay-at-home parent (usually with a second parent working outside the home to support the family) or enjoyed part-time, flexible, or self-structured professional schedules. The labor involved fell disproportionately to women, though perhaps as compared with many American settings it was less exclusively on the shoulders of mothers at Hometown (see DeVault 1991; Cook 2009b; see also Rosen and Twamley 2018).

While Hometown adults often recognized that not all households in their greater communities enjoyed the same resources, many nonetheless held "engagement" and "community" as key, almost transcendent and indisputable values. Schools with less parental engagement were less successful, it was assumed. This may be true, by certain measures, but this framing could also be a way of talking about the communities of which one would *not* want to be part, while remaining seemingly neutral or silent on issues of class or race. While being highly aware of issues of racial and economic diversity and justice on one level, some adults also imagined other adults as "just checked out" or doing what was "just easy and available," as though a deficit of care and commitment primarily explained their perceived shortcomings. In this way, intentions toward inclusion and understanding could be undermined by the tendency to foreground individual motivations over structural factors. In short, while those same intentions should be not be dismissed as superficial covers for classism or racism, we must also consider how individualized, moralized consumer strategies for the protection of children end up reinforcing dynamics of inequality in unintended ways.

In one of his blogs, Scott acknowledged that Hometown's rezoning issue would be contentious since the admission waiting list was already long and changes might mean even more competition. "And talking about race and class can no doubt be messy and complicated. But the alternative—of keeping with the status quo and avoiding this work—does a disservice to our students now and in their futures." Ultimately, Hometown's board voted to strike a balance by placing the two immediate neighborhoods in the priority zone, along with a third, gentrifying neighborhood that was walkable to the school. This plan expanded the priority pool for the elementary grades while narrowing it somewhat for the middle campus. More important to us here, though, is Scott's recognition that talking about class and race was both messy and crucial. Hometowners were situated within this complexity and commitment, where various kinds of social diversity could be sincerely, persistently sought even as the anxiety of protecting one's own child from perceived dangers was in ongoing, implicit or explicit tension with those same values.

Conclusion

Rethinking the Politics of Care and Consumption

At Hometown, middle-class parents worked to provide high-quality nutrition for their children while remaining moderate rather than "crazy." Their concerns arose in a context of industrialized food production where neither the ingredients and processing methods used to create food commodities nor their short- and long-term health effects were transparent or fully known. But these practices were also bound up with specific ways of thinking about the self and about well-being. Autonomy and self-determination were implicit ideals, and individuals were felt to be responsible in large measure for their own physical and emotional health, especially through the power of consumer choice. In parenting, the need to monitor children's consumption and to guide them actively toward practices of self-regulation (of which, as children, they were assumed to be not yet capable) came into tension with the idea that a healthy, socially appealing person effortlessly controlled herself but should not come across as overly controlling of others, even of children.

For all these reasons adults at Hometown, and doubtless in many similar communities across the United States, have directed a great deal of mental and emotional labor toward decisions about their children's eating, with some of that labor being spent in attempting to accomplish desirable kinds of moderation, effortlessness, and open-mindedness. But as we saw in the last chapter, parents' active intentions toward inclusion and cross-class understanding were sometimes at cross-purposes with other moral discourses through which they attributed others' differing priorities and possibilities to lack of attention or lack of care.

Concerns about lack of care—or to put it otherwise, the notion that to do parenting and children's food right, one must primarily *care enough*— are connected tightly with the "rhetoric of individual choice that permeates every aspect of U.S. culture. Raising children is largely defined as a private arrangement that parents choose and thus are fully responsible for managing. This rhetoric of choice obscures larger social forces while instilling the idea that individuals have autonomy and freedom . . . [leaving room for] very little analysis about how such choices are constrained by larger external factors such as social class, neoliberal economic pressures that emphasize the individual responsibility and privatization, and the persistent wage gap between men and women" (Huisman and Joy 2014, 100). Hometowners featured in this book found it unremarkable and uncontentious to claim that it was parental involvement, or the lack thereof, that could make or break how well a school was educating (and feeding) its charges, and I daresay the same would be true for many Americans. Yet this claim places the onus for producing desirable outcomes on the (individual and collected) efforts of adults qua parents, as opposed to all people as civic actors or to public institutions. Parents' choices, the problems they perceive, and the resources they bring to bear are embedded within larger structures of inequality that are sometimes acknowledged but appear less salient when individualized motivations are foregrounded. This reinforces a neoliberal situation in which responsibility for well-being and advancement rests on individual actors and how much they "care."

This view of reality should be highlighted, contextualized, and indeed challenged; for differential resources as well as the longer term effects of class habitus make parental "engagement" with food, education, and child-rearing matters of much more than individual commitment. To draw attention to this is to repeat a rather familiar critique of neoliberalism: deregulation and the retrenchment of social welfare programs mean that more than ever, individuals across the socioeconomic spectrum are charged with the protection of their own and their family members' physical well-being and security in a privatized economy. They bring highly variable economic and social resources to this task, and "a geography of poverty and inequality . . . reflects who has access to care and who undertakes that care-work," and for whom (Milligan and Wiles 2010). Meanwhile, expectations of personal responsibilization moralize those efforts and outcomes, such that failure to offer (what someone deems) adequate care can seem to be a matter of simply not making "good choices" or paying enough attention, as though the desire to do so is all it really takes.

But let us go further than this and consider my observation that Hometown parents were cautious not to appear as though they cared *too* much. They worried about being helicopter parents, appearing "crazy" about food, or being too controlling of their children or judgmental of others. What are the implications of the fact that parents who have the resources to do so take on this work, yet also feel that it is important not to appear to care overly much about it, nor to restrict excessively the autonomy of their children as emerging consumers and pleasure seekers? These fears reveal a view of consumer desire as both essential and dangerous. As we have seen, they also reflect a model of selfhood that is preoccupied with preserving the autonomy and separateness of individuals: a model that aligns well with the conditions of neoliberalism, but which is also part of a deeper history of modern life and post-Enlightenment individualism, on one hand, and situated as a locally specific, urban style of middle classness on the other (Kondo 1990; Giddens 1991; Mauss 1938/1985; Obadia 2018). There are inherent tensions here between simultaneous imperatives to respect each individual's consumer sovereignty *and* to take active responsibility for the well-being of one's family as part of a gendered politics of care.

But beyond all that, this middle-class emotional style acts to depoliticize and to obscure parents' protective labor as such. It demands that adults exercise persistent attention, knowledge, and conscientiousness; but it simultaneously prizes flexibility, nonjudgment, and apparent ease. It questions and condemns what is readily coded as neurotic behavior. The protective labor of parents like those at Hometown circulates as less justified and less visible than it might otherwise, as people imagine that their attainment of the proper kinds of control over themselves, their children, and the products of the industrial marketplace can, and should ideally be, rather effortless. The significant weight of that labor of care and caution thus can be felt by those who enact it (who are disproportionately, but not exclusively, women) not as structural burdens or systemic failings but often, again, as matters of personal failure or excess—whether one's own or one's neighbor's.

An anthropological perspective reminds us that these questions of responsibility and care can be imagined differently. In just one revealing comparison, Yuson Jung (2016) juxtaposed food discontents and activism in postindustrial Detroit with those in postsocialist Bulgaria:

Postsocialist citizens would ask: Who can I hold accountable for the additives, chemicals and other artificial or hazardous stuff in the food I purchased? How do I trust that what I buy is safe for my body and my health? To them, individual responsibility at the point of purchase is not a complete answer because they do not believe structural problems can be fixed only through individual consumption practices. From this postsocialist perspective, it appears deeply problematic that many proponents of ethical foods in advanced capitalist societies privilege individual consumption as the productive point for alternative food practices to overcome structural problems. (301)

Echoing Jung, cultural studies scholar Eliot Borenstein (2019) explains that while post-Soviet Russia has experienced economic transformations that look very "neoliberal,"

neoliberalism as an ideology has been nowhere near as hegemonically successful in Russia as in some Western countries. In the United States, neoliberalism has become so naturalized that it is practically the air we breathe; the ethics of "personal responsibility" distract from what would otherwise obviously be systemic injustices. This is not the case in Russia, where the total transformation of the economy was never accompanied by widespread ideological buy-in. Witness the protests when the government tried to monetize social benefits (setting set amounts in rubles rather than indexing them), or, more recently, the pension reforms. Russian citizens still believe that the state should *provide*. Meanwhile, the super-rich in Russia are not beloved or admired, but assumed to be criminal as a matter of course.

This is not to say that postsocialist European and U.S. capitalist worldviews are entirely opposed to one another, nor that either is essentially unchanging. For example, when I conducted fieldwork in Russia in 2003 (a stint of follow-up research complementing and updating my work in 1998–1999), I noted that Saint Petersburg teachers seemed to be railing less against the immorality and irresponsibility of the new Russian capitalism than they had been just a few years previously (Patico 2008; see also Patico 2016). I interpreted this as a sign not only that their labor and commodity environments had become slightly less stressful during that particular interim, but also that income disparity had become more normalized and that the idea of advancing through individual effort had become somewhat more idealized and naturalized. Forms of predictable security once provided by the Soviet state, such as universal employment and a reasonable living wage, now were rued less acutely, already somewhat less assumed. Shifted, less equitable relationships among markets, households, and the state had begun to be more imaginable and slightly more morally defensible.

The Soviet socialist state is not itself a plausible or instructive alternative to U.S. neoliberalism. Still, postsocialist Russian and Bulgarian citizens offer a usefully disruptive point of view, one where (despite certain forms of economic development in a "neoliberal" direction) the beliefs about selfhood that underlie Hometowners' experiences hold far less sway. This can help us gain purchase on the cultural air Hometowners (and perhaps many readers of this book) breathe and to entertain how things might be otherwise. Not only can we think differently about who should be held responsible for food safety, but we can also interrogate ideas about parental engagement and community politics through less individualizing lenses. Who is held responsible for perceived successes and failures in school and neighborhood communities, and who is held at blame? Who is in control, or felt to be in control? People may distrust public institutions (though Hometowners typically were proud of their school), but what paths may be closed off when they assume that individual fixes that attempt to offset industrial evils or state vacuums are the primary available solutions?

Moreover, where does the assumption of parental responsibility leave parents like those at Hometown, many of whom, it seemed to me, explicitly wished to welcome and support parents who enjoyed fewer resources of available time, money, and energy? While on the face of it, engagement and inclusion seemed to be two sides of one coin— interdependent aspects of an intentional effort at community building—we have seen how "engagement" can actually be in tension or even conflict with "inclusion" because it depends upon time availability and priorities not equally shared by all households, and particularly scarce for some families with whom concerned parents and administrators truly want to collaborate. However, it is not helpful or accurate to discount Hometowners' interest in such inclusion as somehow meaningless or hypocritical. Rather, the coexistence of those desires together with their more classically "neoliberal," self-responsibilized commitments to their own families' health shows the messiness and complexity of how they live with and against their political economy's anxiety-provoking, socially atomizing effects. For academics interested in theorizing neo-liberalism and middle classness, awareness of such tensions is a useful reminder not to indulge overly monolithic visions of what neoliberal or middle-class styles of selfhood are and entail.

But to push this conversation from the walls of academia into realms of more immediate experience, I ask, how might all this go differently if we did not believe or accept that the responsibility for protecting children in all these ways lay so heavily on us as individuals, rather than upon us in some more collective way? I turn now to "we" not because I count myself as part of the Hometown world, though I do identify with many of its sensibilities and this inevitably shapes my analysis, but more importantly because I believe these questions will resonate for many Americans. In fact, they may speak in certain ways to middle-class people around the world, and thus to many of my readers. How much labor do they/we spend in the tension between individual responsibility and the imperative to appear low-key and moderate, to exercise great care while disavowing excessive worry? If the kind of anxiety around children's food described in this book is not personal pathology but a situated form of conspicuous labor, what/whom/how does that labor serve? Where else could that labor be placed, and how else might it be directed in support of our values and hopes, not only for our individual children and their bodies, but for the social worlds we wish for them to inherit? And how might those worlds be variously imagined by those already unable or uninterested in pursuing the kind of conspicuous production this ethnography has described—people who may have far more imme-diately pressing concerns for their own safety and well-being?

A few scholars have suggested some broad metaphors for the work of such reconceptualization. For example, environmental sociologist E. Melanie DuPuis (2015, 156–157) argues that while "modern ideas of self, body, and society have been built around powerful material and conceptual boundaries and dichotomies," "purity politics"—approaches that prioritize monitoring the boundaries of the individual body to keep what is inside pure—have failed and will not provide us with new, more sustainable solutions for safer eating. Instead, she proposes that a metaphor of fermentation guide our thinking about food politics, for fermentation implies a productive mixing of elements: not a banishment of what is foreign or impure nor "a romantic embrace of the outside as salvation," but rather "a collaborative engagement" (157). In the "imperfect politics" of food she envisions, "people can accept a world in which trade-offs and risks are unavoidable, and then go about making the necessary but messy bargains about how they will share those risks. . . . Maybe this new way of looking at the body will allow a certain abandonment of the treadmill of control and purification, of the maintenance of 'bodily essence': relief from the idea of an intact self. But it will require good processes, new kinds of inclusive and just governance that we must build to create a better future" (158, 160) Similarly, sociologist Alexis Shotwell (2016, 5–7, 113) points out that when food ethics are treated as individual problems, only those who can afford to eat "ethically" can qualify as ethical. Because we are always already complicit in broader webs of suffering and embedded within environments that will never be pure, Shotwell argues, we need to move beyond notions of individual boundedness and toward understandings that foreground how we as individuals are co-constituted with our social others and with our environment.

What could this look like in communities like Hometown? Would it involve renewing a commitment to "honoring the cheese puffs"—to taking the overall well-being, measured in a diversity of ways, of a broad, cross-class community as more valuable than the immediate but elusive protection of one's own child's body through consumer choice? Would, for example, middle- and upper-middle-class families eating more cheese puffs or sugar cereal in the name of flexibly and commensally sharing risks in a broader community make any kind of sense, or any meaningful difference? Would it involve some other kind of grassroots redistribution of the safest, most desirable foods available? And who would decide what these even are, let alone carry it out? How can the humanity, agency, and hard work of those who may be most vulnerable to industrial food problems best be respected, even as the systemic problems themselves continue to be called out and fended off, and as people across the class spectrum continue to feel vulnerable, albeit in divergent ways? What would a social activism for children's food that does not rely on moralized notions of individualized, affectively intensive parental care look like? And how might such a reconceptualization shift our very understandings of childhood itself? Indeed, if our fears for the vulnerability of children are in intimate, yet fraught and often conflictual, relationship with our ideas about social diversity and justice, how can we upset and refigure that relationship?

Such questions are both stimulating and unsettling, and how they may yet translate into transformed and transforming practices at the local level is not clear. In some ways, these countervailing efforts might already be under way. As we have seen, Hometowners do think about ways to be "moderate" in parenting and feeding/eating, which inevitably involves compromising any sense of utter purity; and many would be open to the idea of thinking about their community as willingly co-constituted with people, processes, and substances that make them uncomfortable, even if this does not in itself guarantee that transformative alliances are formed or nurtured.

Yet I do not want to suggest that if (some version of) "we" just thought about these things a bit differently, life would be easier and our communities would be more just and inclusive. To some extent this might be true, but I tend to believe that such structures of belief change most meaningfully alongside, and in (tense, frictive, imperfect) coordination with, larger scale shifts in capitalist labor conditions, corporate-led commodity markets, state institutions, and the relationships among those. Thus I take as salutary the suggestions of sociologists such as Janet Poppendieck (2010), who has called for universal free school lunch in the United States; Norah MacKendrick (2018, 156–158), who argues that the burdens of "precautionary consumption" are best addressed through stronger government regulation and greater transparency concerning potential environmental toxins and industrial manufacturing procedures; and Annette Lareau (2003), who reminds us that federal and state safety nets, such as child welfare allowances or transportation support for children's recreation activities, could help to make the conditions of child rearing in the United States more equitable. I would add that agencies such as the Centers for Disease Control and Prevention should critically reexamine how programs centered on "parent engagement," designed to improve children's health outcomes, are likely to reinforce moral condemnations of lower income working parents—and especially mothers. Structural, as opposed to individual, interventions are likely the most effective routes to addressing problems that fundamentally are structural in nature, and the morally loaded language of "engagement" helps to obscure this.

Meanwhile, as we saw in chapter 3, exhortations for middle-class parents to be less anxious, more compromising, less picky, or more "free-range" about children's food present parents with new kinds of double binds, new ways to do it "right," and do not necessarily allay sources of stress and uncertainty. When it comes to food and consumption, women in particular already navigate a thin line between performances of femininity that are considered hegemonic and those that are pathologized, such that they must engage in constant calibrations to avoid the appearance of any extremes (Cairns and Johnston 2015, 35; see also Maher, Fraser, and Wright 2010). I do not want to add fuel to that fire, and this book does not impugn anyone's anxiety as misplaced.

Still, I invite readers to consider what their own answers may be to the questions I have raised, whether because their own communities of practice are similar to the one described here or because the case of Hometown has jogged new thoughts and observations about their own, distinct settings. This book is an encouragement to reflect upon the ways some of us are living through this moment in capitalism, and especially to consider how people take its tensions into their own bodies and self-presentations, as well as into their attempts to care properly for their own children, while also envisioning a future that is more just for a broader circle of humans beyond their own families. Reflecting this way does not fix conditions of fear, stress, or inequity, but it might open small ways to relieve struggle and miscommunication, foster new ideas for seeking structural change, or create fracture lines that can grow into fresh opportunities for compassion and collaboration.

ACKNOWLEDGMENTS

This book would not have been possible had it not been for the graciousness and openness of administrators, teachers, parents, and students at the Atlanta school community I call "Hometown." Hometown's staff welcomed me to school events, classroom discussions, and lunch lines, giving me the opportunity to meet their students' parents, to get a sense of how food issues were part of the daily life of the school, and to become a participant observer in multiple ways. A special thank-you goes to "Carl," Hometown's chef, who co-taught a middle school course on food with me and shared many of his observations as he (then new to the job) got to know the school's pupils from his special vantage point. Students in our class enriched this book by providing enlightening reflections about the significance of food in their own lives. Meanwhile, Hometown parents volunteered their time, often during the school and work day, to talk with me about their parenting routines and worries. They welcomed me into their after-school committees and, in several cases, into their homes for family dinners. Their narratives are the heart of this book, and I can only hope that they will discover something useful and fresh within it that also rings true to their experiences.

The research conducted for this book was funded by the National Science Foundation under Grant BCS-1330988. All findings, conclusions, and opinions expressed here are my own and do not necessarily reflect the views of the National Science Foundation. Internal awards from Georgia State University provided me with releases from teaching that were crucial to the completion of this book. Both NSF and Georgia State funded graduate assistants whose research support was invaluable at various stages of the project. Liz Barnett, Jessie Burnette, and Katie Coleman spent time "in the field" at Hometown, providing volunteer support in its lunchroom or after-school program, attending parent meetings, recruiting new interviewees, and occasionally conducting and transcribing interviews. Several other students, including Allyson

Korb, Lily Green, Emma Mason, Brandice Evans, and Su Choe, ably performed tasks such as transcribing interview tapes and conducting literature searches.

A number of colleagues deserve my thanks for the many ways in which they helped to inspire and make space for this endeavor. My coworkers in the Department of Anthropology at Georgia State helped bring this book to fruition by providing the sane, supportive, professional home base that nourishes all my intellectual pursuits. Special thanks go to Kathryn Kozaitis for her skillful work as department chair, which helped maintain such an environment. I also heartily thank the members of my reading group (Emanuela Guano, Faidra Papavasiliou, Katherine Hankins, and Megan Sinnott), whose camaraderie, sharp minds, and good cheer have been a source of energy over the life of this project. Participants in a seminar at Georgia State's Humanities Center provided helpful commentary and a fresh audience in the final stages of writing. Beyond Georgia State, panels, workshops, and volumes organized by Rachael Stryker, Elsa Davidson, Charlotte Faircloth, and Rachel Rosen invigorated my writing and gave excellent opportunities for feedback. Jennifer Hammer, my editor at NYU Press, provided timely, clear, insightful, and cheerful guidance at every step of the preparation of the manuscript.

I also must thank many friends and family members, too many to name here, who supported my well-being in all kinds of indispensable ways during the years I spent researching and writing this book. Among these are my parents, Alexander and Elaine Patico, who were sources of unflagging encouragement. During some particularly difficult years for our family, Jeff Young and Shelly Moorfield volunteered to spend time with my children regularly, helping me to maintain a balanced life (among other gifts of friendship). Tom McKlin provided persistent emotional support over much of the time I was engaged in this writing, and Melissa Checker was an ever-incisive and witty sounding board for matters anthropological and not. As the finishing touches were placed on this book, Joel Zivot inspired me to look into the future and toward new projects of all kinds. Last but certainly not least, my children, Eliza and Clem, made possible many of the life experiences that drew me to these topics in the first place. They constantly impress me and challenge me to be better, and their spiritedness, companionship, provocations, and patience are at the very center of my life and work.

NOTES

INTRODUCTION

1 "6 Ways to Be an Effective Parent in 2019," *New York Times*, December 25, 2018, www.nytimes.com.

2 An individual's habitus can change over time and is affected by ongoing, interrelated social, economic, and aesthetic experiences, but for Bourdieu it is generally highly informed by childhood tastes.

3 No particular practice has an inherent class meaning, though conditions of access (such as cost) help to create some as more exclusive than others. The question, rather, is how a practice or commodity fits into a broader repertoire of ideologies and tastes. For example, as Halley (2007, 12) has noted, white middle-class Americans also emphasize "natural" instincts and practices in certain contexts, such as child-led feeding and cosleeping (see also Sears 2019a).

4 According to Kochhar (2018), the median income of middle-class American adults was $74,015 in 2010 and $78,442 in 2016, reflecting a slower rate of growth than for those in the upper income bracket (for whom income grew from $172,152 to $187,872 during the same period). Incomes were scaled to reflect three-person households.

5 Self-reported annual incomes for African Americans ranged from $12,000 (the individual income of a young teaching assistant who lived with her parent) to over $90,000 (the household income of a married teacher). The lowest reported household income among white interviewees was $14,000; this was a case in which a former primary breadwinner was ill and no longer working her professional job. Only three answers below $55,000 were given overall. The median African American / Black income was lower (at $61,000) than the median non-Black income ($120,000) in my sample. Even so, it is worth highlighting that all of the African American interviewees were college-educated (two at Atlanta's historically Black colleges), a factor that contributes to class identity across race and income.

6 In a recent *New York Times* opinion column, David Leonhardt (2019) defined the U.S. "upper middle class" as the 90th to 99th percentile of wage earners, who earn roughly $120,000 to $425,000 *after taxes* per year. According to research posted by the Pew Research Center (Kochhar 2018), the median income of middle-class American adults was $78,442 in 2016. The U.S. poverty line was set at $21,330 for a family of three in 2019 (U.S. Department of Health and Human Services n.d.).

CHAPTER 1. DISCERNING THE "REAL" FROM THE "JUNK"

1 For comparative cases of how similar consumer shifts took place and were entangled with labor processes, growing inequalities, and local cultural practice, see Petrov (2012), Baglar (2013), and Merleaux (2015).

2 In connection with the "obesity epidemic" and other dietary worries, the question of whether cupcakes should be allowed in classroom birthday celebrations has been debated in school districts across the country over the past decade (Isoldi et al. 2012; Schulte 2006). Schools that participate in the National School Lunch Program are required to maintain local wellness policies that articulate approaches to such issues. See U.S. Department of Agriculture, Food and Nutrition Service (2016).

3 Pollan draws on Scrinis's critique of nutritionism, the tendency to focus on the health implications of specific food components rather than acknowledging the synergy of foods that make up a diet or a traditional cuisine. Yet Scrinis himself argues that Pollan misunderstands his critique and tends to reinforce nutritionist thinking in his own ways; see Scrinis (2015, 18–19, 238–239).

4 In fact, I noticed few children I subjectively would have characterized as heavy or overweight at Hometown, though there were a few. Even in cases where parents admitted to slight worry about their children's weight, they also expressed caution about talking about weight gain directly with their children: for example, two separate parents mentioned that they had been annoyed that doctors had mentioned weight issues in front of their children during appointments, as parents preferred to keep the focus of the conversation on overall health as opposed to body appearance.

5 Westin A. Price recommends a diet rich in animal broths and animal fats. His program is mentioned by Scrinis (2015) as a contemporary alternative to functional nutritionism.

6 Goldfish are the focus of nutritional line-drawing debates in contexts beyond Hometown: while the snack has come under fire for marketing saturated fat, salt, and white flour (in some varieties) to children, a spokeswoman for Campbell's remarked that the company had made the recipe more healthful by taking out trans fats, reducing salt content in some cases, eliminating artificial colors, and providing whole wheat versions. She argued that these changes could go only so far however, for "if people don't enjoy their food, they don't eat it and they make other choices" (Neumann 2011).

7 Annie's, "About Annie's: Our Mission," www.annies.com.

8 See www.annies.com/our-mission/about-annies. Annie's is identified by food researcher Charlene Elliott (2012) as one of the brands that qualifies as a "better for you" or "healthier for you" brand of children's food, inasmuch as its health claims are intrinsic to the line and not simply isolated claims marked on the box (more in line with Kraft's approach). In a study of 354 children's foods purchased, 82 were in the "better for you" group and did fare better nutritionally according

to the measures of the study: 65 percent were considered high in sugar, fat, or sodium compared with 91 percent of the other kid-marketed foods, though results varied. In one example, EnviroKidz Koala Crisp cereal had a similar amount of sugar (around 40 percent) to the classically sugared and colorful Lucky Charms and Froot Loops. For nutrition information on one variety of Annie's mac and cheese (organic shells with white cheddar), see www.annies.com/products/pastas/organic-shells-white-cheddar.

9   See www.kraftmacandcheese.com/products/bluebox/original-cheese. After this ethnographic research had concluded, a well-publicized study showed that a number of processed cheese products, including Kraft macaroni and cheese, contained troubling levels of phthalates, chemicals whose use had been banned in children's toys a decade earlier (Rabin 2017).

10   Kraft Mac and Cheese, "Home Page," www.kraftmacandcheese.com.

11   See www.traderjoes.com/faqs/product-information. Trader Joe's also markets itself with a vibe of neighborhoodiness, with murals referencing local landmarks and neighborhoods, hand-drawn signs announcing new products, and smiling staff dressed in Hawaiian shirts. As the company's website explains, "We're traders on the culinary seas, searching the world over for cool items to bring home to our customers. And when we return home, we think grocery shopping should be fun, not another chore. So just relax and leave your worries at the door. We'll sail those seven seas, you have some fun with our finds at your neighborhood Trader Joe's" (www.traderjoes.com/faqs/general-information).

12   On arsenic in rice and parenting, see Abel (2015).

13   There were occasional mentions of high-fructose corn syrup as one of the forms of sugar especially to be avoided, as when Renee remembered that she had heard papers about it at an academic conference and that "I can't even remember a whole bunch of the details, but the take-home message I got was like: oh my God! [laughs] bad, bad, bad, it's so much worse than sugar and um—or it wasn't— yeah, it was just like bad, bad, bad, bad . . . so yeah, high fructose corn syrup I've made a real effort to avoid that." Wendy explained why her husband and she sought to avoid high fructose corn syrup: "I mean just that it's empty, like empty sugar and high—yeah, I guess it's like empty calories. I don't know if there is any health—like I don't know if there is any uh, it's not like a carcinogen or anything I don't think . . . but I think just that you know more you've heard it's not good for you, for whatever reason." The "why" of high fructose sugar avoidance was often vague, then, but parents had absorbed from media and academic sources that it was particularly harmful; these reports apparently packed an affective more than a scientifically specific punch to parents' guts. In fact, the question of whether it is significantly more harmful or more obesogenic than other forms of sugar has been contested, though to date some research has found that high concentrations of fructose in the body have long-term effects on the liver and other organs (Beil 2013).

14 One fitness site compares sugar to cocaine for its parallel effects on dopamine levels and negative health results. "It is a scary thought that maybe some of those children popping Ritalin don't actually need the little white pills, but rather a breakfast filled with more proteins and fats (that's right, I said fats) than sugars and carbohydrates. Such a breakfast would provide a sustained energy release throughout the day, increase concentration, and prevent their bodies from becoming dulled to the release of dopamine neuro-transmitters" (Precel n.d.).

CHAPTER 2. HELICOPTERS AND NAZIS

1 Chua observed that a rise in child suicide was being interpreted as a middle-class problem of rising consumerist expectations and children's inability to defer gratification (Chua 2011). In this context, self-control is construed as the missing element that children must gain as they prepare for uncertain futures; children of the elite must learn to endure frustrations such as consumer deferrals as a form of "suicide inoculation," while others such as labor migrants must endure other forms of waiting, instability, and insecurity (2011, 116–117). In this sense, what Chua calls "self-temporalization practices" became a "governing surface for experts to manage how we invest in the future as an unfolding of social and material possibility and who is accused of inappropriate pretensions of behaving recklessly when they do. To tolerate contingency with cultivated skill alchemically transforms the ontological insecurities of late capitalism into a rousing cry to be modern enough to endure modern life well" (130–131).

2 Anthropologist Emily Martin (2010) has asked why brain-based models of subjectivity are so popular currently. She offers that such an approach relieves guilt in some cases, in that an individual's state is "not my fault" (378). On the other hand, she wonders whether people's resistance to brain-based explanations can also be part of a fantasy of unique individual identity in neoliberalism (379).

3 Similar explanations depending upon neuroscience would come up in other school contexts, such as when school psychologists explained to a group of parents, over coffee and pastries, how teens' cognitive development, while rapid in terms of new brain cell production from puberty into the early twenties, often kept them from taking in information or making decisions in the same ways their parents did and expected them to. Their skills were slow, emerging, and inconsistent, aided by adequate sleep. The principal chimed in to explain how they were working on meditation skills in a "Finding Center" group with the middle school students, and some of them had come back saying it had helped them fall asleep.

4 www.sesameworkshop.org/season44/about-the-show/curriculum/ (accessed ca. 2015; link inactive as of March 21, 2019).

5 Further attesting to its growing ubiquity, self-regulation was discussed in the *Washington Post* in an editorial criticizing Donald Trump during his presidential campaign. Clinical psychologist Helena Duch (2016) argued that Trump's public behavior displayed a lack of self-regulation that was setting a detrimental example for the nation's youth. In a *Psychology Today* blog, Steve Stosny (2011) offered this

definition: "Behaviorally, self-regulation is the ability to act in your long-term best interest, consistent with your deepest values. . . . Emotionally, self-regulation is the ability to calm yourself down when you're upset and cheer yourself up when you're down." See also Murray et al. (2015). A guest blogger on a "Mind Positive Parenting" site makes a direct connection between how parents nurture self-regulation—which involves interacting attentively with children without being overly controlling—and children's eating: "Providing consistent messaging and following through with promises also helps children establish self-discipline and a willingness to delay gratification. These executive function skills set our kids up for success in school and life AND are important for establishing healthy eating behaviors" (Duffey 2013).

6 Hoffman (2013, 234–235, 238–239) argues that those who espouse such child-centered child-rearing approaches understand themselves to be superior to a putatively mainstream, more authoritarian parent; but in reality, these principles are reflected in popular child-rearing literature and in that sense are not particularly countercultural.

7 Wiktionary, "Helicopter Parents," https://en.wiktionary.org.

8 Lenore Skenazy, www.freerangekids.com.

9 For example, one *New York Times* article warned that picky eating could be a sign of childhood depression and other behavioral and emotional disorders (Peachman 2015). For another *New York Times* critique of "hovering," see Dell'Antonia (2015).

10 See also Druckerman's (2019) update, "The Bad News about Helicopter Parenting: It Works."

11 On the lack of consumer trust in food corporations, see Lavin (2013, xxv) and Brownell and Harris (2012). For a contrasting view, see Gerrard (2015).

12 Adopting corporate/institutional language more explicitly, a website called Slow Family Living (n.d.) sold "family mission statement workbooks" for $7.50. They are designed to help families "determine who you are, why you entered family life in the first place and where you want to go from here. It is our hope that the questions in this booklet will help bring you and your family to a clear understanding of your desires, needs and values as a family unit—from which you can begin the process of allowing your own mission to unfold."

CHAPTER 3. "HE DOESN'T LIKE ANYTHING HEALTHY!"

1 According to the USDA (2013), in 2013–2014 the reimbursement rates for school lunches ranged from $0.28 (reimbursement for students who pay) to $3.16 (maximum rate for free lunches), with some variation depending on the proportion of children at the school (either more or less than 60 percent) who qualified for free and reduced lunch—the greater the percentage, the greater the reimbursement rate. For 2014–2015, the rates ranged from $0.28 to $3.21. On the advantages of leaving the National School Lunch Program, school administrator Tina pondered, "Okay well do we just chuck the whole . . . school lunch program and you know,

as in regards to being beholden to a state or the federal government and just say 'okay we're going to still take applications but we're not going to send them anywhere, we're not going to use them other than determining whether we'll cover the cost for you as free and reduced' . . . and just still taking care of those kids and paying for their meals or providing them a discounted rate but then not being beholden to any rules and regulations. . . . I really like that idea because it allows you to feed the kid in front of you."

2 For comparison, in 2014–2015, 70.2 percent of school lunches served in Georgia were free, 6.4 percent were reduced-price lunches, and 23.5 percent were fully paid lunches (Georgia Department of Education 2016).

3 See U.S. Department of Agriculture, Food and Nutrition Service (2014).

4 See U.S. Department of Agriculture, Food and Nutrition Service (2012).

5 This was another chance for me to make a connection with anthropology: I noted to them that anthropologists have looked at the same dynamic with gifts, arguing that even if one does not have a conscious or explicit strategy, gift-giving and gift-receiving are still bound by social rules, affect one's relationships, and create positive feeling as well as obligation between participants (Mauss 2000).

CHAPTER 4. HONORING THE CHEESE PUFFS

1 Centers for Disease Control and Prevention (2018b). On the other hand, Lareau, Weininger, and Cox (2018) suggest that the overzealous interventions of affluent parents in school issues such as attendance zoning can have negative impacts including increasing administrator workloads, lessening educators' authority, and worsening economic segregation.

2 See Centers for Disease Control and Prevention (2019).

REFERENCES

Abel, Heather. "Free of Gluten, but Not of Arsenic (or of Guilt)." *New York Times Motherlode*, January 21, 2015. https://parenting.blogs.nytimes.com.

Abu-Lughod, Lila. "The Romance of Resistance: Tracing Transformations of Power through Bedouin Women." *American Ethnologist* 17, no. 1 (1990): 41–55.

———. *Veiled Sentiments: Honor and Poetry in a Bedouin Society*. Berkeley: University of California Press, 1986.

Abu-Lughod, Lila, and Catherine A. Lutz. "Introduction: Emotion, Discourse, and the Politics of Everyday Life." In *Language and the Politics of Emotion*, edited by Catherine Lutz and Lila Abu-Lughod, 1–23. Cambridge: Cambridge University Press, 1990.

Allen, Patricia, and Julie Guthman. "From Old School to Farm to School: Neoliberalization from the Ground Up." *Agriculture and Human Values* 23, no. 4 (2006): 401–415.

Allison, Anne. "Japanese Mothers and Obentos: The Lunch-Box as Ideological State Apparatus." *Anthropological Quarterly* 64, no. 4 (1991): 195–208.

Anagnost, Ann. "Maternal Labor in Transnational Circuits." In *Consuming Motherhood*, edited by Janelle S. Taylor, Danielle F. Wozniak, and Linda L. Layne, 139–167. New Brunswick, NJ: Rutgers University Press, 2004.

Aronson, Matt, and Steve Bialostok. "'Do Some Wondering': Children and Their Self-Understanding Selves in Early Elementary Classrooms." *Symbolic Interaction* 39, no. 2 (2016): 229–251.

Aubrey, Allison. "A Better Breakfast Can Boost a Child's Brainpower." *Morning Edition*, National Public Radio, September 4, 2006. www.npr.org.

Backett-Milburn, Kathryn, Wendy Wills, Mei-Li Roberts, and Julia Lawton. "Food and Family Practices: Teenagers, Eating and Domestic Life in Differing Socio-economic Circumstances." *Children's Geographies* 8, no. 3 (2010): 303–314.

Baglar, Rosslyn. "'Oh God, Save Us from Sugar': An Ethnographic Exploration of Diabetes Mellitus in the United Arab Emirates." *Medical Anthropology* 32, no. 2 (2013): 109–125.

Bailey, Becky. *Easy to Love, Difficult to Discipline: The Seven Basic Skills for Turning Conflict into Cooperation*. New York: Harper, 2000.

———. *There's Got to Be a Better Way: Discipline That Works!* Oviedo, FL: Loving Guidance, 1997.

Bayor, Ronald H. *Race and the Shaping of Twentieth-Century Atlanta*. Chapel Hill: University of North Carolina Press, 1996.

Beck, Ulrich. *Risk Society: Towards a New Modernity*. Thousand Oaks, CA: SAGE, 1992.

Beil, L. "Does High Fructose Corn Syrup Deserve Such a Bad Rap?" *Science News* 183, no. 11 (2013): 22–25.

Bentley, Amy. *Inventing Baby Food: Taste, Health, and the Industrialization of the American Diet*. Berkeley: University of California Press, 2014.

Bialostok, Steven M., and Matt Aronson. "Making Emotional Connections in the Age of Neoliberalism." *Ethos* 44, no. 2 (2016): 96–117.

Biltekoff, Charlotte. *Eating Right in America: The Cultural Politics of Food and Health*. Durham, NC: Duke University Press, 2013.

———. "Nutrition as a Social Reform Project." *Gastronomica* 14, no. 3 (2014): 34–37.

Bluebond-Langner, Myra, and Jill E. Korbin. "Challenges and Opportunities in the Anthropology of Childhood: An introduction to 'Children, Childhoods, and Childhood Studies.'" *American Anthropologist* 109, no. 2 (2007): 241–246.

Borenstein, Eliot. "Neoliberalism and Other Dirty Words (Russia's Alien Nations)." NYU Jordan Center for the Advanced Study of Russia Blog. February 21, 2019. http://jordanrussiacenter.org.

Borovoy, Amy Beth. *The Too-Good Wife: Alcohol, Codependency, and the Politics of Nurturance in Postwar Japan*. Berkeley: University of California Press, 2001.

Bourdieu, Pierre. *Distinction: A Social Critique of the Judgment of Taste*. Translated by Richard Nice. Cambridge, MA: Harvard University Press, 1984.

Bristow, Jennie. "The Double Bind of Parenting Culture: Helicopter Parents and Cotton Wool Kids." In *Parenting Culture Studies*, edited by Ellie Lee, Jennie Bristow, Charlotte Faircloth, and Jan Macvarish, 200–215. London: Palgrave Macmillan, 2014.

Broad, Garrett. "Narrowcasted Nutrition Sciences." *Gastronomica* 14, no. 3 (2014): 11–14.

Broady, Kristen E., and Aisha G. Meeks. "Obesity and Social Inequality in America." *Review of Black Political Economy* 42 (2015): 201–209.

Brown, Solveig. "Intensive Mothering as an Adaptive Response to Our Cultural Environment." In *Intensive Mothering: The Cultural Contradictions of Modern Motherhood*, edited by Linda Ennis, 27–46. Bradford, ON: Demeter Press, 2014.

Brownell, Kelly, and Jennifer Harris. "Sugar Rush: Why We Can't Trust Sugar Companies to Self-Regulate." *Atlantic*, June 22, 2012. www.theatlantic.com.

Cairns, Kate, and Josee Johnston. *Food and Femininity*. New York: Bloomsbury, 2015.

Carrier, James G. "People Who Can Be Friends: Selves and Social Relationships." In *The Anthropology of Friendship*, edited by S. Bell and S. Coleman, 21–38. New York: Berg, 1999.

Carsten, Janet. *After Kinship*. Cambridge: Cambridge University Press, 2012.

Castagna, Angelina. *Educated in Whiteness*. Minneapolis: University of Minnesota Press, 2014.

Centers for Disease Control and Prevention. "Childhood Obesity Facts." 2018a. www.cdc.gov.

———. "Parent Engagement in Schools." August 7, 2018b. www.cdc.gov.

———. "Whole School, Whole Community, Whole Child." May 29, 2019. www.cdc.gov.

Chin, Elizabeth. *Purchasing Power: Black Kids and American Consumer Culture*. Minneapolis: University of Minnesota Press, 2001.

Chua, Jocelyn Lim. "Making Time for the Children: Self-Temporalization and the Cultivation of the Antisuicidal Subject in South India." *Cultural Anthropology* 26, no. 1 (2011): 112–137.

Clarke, Alison J. "Consuming Children and Making Mothers: Birthday Parties, Gifts and the Pursuit of Sameness." *Horizontes Antropológicos* 13, no. 28 (2007): 263–287.

Cohen, Lawrence J. *Playful Parenting: An Exciting New Approach to Raising Children That Will Help You Nurture Close Connections, Solve Behavior Problems, and Encourage Confidence*. New York: Ballantine Books, 2002.

Collins, Patricia Hill, and Sirma Bilge. *Intersectionality*. Cambridge: Polity Press, 2016.

Confessore, Nicholas. "How School Lunch Became the Latest Political Battleground." *New York Times Magazine*, October 7, 2014.

Cook, Daniel Thomas. "Children's Subjectivities and Commercial Meaning: The Delicate Battle Mothers Wage When Feeding Their Children." In *Children, Food, and Identity in Everyday Life*, edited by Allison James, Anne Kjorholt, and Vebjorg Tingstad, 112–129. New York: Palgrave Macmillan, 2009a.

———. *The Commodification of Childhood: The Children's Clothing Industry and the Rise of the Child Consumer*. Durham, NC: Duke University Press, 2004.

———. "The Missing Child in Consumption Theory." *Journal of Consumer Culture* 8, no. 2 (2008): 219–243.

———. "Semantic Provisioning of Children's Food: Commerce, Care and Maternal Practice." *Childhood* 16, no. 3 (2009b): 317–334.

Counihan, Carole. *The Anthropology of Food and Body: Gender, Meaning and Power*. New York: Routledge, 1999.

Coutant, Alexandre, Valerie-Ines de La Ville, Malene Gram, and Nathalie Boireau. "Motherhood, Advertising, and Anxiety: A Cross-Cultural Perspective on Danonino Commercials." *Advertising and Society Review* 12, no. 2 (2011).

Crooks, Deborah L. "Food Consumption, Activity and Overweight among Elementary School Children in an Appalachian Kentucky Community." *American Journal of Physical Anthropology* 112 (2000): 159–170.

———. "Trading Nutrition for Education: Nutritional Status and the Sale of Snack Foods in an Eastern Kentucky School." *Medical Anthropology Quarterly* 17, no. 2 (2003): 182–199.

Crowther, Gillian. *Eating Culture: An Anthropological Guide to Food*. Toronto: University of Toronto Press, 2013.

Curtis, Penny, Allison James, and Katie Ellis. "Children's Snacking, Children's Food: Food Moralities and Family Life." *Children's Geographies* 8, no. 3 (2010): 291–302.

de Kramer, Neri. "Feeding the Squeezed Middle-Class Family: Maternal Stress, Dilemmas, Contradictions, and the Third Shift." In *Mothers and Food: Negotiating Foodways from Maternal Perspectives*, edited by F. P. Guignard and T. Cassidy, 28–40. Bradford, ON: Demeter Press, 2016.

Dell'Antonia, K. J. "If Pressure and Hovering Don't Help Children Succeed, Why Is It So Hard to Stop?" *New York Times*, July 27, 2015. http://parenting.blogs.nytimes.com.

———. "Research Suggests Students Adjusting to New School Lunches." *New York Times*, July 21, 2014a.

———. "Weekly Quandary: Revisiting Limits on Screen Time." *New York Times*, August 25, 2014b. https://parenting.blogs.nytimes.com.

DesMaisons, Kathleen. *Little Sugar Addicts: End the Mood Swings, Meltdowns, Tantrums, and Low Self-Esteem in Your Child Today*. New York: Three Rivers Press, 2004.

DeVault, Marjorie. *Feeding the Family: The Social Organization of Caring as Gendered Work*. Chicago: University of Chicago Press, 1991.

DiSalvo, David. "What Eating Too Much Sugar Does to Your Brain." 2012. www.psychologytoday.com.

Dorfman, Kelly. *Cure Your Child with Food*. New York: Workman, 2013.

Druckerman, Pamela. "The Bad News about Helicopter Parenting: It Works." *New York Times*, February 7, 2019. www.nytimes.com.

———. *Bringing Up Bébé: One American Mother Discovers the Wisdom of French Parenting*. New York: Penguin, 2014b.

———. "A Cure for Hyper-Parenting." *New York Times*, October 12, 2014a. www.nytimes.com.

Duch, Helena. "Kids Need to Learn Self-Regulation to Succeed. Trump Is Teaching Them the Opposite." *Washington Post*, March 10, 2016. www.washingtonpost.com.

Duffey, Kiyah. "How to Build Your Child's Self-Regulation at the Dinner Table." Dr. Dave Mind Positive Parenting, August 15, 2013. http://drdavewalsh.com.

DuPuis, E. Melanie. *Dangerous Digestion: The Politics of American Dietary Advice*. Berkeley: University of California Press, 2015.

Elliott, Charlene. "Eatertainment and the (Re)classification of Children's Foods." *Food, Culture, and Society* 13, no. 4 (2010): 539–553.

———. "Marketing Fun Foods: A Profile and Analysis of Supermarket Food Messages Targeted at Children" *Canadian Public Policy* 34, no. 2 (2008): 259–273.

———. "Packaging Health: Examining 'Better-for-You' Foods Targeted at Children." *Canadian Public Policy* 38, no. 2 (2012): 265–281.

Eriksen, Thomas Hyllen. "Opposing the Motion: The Neoliberal Person." In "Debate: The Concept of Neoliberalism Has Become an Obstacle to the Anthropological Understanding of the Twenty-First Century," edited by Soumhya Venkatesan. *Journal of the Royal Anthropological Institute* 21 (2015): 914–917.

Faircloth, Charlotte, Diane M. Hoffman, and Linda L. Layne. "Introduction." In *Parenting in Global Perspective: Negotiating Ideologies of Kinship, Self and Politics*, edited by Charlotte Faircloth, Diane M. Hoffman, and Linda L. Layne, 1–18. London: Routledge, 2013.

Foster, Robert J. "The Work of the New Economy: Consumers, Brands and Value Creation." *Cultural Anthropology* 22, no. 4 (2007): 707–731.

Foucault, Michel. *The Foucault Reader*. Edited by Paul Rabinow. New York: Pantheon, 1984.

Frankel, Leslie A., Sheryl O. Hughes, Teresia M. O'Connor, Thomas G. Power, Jennifer O. Fisher, and Nancy L. Hazen. "Parental Influences on Children's Self-Regulation of Energy Intake: Insights from Developmental Literature on Emotion Regulation." *Journal of Obesity* (2012). doi:10.1155/2012/327259.

Fredricks, Jennifer, Phyllis C. Blumenfeld, and Alison Paris. "School Engagement: Potential of the Concept, State of the Evidence." *Review of Educational Research* 74, no. 1 (2004): 59–109.

Furedi, Frank. *Paranoid Parenting: Why Ignoring the Experts May Be Best for Your Child*. Chicago: Chicago Review Press, 2002.

Ganti, Tejaswini. "Neoliberalism." *Annual Review of Anthropology* 43 (2014): 89–104.

Georgia Department of Education. "Facts and Figures 2014–2015 Georgia's School Nutrition Program." January 19, 2016. www.gadoe.org.

Gerrard, Jeremy. "Self-Regulation Improves Nutrition in Children's Cereal." *Food Engineering*, November 13, 2015. www.foodengineeringmag.com.

Giddens, Anthony. "Affluence, Poverty and the Idea of a Post-Scarcity Society." United Nations Research Institute for Social Development Discussion Papers, May 1995.

———. *Modernity and Self-Identity: Self and Society in the Late Modern Age*. Stanford: Stanford University Press, 1991.

Gillies, Val. "Raising the 'Meritocracy': Parenting and the Individualization of Social Class." *Sociology* 39, no. 5 (2005): 835–853.

Graeber, David. *Toward an Anthropology of Value: The False Coin of Our Own Dreams*. New York: Palgrave, 2001.

Gregg, Melissa, and Gregory J. Seigworth. *The Affect Theory Reader*. Durham, NC: Duke University Press, 2010.

Grieshaber, Scott. "Mealtime Rituals: Power and Resistance in the Construction of Mealtime Rules." *British Journal of Sociology* 48, no. 4 (1997): 649–666.

Guthman, Julie. "Introducing Critical Nutrition: A Special Issue on Dietary Advice and Its Discontents." *Gastronomica* 14, no. 3 (2014): 1–4.

———. *Weighing In: Obesity, Food Justice, and the Limits of Capitalism*. Berkeley: University of California Press, 2011.

Hackworth, Jason. *The Neoliberal City: Governance, Ideology, and Development in American Urbanism*. Ithaca, NY: Cornell University Press, 2007.

Hallett, Vicky. "School Food Gets Smarter and Snazzier: Cafeterias Becoming Creative in Cutting Fat." *Washington Post*, Southern Maryland Extra, T03, August 31, 2003.

Halley, Jean O'Malley. *Boundaries of Touch: Parenting and Adult-Child Intimacy*. Urbana: University of Illinois Press, 2007.

Hammond, Claudia. "Does Sugar Make Kids Hyperactive?" BBC, July 23, 2013. www.bbc.com.

Hankins, Katherine. "The Final Frontier: Charter Schools as New Community Institutions of Gentrification." *Urban Geography* 28, no. 2 (2007): 113–128.

Hardt, Michael. "Affective Labor." *boundary* 26, no. 2 (1999): 89–100.

Hays, Sharon. *The Cultural Contradictions of Motherhood*. New Haven, CT: Yale University Press, 1996.

Heiman, Rachel, Mark Liechty, and Carla Freeman. "Introduction: Charting an Anthropology of the Middle Classes." In *The Global Middle Classes: Theorizing through Ethnography* (School for Advanced Research Advanced Seminar Series), edited by Rachel Heiman, Mark Liechty, and Carla Freeman, 3–30. Santa Fe, NM: School for Advanced Research Press, 2012.

Henry, Elizabeth E., and Katherine Hankins. "Halting White Flight: Parent Activism and the (Re)shaping of Atlanta's 'Circuits of Schooling,' 1973–2009." *Journal of Urban History* 38, no. 3 (2012): 532–552.

Hewitt, Paige. "Diversity in School Lunches: New Menus Offer Better Food, Bigger Selection." *Houston Chronicle*, October 1, 2001, A24.

Hite, Adele. "Unquestioned Assumptions, Unintended Consequences." *Gastronomica* 14, no. 3 (2014): 5–11.

Hochschild, Arlie R. *The Commercialization of Intimate Life: Notes from Home and Work*. Berkeley: University of California Press, 2003.

———. *The Second Shift*. New York: Penguin, 1990.

Hoffman, Diane. "How (Not) to Feel: Culture and the Politics of Emotion in the American Parenting Advice Literature." *Discourse: Studies in the Cultural Politics of Education* 30, no. 1 (2009): 15–31.

———. "Power Struggles: The Paradoxes of Emotion and Control among Child-Centred Mothers in Privileged America." In *Parenting in Global Perspective: Negotiating Ideologies of Kinship, Self and Politics*, edited by Charlotte Faircloth, Diane M. Hoffman, and Linda L. Layne, 229–243. London: Routledge, 2013.

Holt, Douglas B. "Does Cultural Capital Structure American Consumption?" *Journal of Consumer Research* 25, no. 1 (1998): 1–25.

Huber, Bridget. "Michelle's Moves Has the First Lady's Anti-obesity Campaign Been Too Accommodating toward the Food Industry?" *Nation* 295, no. 18 (2012): 11–17.

Huisman, Kim, and Elizabeth Joy. "The Cultural Contradictions of Motherhood Revisited: Continuities and Changes." In *Intensive Mothering: The Cultural Contradictions of Modern Motherhood*, edited by Linda Ennis, 86–103. Bradford, ON: Demeter Press, 2014.

Huynh, Nancy. "Does Sugar Really Make Children Hyper?" *Yale Scientific*, September 1, 2010. www.yalescientific.org.

Illouz, Eva. *Saving the Modern Soul: Therapy, Emotions, and the Culture of Self-Help*. Berkeley: University of California Press, 2008.

Inglis, Victoria, Kylie Ball, and David Crawford. "Does Modifying the Household Food Budget Predict Changes in the Healthfulness of Purchasing Choices among Low- and High-Income Women?" *Appetite* 52 (2008): 272–279.

Isoldi, Kathy, Sharron Dalton, Desiree Rodriguez, and Marion Nestle. "Classroom 'Cupcake' Celebrations: Observations of Foods Offered and Consumed." *Journal of Nutrition Education and Behavior* 44, no. 1 (2012): 71–75.

James, Allison. "Confections, Concoctions, and Conceptions." In *The Children's Culture Reader*, edited by Henry Jenkins, 394–405. New York: New York University Press, 1998.

———. "Giving Voice to Children's Voices: Practices and Problems, Pitfalls and Potentials." *American Anthropologist* 109, no. 2 (2007): 261–272.

James, Allison, Anne Trine Kjorholt, and Vebjorg Tingstad. "Introduction: Children, Food and Identity in Everyday Life." In *Children, Food, and Identity in Everyday Life*, edited by Allison James, Anne Kjorholt, and Vebjorg Tingstad, 1–12. New York: Palgrave Macmillan, 2009.

Janes, Craig R., and Oyuntsetseg Chuluundorj. "Free Markets and Dead Mothers: The Social Ecology of Maternal Mortality in Post-socialist Mongolia." *Medical Anthropology Quarterly* 18, no. 2 (2004): 230–257.

Julier, Alice. "Hiding Gender and Race in the Discourse of Commercial Food Consumption." In *From Betty Crocker to Feminist Food Studies: Critical Perspectives on Women and Food*, edited by Arlene Voski Avakian and Barbara Haber, 163–184. Amherst: University of Massachusetts Press, 2005.

Jung, Yuson. "Food Provisioning and Foodways in Postsocialist Societies: Food as Medium for Social Trust and Global Belonging." In *Handbook of Food and Anthropology*, edited by Jakob Klein and James Watson, 289–307. New York: Bloomsbury, 2016.

Katz, Cindi. "Childhood as Spectacle: Relays of Anxiety and the Reconfiguration of the Child." *Cultural Geographies* 15, no. 1 (2008): 5–17.

Kipnis, Andrew. "Neoliberalism Reified: Suzhi Discourse and Tropes of Neoliberalism in the People's Republic of China." *Journal of the Royal Anthropological Institute* 13, no. 2 (2007): 383–400.

Kochhar, Rakesh. "The American Middle Class Is Stable in Size, but Losing Ground Financially to Upper-Income Families." Pew Research Center, September 6, 2018. www.pewresearch.org.

Kondo, Dorinne K. *Crafting Selves: Power, Gender, and Discourses of Identity in a Japanese Workplace*. Chicago: University of Chicago Press, 1990.

Kruse, Kevin. *White Flight: Atlanta and the Making of Modern Conservatism*. Princeton, NJ: Princeton University Press, 2005.

Kuan, Teresa. *Love's Uncertainty: The Politics and Ethics of Child Rearing in Contemporary China*. Berkeley: University of California Press, 2015.

Kusserow, Adrie. *American Individualisms: Child Rearing and Social Class in Three Neighborhoods*. New York: Palgrave Macmillan, 2004.

Laidlaw, James. "Proposing the Motion: A Slur for All Seasons." In "Debate: The Concept of Neoliberalism Has Become an Obstacle to the Anthropological Understanding of the Twenty-First Century," edited by Soumhya Venkatesan. *Journal of the Royal Anthropological Institute* 21 (2015): 912–914.

Lareau, Annette. *Unequal Childhoods: Class, Race, and Family Life*. Berkeley: University of California Press, 2003.

Lareau, Annette, Elliott B. Weininger, and Amanda Barrett Cox. "How Entitled Parents Hurt Schools." *New York Times*, June 24, 2018. www.nytimes.com.

Lavin, Chad. *Eating Anxiety: How the Experience of Eating Influences Our Politics*. Minneapolis: University of Minnesota Press, 2013.

Lawson, Michael A., and Hal A. Lawson. "New Conceptual Frameworks for Student Engagement Research, Policy, and Practice." *Review of Educational Research* 83, no. 3 (2013): 432–479.

Lee, Ellie. "Introduction." In *Parenting Culture Studies*, edited by Ellie Lee, Jennie Bristow, Charlotte Faircloth, and Jan Macvarish, 1–22. London: Palgrave Macmillan, 2014.

Leonhardt, David. "How the Upper Middle Class Is Really Doing: Is It More Similar to the Top 1 Percent or the Working Class?" *New York Times*, February 24, 2019. www.nytimes.com.

Levine, Susan. *School Lunch Politics: The Surprising History of America's Favorite Welfare Program*. Princeton, NJ: Princeton University Press, 2008.

Liechty, Mark. "Middle Class Deja-Vu: Conditions of Possibility, from Victorian England to Contemporary Kathmandu." In *The Global Middle Classes: Theorizing through Ethnography* (School for Advanced Research Advanced Seminar Series), edited by Rachel Heiman, Mark Liechty, and Carla Freeman, 271–300. Santa Fe, NM: School for Advanced Research Press, 2012.

———. *Suitably Modern: Making Middle-Class Culture in a New Consumer Society*. Princeton, NJ: Princeton University Press, 2002.

Lutz, Catherine A. *Unnatural Emotions: Everyday Sentiments on a Micronesian Atoll and Their Challenge to Western Theory*. Chicago: University of Chicago Press, 1988.

Maccoby, Eleanor E. "The Role of Parents in the Socialization of Children: An Historical Overview." *Developmental Psychology* 28, no. 6 (1992): 1006–1017.

MacKendrick, Norah. *Better Safe Than Sorry: How Consumer Navigate Exposure to Everyday Toxics*. Berkeley: University of California Press, 2018.

———. "Media Framing of Body Burdens: Precautionary Consumption and the Individualization of Risk." *Sociological Inquiry* 80, no. 1 (2010): 126–149.

———. "More Work for Mother: Chemical Body Burdens as a Maternal Responsibility." *Gender & Society* 28, no. 5 (2014): 705–728.

Maher, JaneMaree, Suzanne Fraser, and Jan Wright. "Framing the Mother: Childhood Obesity, Maternal Responsibility and Care." *Journal of Gender Studies* 19, no. 3 (2010): 233–247.

Martin, Emily. *Bipolar Expeditions: Mania and Depression in American Culture*. Princeton, NJ: Princeton University Press, 2007.

———. *Flexible Bodies: Tracking Immunity in American Culture from the Days of Polio to the Age of AIDS*. Boston: Beacon, 1994.

———. "Self-Making and the Brain." *Subjectivity* 3 (2010): 366–381.

Martin, Leslie. "Fighting for Control: Political Displacement in Atlanta's Gentrifying Neighborhoods." *Urban Affairs Review* 42, no. 5 (2007): 603–628.

Matza, Tomas. "Good Individualism? Psychology, Ethics and Neoliberalism in Postsocialist Russia." *American Ethnologist* 39, no. 4 (2012): 805–819.

Mauss, Marcel. "A Category of the Human Mind: The Notion of Person; The Notion of Self" (1938). In *The Category of the Person: Anthropology, Philosophy, History*, edited by Michael Carrithers, Steven Collins, and Steven Lukes, 1–25. Cambridge: Cambridge University Press, 1985.

———. *The Gift*. New York: Norton, 2000.

McClelland, Megan M., G. John Geldhof, Claire E. Cameron, and Shannon B. Wanless. "Development and Self-Regulation." In *Handbook of Child Psychology and Developmental Science*, edited by Richard M. Lerner, 1–43. Hoboken, NJ: John Wiley, 2015.

McKay, Sharon. *The Picky Eater*. New York: HarperCollins, 1993.

Merleaux, April. "Sweetness, Power, and Forgotten Food Histories in America's Empire." *Labor* 12, nos. 1–2 (2015): 87–114.

Metcalfe, Alan, Jenny Owen, Geraldine Shipton, and Caroline Dryden. "Inside and Outside the School Lunchbox: Themes and Reflections." *Children's Geographies* 6, no. 4 (2008): 403–412.

Miller, Claire Cain. "The Relentlessness of Modern Parenting." *New York Times*, December 25, 2018. www.nytimes.com.

Miller, Daniel. *A Theory of Shopping*. Ithaca, NY: Cornell University Press, 1998.

Milligan, Christine, and Janine Wiles. "Landscapes of Care." *Progress in Human Geography* 34, no. 6 (2010): 736–754.

Mintz, Sidney. *Sweetness and Power: The Place of Sugar in Modern History*. New York: Penguin, 1986.

———. *Tasting Food, Tasting Freedom: Excursions into Eating, Culture, and the Past*. Boston: Beacon, 1996.

Moffat, Tina. "The 'Childhood Obesity Epidemic': Health Crisis or Social Construction?" *Medical Anthropology Quarterly* 24, no. 1 (2010): 1–21.

Mooney, Carol G. *Theories of Childhood: An Introduction to Dewey, Montessori, Erikson, Piaget and Vygotsky*. 2nd ed. St. Paul, MN: Redleaf Press, 2013.

Munn, Nancy D. *The Fame of Gawa: A Symbolic Study of Value Transformation in a Massim (Papua New Guinea) Society*. Durham, NC: Duke University Press, 1986.

Murray, Desiree W., Katie Rosanbalm, Christina Christopoulos, and Amar Hamoudi. "Self-Regulation and Toxic Stress: Foundations for Understanding Self-Regulation from an Applied Developmental Perspective." OPRE Report 2015-21. Duke University Center for Child and Family Policy, January 2015. www.acf.hhs.gov.

Mustich, Emma. "Cookie Monster Learns to Self-Regulate so Kids Can Too." *Huffington Post*, September 13, 2013. www.huffpost.com.

Namie, Joylin. "Public Displays of Affection: Mothers, Children, and Requests for Junk Food." *Food, Culture, and Society* 14, no. 3 (2011): 393–411.

Narayan, Kirin. "How Native Is a 'Native' Anthropologist?" *American Anthropologist* 95, no. 3 (1993): 671–686.

National Institutes of Health. "Chronic High Blood Sugar May Be Detrimental to the Developing Brain of Young Children." December 17, 2014. www.nih.gov.

Neumann, William. "Food Makers Push Back on Ads for Children." *New York Times*, July 14, 2011. www.nytimes.com.

Ngai, Sianne. *Ugly Feelings*. Cambridge, MA: Harvard University Press, 2005.

Obadia, Julienne. "Contracting Intimate Futures: 'Do What You Love' and Other La-
bored Perversions." Paper presented at the American Anthropological Association
Annual Meeting, Minneapolis, 2016.

———. "Paying in Processing Time: The Contract Complex, Polyamory, and the Shifting Labor of Love in American Late Liberalism." Manuscript, 2018.

Ochs, Elinor, Clotilde Pontecorvo, and Alessandra Fasulo. "Socializing Taste." *Ethnos*
61, nos. 1–2 (1996): 7–46.

Ochs, Elinor, and Merav Shohet. "The Cultural Meaning of Mealtime Socialization."
New Directions for Child and Adolescent Development 111 (2006): 35–49.

O'Connell, Rebecca, and Julia Brannen. "Children's Food, Power and Control: Negotiations in Families with Younger Children in England." *Childhood* 21, no. 1 (2014):
87–102.

Oppenheimer, Mark. "Let Them Drink Chocolate." *New York Times*, April 19, 2014.
www.nytimes.com.

Patico, Jennifer. *Consumption and Social Change in a Post-Soviet Middle Class*. Washington, DC: Woodrow Wilson Center Press and Stanford University Press, 2008.

———. "Culturedness, Responsibility and Self-Help: Contexts of Middle Classness
in Postsocialist Russia." In *The Middle Class in Emerging Societies: Consumers,
Lifestyles and Markets*, edited by Leslie Marsh and Hongmei Li, 19–32. New York:
Routledge, 2016.

———. "The Real World in a Honey Bun." *Gastronomica* 13, no. 3 (2013): 42–46.

———. "Spinning the Market: The Moral Alchemy of Everyday Talk in Postsocialist
Russia." *Critique of Anthropology* 29, no. 2 (2009): 205–224.

———. "To Be Happy in a Mercedes: Culture, Civilization and Transformations of
Value in a Postsocialist City." *American Ethnologist* 32, no. 3 (2005): 479–496.

Patico, Jennifer, and Eriberto Lozada. "Children's Food." In *Handbook of Food and Anthropology*, edited by Jakob Klein and James Watson, 200–226. New York: Bloomsbury, 2016.

Paugh, Amy, and Carolina Izquierdo. "Why Is This a Battle Every Night? Negotiating Food and Eating in American Dinnertime Interaction." *Journal of Linguistic
Anthropology* 19, no. 2 (2009): 185–204.

Paxson, Heather. "Post-Pasteurian Cultures: The Microbiopolitics of Raw-Milk Cheese
in the United States." *Cultural Anthropology* 23, no. 1 (2008): 15–47.

Peachman, Rachel Rabkin. "Picky Eating in Children Linked to Anxiety, Depression,
and A.D.H.D." *New York Times*, August 3, 2015. https://parenting.blogs.nytimes.
com.

Peters, Michael A. "Education, Neoliberalism, and Human Capital: Homo Economicus
as 'Entrepreneur of Himself.'" In *The Handbook of Neoliberalism*, edited by Simon
Springer, Kean Birch, and Julie MacLeavy, 297–307. New York: Routledge, 2016.

Petrov, Kristian. "From Blood-Stained Colonial Sugar to Life-Essential Blood Sugar.
Swedish-European Themes in the Global Cultural History of Sugar." *RIG: kulturhis-
torisk tidskrift* 95, no. 3 (2012): 129–154.

Pfeiffer, James, and Rachel Chapman. "Anthropological Perspectives on Structural Adjustment and Public Health." *Annual Review of Anthropology* 39 (2010): 149–165.

Pigeron, Elisa. "Parents' Moral Discussions about Strategies for Monitoring Children's Media Exposure." *Novitas-ROYAL (Research on Youth and Language)* 6, no. 1 (2012): 15–32.

Pike, Jo. "Foucault, Space and Primary School Dining Rooms." *Children's Geographies* 6, no. 4 (2008): 413–422.

———. "'I Don't Have to Listen to You! You're Just a Dinner Lady!' Power and Resistance at Lunchtimes in Primary Schools." *Children's Geographies* 8, no. 3 (2010): 275–287.

Pike, Jo, and Deanna Leahy. "School Food and the Pedagogies of Parenting." *Australian Journal of Adult Learning* 52, no. 3 (2012): 434–459.

Pollan, Michael. *In Defense of Food: An Easter's Manifesto.* New York: Penguin, 2008.

Pomeranz, Jennifer L., Tim Lobstein, and Kelly D. Brownell. "A Crisis in the Marketplace: How Food Marketing Contributes to Childhood Obesity and What Can Be Done." *Annual Review of Public Health* 30 (2009): 211–225.

Poppendieck, Janet. *Free for All: Fixing School Food in America.* Berkeley: University of California Press, 2010.

Povinelli, Elizabeth A. *The Empire of Love: Toward a Theory of Intimacy, Genealogy, and Carnality.* Durham, NC: Duke University Press, 2006.

Precel, Jonathan. "The Deadly Ways Excess Sugar Is Stunting Your Child." *Breaking Muscle*, n.d. http://breakingmuscle.com.

Pugh, Alison. *Longing and Belonging: Parents, Children, and Consumer Culture.* Berkeley: University of California Press, 2009.

Ramaekers, Stefan, and Judith Suissa. *The Claims of Parenting: Reasons, Responsibility and Society.* Dordrecht: Springer, 2012.

Rabin, Roni Caryn. "The Chemicals in Your Mac and Cheese." *New York Times*, July 12, 2017. www.nytimes.com.

Reinolds, Chris. "What's for Lunch? Crafty Cafeteria Planners Nourish Students' Taste for Healthy Food." *Atlanta Journal Constitution*, October 20, 2005, 1JQ.

Richard, Analiese, and Daromir Rudnyckyj. "Economies of Affect." *Journal of the Royal Anthropological Institute* 15, no. 1 (2009): 57–77.

Rickett, Joel, and Spencer Wilson. *Q Is for Quinoa: A Modern Parent's ABC.* New York: Overlook Press, 2014.

Rosaldo, Michelle Z. "Toward an Anthropology of Self and Feeling." In *Culture Theory: Essays on Mind, Self, and Emotion*, edited by Richard A. Shweder and Robert A. LeVine, 137–157. Cambridge: Cambridge University Press, 1984.

Rosen, Rachel, and Katherine Twamley. "The Woman-Child Question: A Dialogue in the Borderlands." In *Feminism and the Politics of Childhood: Friends or Foes?*, edited by Rachel Rosen and Katherine Twamley, 1–20. London: University College London Press, 2018.

Rosenberg, Merri. "In the Schools: Lesson Plans for Better Lunches." *New York Times*, March 23, 2003. www.nytimes.com.

Rothman, Barbara Katz. *A Bun in the Oven: How the Birth and Food Movements Resist Industrialization*. New York: New York University Press, 2016.

Salmenniemi, Suvi, ed. *Rethinking Class in Russia*. Abingdon: Routledge, 2016.

Schulte, Brigid. "More Nutritious, Less Delicious: Montgomery Schools to Slim Down Cafeteria Offerings." *Washington Post*, January 27, 2002, B01.

———. "Once Just a Birthday Treat, the Cupcake Becomes a Cause." *Washington Post*, December 11, 2006. www.washingtonpost.com.

Scrinis, Gyorgy. *Nutritionism: The Science and Politics of Dietary Advice*. New York: Columbia University Press, 2015.

Sears. "Attachment Parenting." 2019a. www.askdrsears.com.

———. "Harmful Effects of Excess Sugar." 2019b. www.askdrsears.com.

Shotwell, Alexis. *Against Purity: Living Ethically in Compromised Times*. Minneapolis: University of Minnesota Press, 2016.

Siegel, Bettina Elias. "As Lobbyists and Politicians Shout It Out over School Lunch, Can Parents Be Heard?" *New York Times*, October 8, 2014.

Siegel, Daniel J. *Brainstorm: The Power and Purpose of the Teenage Brain*. New York: Penguin Putnam, 2013.

Slow Family Living. "Family Mission Statement Workbook." N.d. http://slowfamilyliving.com.

Sparke, Matthew. "Health and the Embodiment of Neoliberalism: Pathologies of Political Economy from Climate Change and Austerity to Personal Responsibility." In *The Handbook of Neoliberalism*, edited by Simon Springer, Kean Birch, and Julie MacLeavy, 237–251. New York: Routledge, 2016.

Stewart, Kathleen. *Ordinary Affects*. Durham, NC: Duke University Press, 2007.

Stosny, Steve. "Self-Regulation: To Feel Better, Focus on What Is Most Important." *Psychology Today*, October 28, 2011. www.psychologytoday.com.

Szinn, Stephen. "New School Lunch Standards Are Working. So Why Does Congress Want to Knock Them Down?" *Washington Post*, March 8, 2016. www.washingtonpost.com.

Thomas, Nigel, and Claire O'Kane. "The Ethics of Participatory Research with Children." *Children and Society* 12 (1998): 336–348.

Trnka, Susanna, and Catherine Trundle. "Competing Responsibilities: Moving beyond Neoliberal Responsibilisation." *Anthropological Forum* 24, no. 2 (2014): 136–153.

U.S. Department of Agriculture, Food and Nutrition Service. "Local School Wellness Policy." March 30, 2016. www.fns.usda.gov.

———. "Nutrition Standards in the National School Lunch and School Breakfast Programs." January 26, 2012. www.fns.usda.gov.

———. "Rates of Reimbursement." August 13, 2013. www.fns.usda.gov.

———. "Whole Grain Resource National School Lunch and Breakfast Programs." February 12, 2014. www.fns.usda.gov.

U.S. Department of Health and Human Services. "Poverty Guidelines." N.d. https://aspe.hhs.gov.

Valentine, Gill. "Being Seen and Heard? The Ethical Complexities of Working with Children and Young People at Home and at School." *Philosophy & Geography* 2, no. 2 (1999): 141–155.

Veblen, Thorstein. *The Theory of the Leisure Class.* 1899. New York: Penguin, 1994.

Warner, Judith. "Junking Junk Food." *New York Times*, November 28, 2010. www.nytimes.com.

———. *Perfect Madness: Motherhood in the Age of Anxiety*. New York: Riverhead Books, 2005.

Weeks, Kathi. "Life Within and Against Work: Affective Labor, Feminist Critique, and Post-Fordist Politics." *Ephemera* 7 (2007): 233–249.

Wentworth, Chelsea. "Good Food, Bad Food, and White Rice: Understanding Child Feeding Using Visual-Narrative Elicitation." *Medical Anthropology* 36, no. 6 (2017): 602–614.

Wright, Jan. "Biopolitics, Biopedagogies, and the Obesity Epidemic." In *Biopolitics and the "Obesity Epidemic,"* edited by Jan Wright and Valerie Harwood, 1–14. New York: Routledge, 2009.

Young, Donna, and Anne Meneley. "Introduction: Auto-ethnographies of Academic Practices." In *Auto-ethnographies: The Anthropology of Academic Practices*, edited by Anne Meneley and Donna Young, 1–21. Toronto: University of Toronto Press, 2005.

Zelizer, Viviana. *Pricing the Priceless Child: The Changing Social Value of Children.* Princeton, NJ: Princeton University Press, 1994.

Zimmerman, Heidi. "Caring for the Middle Class Soul: Ambivalence, Ethical Eating and the Michael Pollan Phenomenon." *Food, Culture and Society* 18, no. 1 (2015): 31–50.

INDEX

actors, boundaries between, 13
Adam (interviewee), 98
addiction, 71–72, 151
ADHD. *See* attention-deficit/hyperactivity
  disorder
admissions lottery, 21, 123, 166–67
adults, 129–30; boundaries between
  children and, 15, 85–86, 87, 93–94, 109;
  perceptions of, 55, 112, 115
allergies, 30–31, 52, 62
Amanda (interviewee), 149, 160; on control, 101; on parental engagement, 179;
  on racial tensions, 164–65
American individualism, 93, 106
Annie's (brand), 63, 64, 117, 202n8; gummy
  fruit snacks, *50*; macaroni and cheese, *65*
anthropologists, 9–10, 19, 29, 115, 206n5
anxiety, 15, 31, 197; empathy conflicting with,
  153, 154, 172; food, 95; parenting, 13–14
Aronson, Matt, 81
assent forms, 114
Atlanta, Georgia, 19, 20, 158
attention-deficit/hyperactivity disorder
  (ADHD), 40, 68, 86
authoritarianism, 84
autonomy: of children, 80, 111; choices
  and, 121; control *versus*, 96; forms of,
  75; of individuals, 189, 190, 191; relatedness and, 107, 108
awareness: emotional, 81; food, 35, 36, 54, 134

"bad" food, compared to "good" food,
  41–42, 138–39
Bailey, Becky, 82–83, 84, 85, 86–87

balance, 128, 148, 188; children's food and,
  5, 59; parenting, 90, 95–96, 109
Barbara (Hometown elementary principle), 152–53
Barnett, Liz, 62, 171–72
Barry (interviewee), 72, 98–99
Beck, Ulrich, 31, 36, 47
behavior: self-regulation and, 89; sugar
  impacting, 67–74
benign neglect, 90, 92, 102
Bialostok, Steve, 81
birthday parties, 32, 69, 102, 119, 121, 173
Borenstein, Eliot, 192
Borovoy, Amy, 105
boundaries: between actors, 13; between
  children and adults, 15, 85–86, 87, 93–
  94, 109; emotional, 4, 105–6; as fuzzy,
  31, 82
boundedness, of community, 195–96
Bourdieu, Pierre, 16, 18, 175
brain states, 83–84
brands: comfort from, 60–64; discounts and, 53; obesity and, 9; trust
  of, 31
breakfast cereals, 56–58
Bringing Up Bébé (Druckerman), 94
Burkehead, Scott, 155, 156–57, 188
Burnette, Jessie, 167–68

capitalist economies, 18, 19, 197; childhood
  and, 116; industrial modernity of, 12;
  labor in, 11, 18, 196; late conditions of,
  9; shifts in, 196
care, 189–90, 191

ABOUT THE AUTHOR

Jennifer Patico is Associate Professor of Anthropology at Georgia State University in Atlanta. She is the author of *Consumption and Social Change in a Post-Soviet Middle Class* (2008). Her ethnographic research in Russia and the United States has been published in journals including *American Ethnologist, Ethnos, Critique of Anthropology*, and *Gastronomica.*